The ORIGINS of CHRISTIANITY

BY

Revilo P. Oliver

THIRD EDITION

COSMOTHEIST BOOKS
MOUNTAIN CITY

ISBN 978-1-7371169-1-2

copyright ©2025
by Kevin Alfred Strom

First edition, July 1999
Second edition, June 2001
Third edition, January 2025

book design and editing by Kevin Alfred Strom

All rights reserved. No part of this book, except for brief excerpts for the purpose of review, may be produced in any form without written permission from the copyright holder.

published by

COSMOTHEIST BOOKS
BOX 4 • MOUNTAIN CITY • TENNESSEE • 37683
COSMOTHEISTCHURCH.ORG

Foreword

Our belief systems, such as religions, have no actual existence except as chemical and electrical activity in our brains. They have no more reality than do dreams. For something so insubstantial, however, they have profound effects upon our lives and upon the race and civilization to which we belong.

Religions produce not only cultural artifacts, such as temples to Athena or Mithras or Jesus, "holy" books, music, and the like; they also often constitute a controlling influence over what men think, and therefore also over what men do, thus defining the structure of our laws and punishments, our wars and crusades, our standards of sexual behavior, and a thousand other things. For all their constant mutations, fantastic improbabilities, and mutually exclusive claims of infallibility, religions remain a powerful factor in determining who shall live and who shall die; and who shall be allowed power and wealth, and who shall be condemned to impotence and penury.

So religions must be taken very seriously, even by — perhaps especially by — those who find it impossible to believe in them. Thus, the study and understanding of the religion currently dominant among members of our race, Christianity, is of the utmost importance.

Dr. Revilo Pendleton Oliver (1908-1994), one of the leading classicists, philologists, and scholars of the 20th century, was uniquely qualified to write on such matters. Dr. Oliver made a special study of religions, ancient and modern, writing often on the subject both for scholarly journals and for the public; and his personal library contained the greatest collection of books on religion that I have seen outside of a large university library.

This volume, Dr. Oliver's last major work, was begun in 1980, around the time that his earlier books, *America's Decline: The Education of a Conservative* and *The Jewish Strategy* were being finished. *The Origins of Christianity* was undergoing final revisions (e.g., the removal of phraseology that had become outdated upon the fall of the Soviet Union, and the addition of a few new amplifications of certain points in the text) at the time of his death.

Dr. Oliver regarded this book as his most important work. In my opinion, no higher recommendation is possible.

Kevin Alfred Strom
Mineral Point, Pennsylvania
7 July, 2024

Introduction

OF THE MANY PROBLEMS that confront us today, none is more vexing than that of the relation of Christianity to Western Civilization. None, certainly, causes more acrimonious controversy and internecine hostility between the members of the race which created that civilization. None more thoroughly counteracts their common interest in its preservation and renders them impotent and helpless. And that is not remarkable: What is in question is the essential nature of our civilization, and if there is no agreement about that, there can be no effective agreement on other questions.

Around 1910, Georges Matisse, in *Les Ruines de l'Idée de Dieu*,[1] predicted that by 1960, at the very latest, the only churches left in the civilized world would be the ones that were preserved as museum pieces for their architectural beauty or historical associations. The scientific and historical knowledge accumulated by our race had rendered belief in supernatural beings impossible for cultivated men, and universal education would speedily destroy the credulity of the masses: "We have climbed out of the dead end of the dungeon into which Christianity cast us. The man of today walks in the open air and the daylight. He has won confidence in himself."

In 1980, especially in the United States, there was a massive "upsurge" of Christianity. In November, one of America's many bawling evangelists, Oral Roberts, had an interview with Jesus and took the opportunity to observe that Jesus is nine hundred feet tall. That datum so impressed his followers that within two weeks, it is said, they supplied him with an extra $5,000,000 to supplement the $45,000,000 they give him annually. A little earlier, another holy man, Don Stewart, reportedly made the big time in evangelism (i.e., an annual take of more than $10,000,000) by distributing to his votaries snippets of his underwear, which True Believers put under their pillows, since the bits of cloth that had been in contact with his flesh had absorbed the *mana* of his holiness. And in the quadrennial popularity contest to determine which actor was to have the star role in the White House, all three of the presidential candidates deemed it expedient to announce that they had "got Jesus" and been "born again."

More significantly, in both England and the United States, a considerable number of men who have received enough technical train-

---

1   Paris, *Mercure de France*, s.a. All translations from foreign languages in these pages are mine, unless otherwise noted.

ing to be called scientists, have been hired or inspired to prove the authenticity of the Holy Shroud of Turin by "scientific" proof that the coarse cloth was discolored by supernatural means, the *mana* of divinity. Some of these scientists, it is true, claim that the vague picture was formed on the fabric because the body of the deceased god was highly radioactive and emitted radiation of an intensity comparable to that produced by the explosion of the atomic bomb at Hiroshima, but obviously only a very supernatural force could have charged the cells of an organic body with such enormous and deadly energy. In many American colleges, professors of reputable academic subjects are teaching courses to demonstrate that human beings cannot be the product of the biological process of evolution, but must have been specially designed and manufactured by a god in a way that they more or less explicitly identify with the well-known account of the descent of mankind from Adam and his spare rib. The divinity school of Emory University (founded in 1836) offers, for the edification of Methodist ministers, a graduate seminar in the theology of America's most distinguished automobile thief and rapist, a Black preacher named King, and, presumably for such exemplary Christianity, was rewarded with a gift of $100,000,000, the largest private benefaction on record.

The United States has always been noted for the multiplicity and fanaticism of its Christian sects, but on a much smaller scale a Christian "outreach" (to use the evangelical term) for souls and funds may be observed in several countries of Europe, even including, it is said, some in Soviet territory. And one wonders whether a survey in England today would maintain the statistics that permitted Professor A.N. Whitehead to conclude, in 1942, that "far less than one-fifth of the population are in any sense Christians today." I hear that the fraction would have to be significantly increased, and that Roman Catholicism, more than other sects, is constantly attracting a significant number of "converts." But the number of persons who attend churches or profess to believe some one of the numerous Christian doctrines is relatively unimportant. The domestic and foreign policies of all the nations of the Western world are based on ideas that their populations as a whole take for granted and accept without reflection or consideration — ideas which are obviously, though sometimes not explicitly, derived from Christian theology and are, so to speak, a residue of the ages when our race was, not inaccurately, called Christendom.

Matisse was egregiously wrong. His spectacular error, however, was a projection logically made from the evidence available to him in 1910, when he concluded that

> the White race has conquered the whole world and slain the Dragon [of superstition]. And the race had to do it. If the human mind had been incapable of that achievement, the most difficult of all its achievements, it would have been doomed. Intellect would have ended in failure on this planet. It was a question of the life or death of intelligence.... The indisputable proof of the innately superior power of the European mind today is atheism.

Matisse, of course, did not foresee the catastrophe of 1914 or sense the subterranean and occult forces that were secretly in operation even in 1910 to precipitate, not just another European war to alter the balance of power on the Continent, but a war that those forces converted into a universal disaster, even more destructive of rationality than of property and life, which may prove to have been the beginning of the end for our civilization and race. The question that Matisse so clearly posed therefore remains, not altered by the calamities he could not foresee, but instead now made even more vital and urgent.

The question is obviously, perhaps fatally, divisive, but it cannot be evaded or ignored. The question is one to which even reticence is an answer; and hypocrisy is demoralizing. I have therefore undertaken the exacting and almost impossible task of presenting in these pages an objective and dispassionate summary of the problem, condensing into a few pages what would more properly be the substance of several volumes, themselves compendious. I have necessarily refrained from debating side issues and from straying into scholarly controversies. I have tried to limit myself to skeletal essentials of what may with confidence be regarded as established fact and logical inference therefrom, and I assume that I need not tell intelligent readers that the subject is one on which it is flatly impossible to make any statement whatsoever that is not contradicted somewhere in the horrendous tonnage of printed paper on the shelves of even a mediocre library.[2]

To view our problem clearly, we must begin with its beginnings and indicate, as summarily as possible, its prehistoric origins, limit-

---

2   I have restricted the documentary notes to a bare minimum, limited to points that may not generally be matters of common knowledge. So far as possible, I have cited only works available in English, selecting from these the one or two that give, so far as I know, the most succinct and perspicuous treatment of the given topic.

ing ourselves to matters directly relevant to our own race, with which alone we need have a rational concern. And since Indo-European is best reserved for use as a linguistic term, and such words as Nordic and Celtic are too restrictive as designations of variations within our species, we shall use the only available word in general use that designates our race as a whole, although the Jews have forbidden us to use it. The word *Aryan*, furthermore, has the advantage that it is not a geographic term, and while some may think it immodest to describe ourselves as *arya*, 'noble,' that word does indicate a range of moral concepts for which our race seems to have instinctively a peculiar and characteristic respect, which differentiates it from other races as sharply as do its physical traits, and, like them, more or less conspicuously, depending on the particular contrast that is made. It is unfortunate that in the present state of knowledge we cannot trace our species, the Aryans, to the species of *Homo erectus* or *Homo habilis* from which it is descended.

Chapter One: Religion

RELIGION, which we may define as a belief in the existence of praeterhuman and supernatural beings, is a phenomenon limited to several human species, since it depends on rudimentary powers of reason and relatively developed powers of imagination. We may agree with Xenophanes that if oxen or horses or lions conceived of gods, each species would, like men, create its gods in its own image, but there is no slightest reason for supposing that mammals other than man have any conception of superior beings other than an instinctive recognition of predatory species that can prey on them and an instinctive suspicion of whatever is unfamiliar and may therefore be dangerous.

Anatole France, to be sure, identified dogs as religious animals, and he had a basis for doing so. A dog does venerate his master as a being with powers vastly superior to his own. He worships his god in his own way, seeking to conciliate his favor with propitiatory motions and caresses, learning to obey his wishes and whims, and even having a sense of sin when he knows that he has yielded to a temptation to do something that will displease his deity. A dog tries to appease his god's anger, as men do, by humility and fawning, and he will fight for his god, even at the risk of his own life. But we must not carry France's analogy too far. The dog's god is a living being, who normally feeds his canine worshipper, punishes him physically on occasion, and, if worthy of devotion, pets him affectionately. No dog ever worshipped a being that he could not see, hear, smell, and touch.

Eugène Marais, whose scientific investigations have at last been accorded the honor they long deserved, made observations of the highest importance for anthropological studies. He discovered that baboons collectively evince a degree of intelligence that, in certain respects, surpasses that of the apes that are usually classified as anthropoid, and, despite their lack of an articulated language, they may favorably be compared to the more primitive species that are classified as human. The chacmas whom Marais so patiently observed undoubtedly have rudimentary powers of reason, to which, indeed, they owe their survival in an environment that became overwhelmingly hostile when farmers and government undertook to exterminate them. In his articles for the general public, which were collected and translated under the title, *My Friends, the Baboons* (London, 1939), Marais describes a highly significant incident that occurred during his prolonged observation of a band of baboons that had, after long observation, come to accept him and his colleague as not hostile members of a species they justly feared. When many of the infant baboons were smitten by an epidemic malady, the elders of the band, its oligarchs, solicited human help and found a way to show that they believed or hoped that kindly members of our species, which, they knew by experience, had the power to inflict death miraculously with a rifle, also had the miraculous power to preserve from death beings they chose to protect. And at least one of the female baboons, mother of a dead infant, unmistakably believed or hoped that men had the power to resurrect the dead and restore them to life.

If the pathetic episode is reported correctly, the chacmas have something of the power of imagination that is requisite for religiosity. But we should not call them religious. They attributed to a mammalian species, which they knew to have powers incomprehensible to them, a power the species did not have. Baboons do fear night and darkness, but if they give a shape to what they fear, they probably think of it as a leopard. There is no evidence to suggest that they have even the most rudimentary notion of gods. No more can be said of some species of anthropoids that are classified as human because they have an articulate, though rudimentary, language. Anthropologists who had opportunities to observe those species before their native consciousness had been much corrupted by "missionaries" or by contact with higher races (which usually excites an almost simian imitativeness), report that the dim consciousness of those species, although possessing certain animal instincts and faculties that are weak or wanting in our race, is strictly animistic, attributing, so far as we can tell, the efficacy of a spear to some power inherent in the spear itself, and being unable to distinguish between animate and inanimate objects. The creatures live in a world of perpetual mystery, incapable of perceiving a relation between cause and effect. Scrupulous observation has shown that the Arunta and other tribes of Australoids, admittedly the lowest species that is classified as human, propagated themselves for at least fifty thousand years without even guessing that there might be some causal relationship between sexual intercourse and pregnancy. For aught we know to the contrary, baboons may have more native intelligence. Obviously, where nothing is either natural or supernatural, there can be no concept that could be called religious.

Such facts should make us chary of trying to reconstruct the unknown prehistory of our race from observation of the primitive races that have survived to our own time. They, like the primitive coelacanth, which has survived much longer, may represent the dead ends of an evolutionary process that can go no farther. The work of Frobenius, best known in the English translation entitled *The Childhood of Man* (London, 1909), encouraged, more by its title than its content, an assumption once generally held as a residue of Christian doctrine. When the dogma that all human beings were the progeny of Adam and his spare rib could no longer be maintained, it was, as happens with all cultural residues, modified as little as possible, and it was replaced with the notion of human descent from a single hypothetical ancestral family. Now that Dr. Carleton Coon, in his *Origin of Races* (New York, 1962), has shown, as conclusively as the exiguous data permit, that the five primary races owe their diversity to the differences between the several pithecanthropoid species from which they respectively evolved, we can no longer assume that, for example, the Hottentots of today represent a stage of evolution through which our ancestors once passed. There is simply no evidence that our race was ever animistic; its religiosity may have appeared in minds of basically different quality.

We have no certain trace of our race before comparatively recent times. If we overrule some dissenting opinions and identify the Cro-Magnon people as Aryan, we have gone as far as we can into our past, and that, for most of our evidence, is less than twenty thousand years. We may think it likely that the Cro-Magnons had a religion, but we have no means of knowing what it was. The confident statements that one so commonly sees are conjectures, formed largely on inadmissible analogies with modern primitives, and based entirely on two kinds of evidence: burials and the cave-paintings that evince an artistic talent that makes the Cro-Magnons unique among the peoples of the world in their time.

We are frequently told that care for the dead and painstaking burials are evidence of some belief in an afterlife and, hence, in ghosts, but that is a guess. Burial may be no more than a manifestation of an instinctive respect or affection for the dead and an unwillingness to see his corpse devoured by beasts or becoming putrescent near the camp. When a man's possessions are buried with him, there may indeed have been some notion (as is attested in Egypt, for example) that the equipment would be useful to him in a post-mortem existence, but it is equally possible that some or many instances of this custom may indicate the emergence of a strong sense of private property: The spear or the beads or the golden drinking horn were the dead man's, and no one should steal from him when he dies and can no longer defend his own.

In the celebrated cave-paintings, we see men who wear the heads and hides of animals, so we are told, on the basis of conjectural analogies, that the figures are shamans making magic for a successful hunt. But the very cave ("Trois-Frères" in Haute-Garonne) that contains the best-known depiction of such a "sorcerer" also contains a painting that shows a man who wears the head and hide of a reindeer while stalking a herd of those animals, and his disguise has an obviously practical purpose. The isolated figures in animal costume that seem to be dancing may be merely cavorting for the amusement of their fellows or, conceivably, exhibiting extravagant joy over luck in hunting.

In one cave (Willendorf) is found a small figurine, carved with noteworthy skill from the tusk of a mammoth, which depicts a very plump woman with an elaborate coiffure in an advanced stage of pregnancy, clearly not her first. Some wit satirically calls it a "Venus," and we soon have our choice between several dissertations about fertility cults and the religion of which they were a part. The fact is that we do not know who carved the figurine or why. It does evince some interest in pregnancy — perhaps that of a husband who hopes for another offspring, perhaps that of a man who had a whim to carve something from a tusk.

We may, of course, form conjectures about the origin of religion. Statius was doubtless right: *Primus in orbe deos fecit timor.* [*The first gods of the world were made by fear*.] Early men did live in a world filled with terrors and dangers that they, no matter how natively intelligent, could not understand. Earthquakes are awesome, even when they are not destructive. Storms arise without perceptible causes; hurricanes and violent lightnings awaken atavistic fears in us, even if we, who know that they are merely natural phenomena, are in places of safety. The very seasons (especially in a time of climatic changes following the retreat of glaciers) seem mysterious at best, and even fearful when accompanied by prolonged rainfall, excessive snow, or desiccating drought. Even luck (that is, unexplained coincidences) makes some of our own contemporaries superstitious and, if adverse, may suggest the activity of mysteriously inimical forces. And, like the baboons, we instinctively dread darkness, which may conceal all the fearsome dangers that the imagination can conceive. Ignorance is terrible. So much is obvious.

We are reduced to precarious speculation, however, when we try to understand why our remote ancestors imagined that the incomprehensible phenomena amid which they had to live could be influenced by their own acts — that they could, for example, appease whatever caused storms or persuade whatever caused rain to end a drought. And was it because phenomena of which the cause is unknown seem capricious, and thus like impulses and whims of men, that they imagined that invisible beings, praeterhuman men, consciously produced the phenomena? Did many bands or tribes spontaneously and independently imagine supernatural beings as the causes of inexplicable phenomena, or did the notion first occur to some visionary individual, whose explanation was accepted and adopted ever more widely because no one could think of a better one? Or did adults transfer to the external world the sentiments excited when they were children and subject to whatever rewards or chastisements a parent chose to bestow or inflict? One may speculate endlessly why men began to attribute natural phenomena to supernatural persons. The only certainty is that they did, and whenever they did so, religion was born. It was an attempt to understand the world by identifying causes and classifying them, and crude as it seems to us, it evinces a more than animal intelligence.

Chapter Two: The Triple Function

WE LIVE IN A TIME in which there is much talk about "religious freedom." It is assumed that beliefs about the supernatural are a "private matter" which every individual has a right to determine for himself. Thus we have the dogma about the "separation of church and state" which was one of the basic principles of the American Constitution and survives today as one of the few bases of that Constitution that have not been officially repudiated or covertly abrogated.

This conception of religion is a recent one. It was a novelty when the Constitution was written, and it was then a compromise that many of our people accepted only reluctantly. It has consequences that very large segments of our population are unwilling to accept today. And it is now a source of infinite sophistry, hypocrisy, chicanery, and befuddlement.

We must therefore remind ourselves that religion is historically a social phenomenon and a concern of the collectivity much more than of the individual. From the earliest history of our race to the present, religion has, in varying degrees, served three distinct purposes: as a political bond, as a sanction for social morality, and as a consolation for individuals. These three functions became so intertwined that at any given time in our history, including the present, they seem inextricably interwoven, but to distinguish them clearly, we may consider them separately.

Cohesion

As all readers of Robert Ardrey's brilliant expositions of biological facts, *The Territorial Imperative* and *The Social Contract*, well know, all animals that hunt in packs must have an instinctive sense of a common purpose and a rudimentary social organization that regulates the relations between individuals and produces, at least temporarily, a cohesion between them by subordinating the individual to the group and its common purpose. Obedience to the law of the pack must be automatic among wolves, *lycaones*, and all species that depend for survival on cooperation between individuals.

We may be certain that that instinctive sense was present in our remote biological antecedents of two or more million years ago, the *Australopitheci*, who hunted in small packs and even learned to use as simple weapons stones and the bones of animals they had killed and devoured. We may assume, however, that they, like wolves, assembled as packs only to hunt larger animals, and that the bond between individuals, other than mates, endured only during the hunt. This instinct for limited confederation must have been present, a million or more years later, in the various prehuman species, commonly called *Homines erecti*, some of which, as Carleton Coon has shown in his *Origin of Races*, survived as distinct species of anthropoids that eventually developed into the extant races of mankind. It is a reasonable and perhaps necessary deduction from the available evidence that the species which survived to become human were those in which the instinct became strong enough to produce more permanent associations, a pack that remained together even after the successful termination of the hunt and the eating of its quarry, while the species that could form no larger permanent groups than do gorillas today were headed for extinction.

We must assume that the several species of *Homines erecti* that became the ancestors of the various races now alive were as intelligent as baboons, hunted in packs of from ten to twelve adult males, remained together as a band or miniature tribe, as do baboons, and communicated with one another by uttering a variety of cries and other sounds, supplemented by gestures, again as baboons do. And it is probable that no association of individuals larger than such a band was possible for many thousands of years.

The Neanderthals[3], whom the Cro-Magnons wisely, though no doubt instinctively, exterminated in Europe and perhaps elsewhere, are now generally regarded as an extinct race of human beings, probably even lower than the Australoids and Congoids of our own time, and most biologists now include them in the taxonomic category that embraces the several races that have been ironically called *Homines sapientes*. Although it is frequently assumed that the Neanderthals formed groups larger than a band of baboons, there is no valid evidence that they did, and such social cohesion as they had must have been entirely instinctive and subconscious. Although some anthropologists have found new grounds for dissent, the majority now believes that the Neanderthals were able to communicate with one another by means of a very crude and rudimentary language, that

---

3   Information which was not yet available when Dr. Oliver wrote indicates that not all of the Neanderthals were exterminated; in fact, all human races today, except sub-Saharan Negroids, possess a small amount of Neanderthal ancestry. It is also increasingly acknowledged that Neanderthals, at least some of them, were of a higher evolutionary grade than previously assumed. — Ed.

is, articulated sounds of definite meaning, as distinct from the variety of inarticulate cries and grunts, supplemented by gestures, by which baboons now communicate, and *Homines erecti* must have communicated, with one another. It is most unlikely, however, that the Neanderthals' language was sufficiently developed to permit either generalizations or statements about the past and future rather than the present.

The success of the Cro-Magnon people in hunting such formidable game as mammoths is sufficient proof that they must have lived together in groups large enough to be called a tribe, and that they had a language that was in some way inflected to form tenses and thus indicate temporal relationships, thereby making possible conscious planning and specific reference to past experiences. This, in turn, permitted the generalizations that are a kind of rough classification and a conscious awareness of tribal unity, which could be communicated to the young by spoken precept and rule, however crude and elementary, thus forming what anthropologists call a culture.

What superstitions the Cro-Magnons had, and what rituals they performed, can only be conjectured by tenuous speculations, but a moment's reflection will show that if they had a religion (as is, of course, likely), it must have been concerned with tribal purposes, such as success in hunting or the mitigation of an epidemic disease or the production of rain. And such religious ceremonies as may have been performed for such purposes were doubtless rituals that required the participation of the whole tribe or the part of it that was immediately concerned, such as all adult males, if hunting was involved, or all females, if fertility and offspring were sought. The ritual thus became an affirmation of tribal unity.

The earliest religions of which we have knowledge are tribal, and their ceremonies are rituals in which the whole tribe (except children) participates or all of the part of the tribe that is concerned (e.g., all men of military age or all married women) or a group that has been selected to perform a dance or a sacrifice on behalf of the tribe as a whole. And when a number of tribes coalesce to form a small state, the demonstration of their effective unity and common purpose by religious unanimity becomes even more necessary, and it is affirmed by festivals in which every citizen is expected to participate, at least by abstaining from other activity and being present as a spectator, and in which aliens, whether visitors or *metics*, are not permitted to participate and from which they may be so excluded that they are forbidden to witness any part of the proceedings. The number of citizens is now so large that active participation of all in a religious ritual is no longer feasible, and comparatively small groups must be selected to act on behalf of the whole state or the whole of a class in it. Alcman's *Partheneion*, for example, was written for a choir of virgins who performed a ceremony on behalf of all the virgin daughters of Spartan citizens to conciliate for them the favor of Artemis. The *Panathenaea*, which celebrated the political unification of Attica, was a series of varied ceremonies (one of which was a reading of the poems of Homer) in honor of the goddess who was the city's patroness, and although a fairly large number of individuals took part in the chariot-races, musical contests, choral performances, cult dances, and other ceremonies, only a small fraction of the citizen body could take an active part in the festival that was held for the benefit of the whole state, and on the last day, traditionally Athena's birthday, *metics* were even permitted to join the grand procession as attendants on citizens. At Rome, the twenty-four *Salii* solicited for the entire nation the favor of Mars and Quirinus by perfoming their archaic dance accompanied by a litany in Latin so archaic that its meaning was only vaguely known. And the *feriae* in honor of Jupiter on the Alban Mount, at which the presence of both consuls was mandatory, celebrated the political unification of Latium.

What many of our uninformed contemporaries overlook is the fact that participation in such ceremonies, including attendance at them, was essentially a political act by which citizens affirmed their participation in their state. It did not in the least matter, for example, whether the individual citizen "believed in" the gods who were propitiated and honored: If he disbelieved in their existence or spoke of them in injurious terms (except during the ceremonies themselves), and if the gods concerned took notice and resented his conduct, it was up to those gods (as Augustus had to remind some of his contemporaries) to take what action they deemed appropriate against him. And it did not really matter whether the rites were really efficacious: The important thing was that persons who refused to participate in them thereby exhibited their alienation from the state and seemed to be renouncing their citizenship. If a Roman who was an atheist was elected consul, his office obliged him to make the appropriate sacrifices to Jupiter at the *Feriae Latinae* and to preside at, or otherwise participate in, other religious rites, but he had no sense of incongruity or hypocrisy: He was performing an essentially political rite for which a religious faith was no more necessary than it was, e.g., for watching a chariot race in the circus, which officially was also a religious ceremony.

This function of religion is to affirm political cohesion. And it has retained that function almost to our own time. When the unity of Christendom was shattered by the Reformation and it became clear that it would not be easy for either the Catholics or the Protestants to exterminate the other party, an early compromise was the doctrine of *cuius regio, eius religio* [*whose realm, his religion*]. By agreeing that the ruler's religion was to be that of all of his subjects (except of course the Jews, who were always given special privileges), men hoped to maintain the effective unity of each state, and that was a political purpose that atheists could and did recognize as expedient. The establishment of the Anglican Church was one of the least unsuccessful applications of the principle, and from the political standpoint, the disabilities of the Catholics in England are less remarkable than the toleration that was accorded them. And it is perverse to refuse to understand the attitude of Louis XIV in Catholic France after he was convinced that Jansenists, although indubitably Catholic, were fracturing the nation's political unity. The story that he at first refused to appoint a man to high office because he had heard the man was a Jansenist, but gladly appointed him as soon as he was reliably informed that the man did not believe in god at all, is undoubtedly true — and was probably true on several occasions. The king was probably quite uninterested in the theological hair-pulling and cut-throat competition that was then making so much noise, but he had the common sense to perceive that by appointing an atheist he was not strengthening a faction of political trouble-makers. If he knew of Cardinal Dubois's famous dictum that God is a bogeyman who must be brandished to scare the populace into some approximation of honesty, he may or may not have thought that the good cardinal was running a risk of post-mortem woe, but he recognized that Dubois's opinions did not detract from his political efficiency in maintaining social stability.

The requirement at Oxford and Cambridge until quite recent times of an oath of affirmation in the Church of England's Thirty-Nine Articles has been perversely misunderstood. Everyone knew for centuries that many did not believe what they affirmed, and there was some truth in the hot-headed Sir William Hamilton's charge that Oxford was a "school of perjury," but he naïvely became excited because he did not perceive that the requirement had not the fantastic theological purpose of pleasing a god in whom many who took the oath did not believe, but the strictly practical one of excluding fanatics who were emotionally attached to dogmas that would inspire trouble-making agitation over questions that, if not totally illusory, were incapable of rational determination. It was regrettable, of course, that adolescents like young Gibbon should, in effect, expel themselves from the university through a waywardness they would later regret, and that intelligent adults like Newman should develop emotional enthusiasms and a zeal for fruitless controversy that, the conservatives felt, was much better than bestowing the prestige of the universities on seditious fanatics.

In the United States, Benjamin Franklin certainly did not believe in any form of Christian doctrine, but that did not prevent him from approving, if he did not inspire, a state constitution which, by requiring an oath of belief in the Trinity, effectively excluded from political influence many of the Jews and such dissidents as the Quakers, who, for example, refused to defend with arms a society whose privileges they wanted to enjoy, and were, at least passively, disturbers of the political cohesion of the state of Pennsylvania. The persecution of the Mormons, which effectively gives the lie to Americans who want to boast about "religious freedom," was led by holy men who wanted to stamp out competition in their business, but some part of that episode was caused by an awareness, probably subconscious in the majority, that the political consensus requisite for national survival would be gravely impaired or destroyed if the population were split into two incompatible groups, one of which believed polygamy divinely ordained while the other insisted on pretending that Christian doctrine forbade every kind of polygamy.

The principle of the separation of church and state, which was one of the bases of the Federal Constitution, has been nullified by the various states and, hypocritically, by the Federal government itself by exempting nominally religious organizations from taxation, and is nullified in practice by the strenuous political activity of virtually all the Christian and other religious sects, which, of course, is laudable when they agitate and intrigue for political ends of which you and I approve, and damnable when they use their power to oppose them, as any theologian can prove in five minutes by reciting selected passages of Holy Writ and tacitly lying by pretending that contradictory passages do not exist. The separation of church and state has proved impossible in practice in the United States, and for all practical purposes the ostensibly religious organizations have become privileged political organizations, most of which are actively engaged in subverting what little cohesion the nation once had and are furthermore avowed enemies of the race to which we and many of their members belong.

The use of religion as an expression of cultural unity and political consensus cannot long survive the first practice of toleration by which the nation's established church, whatever it is, is tacitly disavowed by failure to suppress openly dissident sects. That function of religion, once the most important of all, has, in little more than a century, been so completely forgotten that some of our contemporaries are astonished when they hear of it.

Immortality

The Greeks, being Aryans, liked to think of human beings as rational and they accordingly tried to trace social phenomena, so far as possible, to the operations of human reason. Critias (Plato's uncle) accordingly explained religion as a calculated device, invented by good minds to create a stable civilization.

Organized society is made possible only by laws to govern the conduct of individuals, but since laws can always be secretly evaded by men who conceal their crime or their responsibility for it, gods were invented, deathless beings who, themselves unseen, observe, by psychic faculties that do not depend on sight or hearing, all the acts, words, and thoughts of men. And the founders of civilization attributed to the imagined gods the natural phenomena, the lightning and the whirlwind, that terrify men. By this noble fiction they replaced lawlessness with law.

Thus far, Critias simply described the theology of Hesiod as the invention of *nomothetes*, and it is at this point that our fragment of his play ends.[4] If he went on (and I do not claim that he did), he added that when men learned by experience that they could still violate the laws secretly with impunity, the lawgivers perfected their invention by claiming that men had souls which were immortal, so that the gods, who failed to use their lightnings to punish crime in this world, would infallibly inflict terrible penalties on the guilty and condignly reward the guiltless after death. Thus they placed their civilizing fiction beyond possible verification or disproof, and provided supernatural sanctions to buttress their laws and scare their people into honesty.

---

4   It is quoted by Sextus Empiricus, *Adv. math.*, IX.55 (= *In phys.*, I.54). A good English translation by R.G. Bury may be found in Vol. III of the edition of *Sextus Empiricus* in the well-known Loeb Library.

Whether or not Critias carried his argument to its logical conclusion, it is clear that the effective use of religion as a political instrument to enforce morality required a doctrine that would promise to individuals after death the justice that the gods failed to administer in this world. This association of ideas has now become commonplace and is so taken for granted that our contemporaries often assume that a religion — any and every religion — must be primarily concerned with the provision of suitable rewards and penalties in an afterlife. This idea, however, was a startling and revolutionary one when it reached the Greeks in the sixth century BC.

The notion that a person's individuality does not wholly perish when he dies is, of course, a very old one and may be older than belief in the existence of gods. Its oldest and most elementary form, which still lingers in our subliminal consciousness, is the supposition that something of the dead man survives him and lives on in his tomb. Only later did men come to believe that the ghost of the dead migrated to a realm of the dead that was located either underground or, more poetically, in the west beyond the sunset. But the dead were phantoms, bodiless shades, doomed forever to an umbratile existence, mourning the life they had known and could never know again. When Ulysses, in the famous *Nekyia*, sailed beyond the Ocean to the sunless land, shrouded in mist and eternal twilight, he found only tenuous wraiths that were voiceless until he permitted them to lap up the blood of freshly slain sheep; and even Achilles, though he was the son of a goddess and half-divine, had become only a shadow in the gloom and could only say fretfully that it were better to be the meanest and most miserable slave among the living than king of all the dead.

Such was the immortality to which the heroes of the Trojan War could look forward — an immortality in comparison with which annihilation would have been a boon. And we may reasonably ask whether any of us today would have the courage to face such a future, to say nothing of the awesome strength to choose, as Achilles did, to die young with honor rather than live a long life of mediocrity.

It is easy to see why a promise of post-mortem comfort fascinated the minds of men and gained their allegiance to religions which promised it as a reward for obedience to a society's moral code. There were, however, two quite different conceptions of the way in which such immortality could be obtained: If, as the Homeric eschatology assumed, our present life on Earth is the only one, even the righteous man must be rescued from the common fate of mankind by some special and miraculous benefaction by gods capable of communicating to him something of their theurgic power; if, on the other hand, we assume that the dead survive by metempsychosis, we can construct an eschatology of the kind familiar to us from the Hindu doctrine of *karma*, assuming that when a man dies the spark of life within him enters another body, so that he will be reincarnated again and again forever and is doomed to repeat endlessly (and without knowing it) the peripeties and sorrows of the life we know, unless he, by exemplary moral conduct, finds a way to escape from the "grievous cycle of rebirth" and thus attain a beatific existence in a transmundane realm of enduring felicity.

The first of these alternative theories was adopted by the numerous mystery-cults of antiquity, the Eleusinian, Samothracian, Andanian, and others.

Despite the oaths of secrecy taken by the initiates and never deliberately violated, we know that the *mystae*, candidates for salvation, had to be guiltless of gross violations of the prevailing moral code, underwent a prolonged initiation into divine mysteries by the *hierophants* — (the professional holy men in charge), and were eventually "born again" through the grace of some god, usually one who had himself experienced mortality by being slain and rising from the dead. Having thus been saved, the *mystes*, sometimes a year after his first initiation, became an *epoptes*, seeing the god (or goddess) and experiencing *enthusiasm* (which, we must remember, was the state of irrationality and rapture that occurred when a mortal was literally possessed by a god). Although such hallucinations often accompany psychotic states that may in turn be provoked by extreme asceticism or overheated imaginations, the number of apparently rational persons who were initiated into the various mysteries is proof that the *hierophants* must have administered hallucinatory drugs to induce the temporary madness.

Aryans are innately suspicious of such "enthusiasm" and similar irrationality, and many of them naturally preferred the alternative.

The most reasonable and most beautiful doctrine of immortality that I have seen was stated in the matchless verse of Pindar's second *Olympian*, composed and declaimed in Sicily soon after 476 BC. When an individual has passed through three or six[5] successive mor-

---

5   Whether three or six depends on the translation of certain disputed words, which I do not know with certainty. Each of the commentators has his idea of what Pindar meant, and so do I, but the fact is that none of us can know the details of the doctrine, presumably "Orphic," that Pindar and Theron of Acra-

tal lives in which he has observed strict justice in all his actions and lived with perfect integrity, he will have emancipated himself from the cycles of reincarnation and will transcend the limits of mortality: He will pass beyond the Tower of Cronus to the fair realm that cannot be reached by land or sea, where the mildly bright sun stands always at the vernal equinox and gentle breezes from a placid ocean blow forever over the fields of asphodel. If you read Pindar, you will think all other Heavens insufferably vulgar. It would be a waste of time to talk about them.

Since we have spoken of Greek conceptions, we should remark that they and our racial kinsmen, the Norse, did not imagine an Elysium.[6] The idea of metempsychosis was not unknown, for some persons expected that a man would be reborn as his grandson or great-grandson, but it commanded little assent. A short passage in the *Hávamál* implies that death is annihilation, but that view was not widely held. The ghost of the dead man was thought to linger in his tomb or to go to *Hel*, where all were equal in wretchedness, although there is one mention of a yet more terrible abode (*Niflhel*) for the spectacularly wicked. Perhaps the most optimistic view was that brave men who die in battle are taken to the halls of Odin, *Valhalla*, where they will feast until the time comes for them and the gods themselves to perish in the final catastrophe, the *Ragnarök*.

Polytheism

If gods exist, a polytheism is the most reasonable form of religion, since it conforms most closely to the facts of Nature and does not raise the almost insoluble problem of constructing a plausible theodicy.

A polytheism assumes the existence of numerous gods, each of whom is essentially the personification of some force of Nature and may, in his or her own province, act independently of other gods in his or her relations with mortals. The gods are thought of as immortal *Übermenschen*, forming, so to speak, an aristocracy unapproachably far above mortal men, but having human character and emotions, so that their acts are readily comprehensible and involve no theological

---

gas took for granted.

6   I am aware that a paradise is mentioned in Ibn Fadlán's description of a funeral he witnessed when negotiating with the Rús on the Volga, but if the Arab is telliing the truth and did not misunderstand his interpreter, the belief, like the ceremony he witnessed, must have been exceptional.

mysteries, and it is natural to imagine them as anthropomorphic in bodily form as well as in mind, so that belief in them does not imply the paradox inherent in religions that try to imagine gods that do not look like men and women.

The members of the divine aristocracy are deathless and are far more powerful than mortals, but they are not omnipotent. As in all aristocracies the gods are not equal, some being more prominent than others, and they have a chief who has a certain authority over them but is himself bound by the social code of divinities. Jupiter/Zeus is styled *pater hominum divômque* and Odin is called *Alfaðir*, but, among the great gods, the Olympians and the Æsir, their chief is only *primus inter pares*, and while he is stronger than any one other god, his authority is limited by political realities and really depends on the voluntary allegiance of his peers. In the *Iliad*, it is clear that Zeus favors the Trojans and wants them to be victorious, and some of the other gods share his sentiments, but he and his sympathizers cannot inhibit the actions of the gods who are partial to the Greeks, and in the end, of course, it is the Greeks who will be victorious.

Each of the great gods has authority over some force of Nature, sets it in motion, and may direct it to favor or harm mortals who have pleased or offended him, but in Aryan religions — and this is most important — all the gods together are not omnipotent. They dwell in a Universe they did not create: One hymn in the *Rig-veda* specifically states that "the gods are later than the creation of the world," and in the following lines the author asks whether the world was created by giving form to what was "void and formless," and whether the creating force, if there was one, was conscious or unconscious. The gods, therefore, although they control such natural phenomena as the winds, the lightning, and sexual attraction, are themselves subject to the natural laws of the Universe, much as among men rulers have power over their subjects but are themselves subject to the laws of Nature. The Greeks and the Norse, with their mythopoeic imaginations and the tripartite modality of our racial mind, personified fate as three women, the *Moerae, Parcae, Nornir*, but their real belief was in an impersonal, inexorable, automatic force that was inherent in the very structure of the Universe and which no god could alter or deflect: *Moros, Fatum, Wyrd, Destiny*. From that causality there was no escape: Behind the capricious gods with their miraculous powers there lay the implacable nexus of cause and effect that is reality.

The gods are essentially personifications of natural forces, and like those forces they are neither good nor evil but operate with a complete indifference to the convenience and wishes of mortals, except in special cases, when some mortal has won a god's favor or incurred his displeasure. One god's goodwill or enmity toward a given mortal does not influence his colleagues: They will remain indifferent or even, if they have cause, help that man. This gives us a fairly rational conception of human life, in which, as we all know, a man who is "lucky" at cards may be "unlucky" in love and on the sea and in battle. And the religious conception, although it does admit of miracles, i.e., the intervention of supernatural beings in natural phenomena, does not too drastically conceal the realities of a Universe that was not made for man. The gods are not only the explanation of natural phenomena of which the causes had not yet been ascertained, but the conceptions of their characters, aside from a few whimsical myths, are really quite rationally drawn, although idealists, such as Plato, often miss the point.

Men always create their gods in their own image, and the gods, although endowed with supernatural powers, remain human in their minds and morality. Idealists whimper about the "immorality" of the gods and want something better, that is to say, something more fantastic, more incredible. Odin is the god of war and of an aristocracy that had a relatively high code of honor, but he is wily, for his votaries know that victory in battle depends less on sheer berserk courage than it does on strategy, which is simply the art of deceiving the enemy. Odin is treacherous, falling below the moral code of his votaries, because it is a simple fact that treachery is often victorious, and it is Odin who gives victory. That is unfortunate, no doubt, and we may wish to be morally superior to our gods, but if we claim that Odin is not treacherous, we are irrationally denying the fact that in this world treason is often so successful that none dare call it treason.

Venus is caught in adultery with Mars. Honorable wives will not imitate the goddess to whom they pray, but it is a fact, deplorable no doubt, that Helen and Paris are by no means the only example of adultery in this world, and it is a notorious fact that dissatisfied wives are apt to be especially attracted to men of military prowess and distinction. It was wrong, no doubt, of Venus to inspire Helen with love and desire for Paris, but it is a sad fact that in this world the force of sexual attraction very commonly operates in disregard of both morality and prudence. It does happen that beautiful women, even if married, are desired by, and attracted to, handsome young men, and it also happens that the young men form liaisons which, in societies that have not completely repudiated sexual morality, bring disaster on themselves and their families. If we imagine a Venus who is ideally chaste, we are lying to ourselves about the power of sexual attraction in the real world in which we live.

The ancient Aryans were often puzzled by themselves, and we, despite the best efforts of sane psychologists, find "in man the darkest mist of all" and admit that "we knowers are to ourselves unknown." Every man of letters is aware that in any creative process, such as the writing of poetry, his best thoughts usually come inexplicably into his conscious mind by "inspiration"; scientists and mathematicians confess that they "suddenly saw" the solution of a problem that long defied their most systematic efforts to solve it; and men of action, including victorious generals, have reported that they were guided by a "hunch" or "instinctively felt" which was the best of alternatives between which conscious planning had not enabled them to choose. The processes of strictly logical reasoning on the basis of ascertained data have their limitations, and the right decisions are often made by intuitive impulses that we now attribute to the subconscious mind, without being able precisely to explain them. In polytheism, thoughts which come to the conscious mind from a source outside itself are ideas injected by some god. When Achilles stayed his hand from drawing his sword on Agamemnon, he was too irate to reason that he would precipitate an irreparable division within the army that would end the Greeks' chances of victory, but an impulse restrained him: Pallas Athena, the goddess of rational activity, took him by his blond hair and held him back, and she, invisible to all but him, soundlessly told him that he should not resort to violence against the commander of the host. Needless to say, the gods, for purposes of their own, may deceive, for "hunches" are often misleading, and Agamemnon will more than once have occasion to complain that Zeus tricked him with "inspirations" that made him blunder. The psychology may seem crude, but it compares favorably with some "scientific" superstitions now in vogue.

Much may be said for polytheism, especially in Aryan religions.

There are many gods — innumerable ones, if we count the minor and local deities who preside over a fountain and make it gush now and barely trickle at another time, or dwell in a river and make it overflow its banks or subside into a rill, or are the spirits of the wildwood and inspire awe or panic in the impressionable traveler. Even major gods are too numerous to be given equal worship, despite the risks of offending some by neglect. An Aryan people, with its tripartite thought, may select a trinity of gods as deserving special honor for their functions, such as the archaic and Capitoline triads at Rome, or the triad of gods that were joint tenants of the great Norse temple at Uppsala, three specialists, as it were, who could care for most needs. If a worshipper wanted success in war, he naturally addressed Odin; if the weather and crops depending on it were his concern, he naturally turned to Thor; and if his problem was sexual, Freyr was there to help him.

Cities naturally selected a god or goddess as their special patron, the focus of their civic cults, and understood that courtesy among immortals precluded jealousy in such cases. Pallas Athena was the patron of Athens, but although Poseidon had hoped to be chosen in her stead, he did not prevent Athens from becoming a thalassocracy, while Athena was not offended by lavish rites in honor of Demeter and Dionysus. Other cities chose other tutelary gods.

The gratitude of worshippers whose prayers had been granted, and sometimes the civic pride of cities that had a local deity, often led to hyperbole that other gods politely overlooked. A few minutes with the great collections of inscriptions will enable anyone to compile an astonishing roster of gods, including even such as Osogoa, the patron of the small and declining town of Mylasa, who are enthusiastically described in Greek or Latin as *maximus deorum*, and when the Norse salute one of their gods as "most august" (*arwurðost*), they are indulging in the same extravagant emotion. The pious men and women who are moved to hyperbole because a god had heard their prayers and wrought some miracle for them are no more hypocritical that you are, when you have really enjoyed a dinner and tell your hostess it was the best you have ever had. Everyone understands such things, and no god feels slighted, while the worshipper will turn from his "greatest of the gods" to another, when he wants something in the other god's special province.

This tendency, however, may lead individuals and even tribes to an odd modification of polytheism, in which, without in the least doubting the existence and power of the other gods, they decide to concentrate their worship on one of them. In individuals this is known as monolatry, and Euripides has shown in his *Hippolytus* the dangers of carrying this tendency to the excess of slighting other deities that represent natural forces: He flattered the virgin Artemis but angered Aphrodite. Such indiscretion was very rare in the Classical world: One would naturally show special devotion to a god who had been particularly beneficent, but it would be very rash to put all of one's supernatural eggs in one basket. The practice was more common among the Norse, a number of whom selected some god as their *fulltrúi* and entrusted to him the care of all their interests, thus ignoring the division of labor among the gods.

I mention this rare oddity only for contrast to an extremely un-Aryan form of polytheism, the Jewish religion shown in what Christians call the "Old Testament." The Jews selected a god, Yahweh, who was at first content to have no competitor associated with him in a temple and worshipped in his presence ("before me," "*coram me*") but eventually demanded exclusive veneration, and entered into a contract with the tribe to assist them in all their undertakings, if they would observe all his taboos and give him, in sacrifices, a share of the profits. According to the "Old Testament," the Semitic god thus chosen for a form of religion that is called henotheism was able to beat up the gods of other peoples whom the Jews wished to exploit, such as Dagon, whom Yahweh decapitated and crippled at night when no one was looking.

Such henotheism is utterly foreign to the Aryan mind, which, as it rejects fanaticism and holy ferocity as manifestations of savagery, naturally does not attribute such jealousy and malevolence to its gods.

Chapter Three: Monotheism

MONOTHEISM is a quite unusual form of religion and one which creates difficulties for even its most adroit theologians. If it is a theism, its god must be a superhuman person, conscious and accessible to his votaries. Thus religions which posit an impersonal force, such as the Classical Fatum or the Hindu's impersonal Brahma (neuter), as the supreme power in the Universe are excluded, as are all forms of pantheism which assume that the whole Universe is a living but unconscious entity that cannot properly be called a god. And if the theism is *mono*, the God must be actually supreme and therefore omnipotent, although he need not be the only supernatural being in the Universe. Men cannot readily imagine a hermit god, so viable monotheisms suppose a god who is indeed absolute master, but has his retinue of associates, companions, and servants who obey him and carry out his orders. But he must be supreme: All other gods must be thought of as his agents, and no other god can be represented as his rival and enemy. That, of course, rules out Christianity for the greater part of its history and as described in its Holy

Book, which provides the Christian god with a rival god, Satan, and assumes that the two gods are slugging it out for mastery now, although it is predicted that one of them will eventually triumph. In quite recent years the clergy of most Christian sects have joined in killing off the Devil to make their religion a monotheism, so that, as an eminent Catholic theologian, Father Jacques Turmel, complained in the work which he published in an English translation under the pseudonym Louis Coulange, "Satan… is now like the Son of Man, of whom the Gospel tells us that He had nowhere to lay His head." But so long as Christianity supposed the existence of a god and an anti-god, it was a ditheism, and that only on the assumption that its tripartite god counted as one and that the anti-god was the sovereign of all other gods, such as Jupiter, Apollo, Venus, and Dionysus, a point on which some of the early Fathers of the Church could not quite make up their minds.

The invention of monotheism is generally credited to Ikhnaton (*Akh-en-Aton*), a deformed and half-mad king, who ruled (and almost ruined), Egypt from c.1369 to 1354 BC, and who cannot have been worthy of his lovely wife, Nefertiti, whom he later so hated that he erased her name from their joint monuments. His portraits show that he suffered from some disease or malformation that produced an enormously distended belly and heavy hips that are in painful contrast to his asthenic limbs and torso. He was a mongrel. His grandmother was a blonde Aryan, perhaps Nordic, princess, whose skull and hair attest her race. His father's features may show some admixture of Semitic blood; the race of his round-faced mother is uncertain: She could have been an octoroon or even a quadroon; and his own protruding negroid lips attest a considerable Black taint in his blood, while his oddly shaped jaw shows some clash of incompatible genes. A mind so divided against itself genetically must have matched the distortion of his body. It is quite certain that he venerated Aton, the solar disk, as the supreme god, and we must grant that heliolatry is a quite rational monotheism, since the sun is obviously the source of all life on Earth. Whether the king admitted the existence of other and subordinate gods is a question on which Egyptologists are divided, but not, as we have indicated above, crucial to his claim to be the first monotheist. There is greater uncertainty as to whether the religious innovation should be credited to his father, Amenhotep III, with whom he may have ruled jointly for a few years.

Ikhnaton's religion, for which he convulsed Egypt and forfeited her empire, must have been well-known to the contemporary Aryans on Crete and in the Mycenaean territories elsewhere, but there is no indication that they were in the least impressed by his monotheism. Some have conjectured that a tradition about him may have reached the Jews, who however, show no tendency toward monotheism until more than a millennium later, when they had quite different models before them.

The first Aryan known as a monotheist was Xenophanes (born c. 570 BC, died c. 470). He certainly repudiated the anthropomorphic gods of polytheism and posited one god, spherical because that is the perfect form, eternal, and unchanging; but we are also told that the god was an infinite sphere and identical with the Universe. Now, was the Universe conscious, and could men, whom Xenophanes thought the products of a kind of chemical reaction between earth and water, pray to the vast being of which they were an infinitesimal part? There is no evidence that Xenophanes thought they could, and I do not see how one could imagine that a man could attract the attention of the Universe. Even assuming that Xenophanes thought of the Universe as a living being (which, of course, is not unchanging), can we imagine one cell in our bodies as praying to us? My guess is that what has been called "the only true monotheism that has ever existed in the world" was, strictly speaking, atheism.[7] If there are no gods whom men can ask to intervene in human affairs, it is simply an abuse of language to call an impersonal, inexorable force 'god.' Xenophanes was certainly one of the great men in whom our race may legitimately take pride, but I do not see how we can properly term him a monotheist, although he may have influenced later Greeks to accept a monotheism.

The spread of Stoicism in the Graeco-Roman world is one of the most remarkable phenomena of history. Many have remarked on the paradox that a Semite, a Phoenician merchant in the export trade, who went to Athens on business and happened to attend lectures by one of the Cynic philosophers and who could not speak grammatically correct Greek, should have set himself up as a philosopher in his own right and, despite his alien features and tongue, attracted a large following of Greeks. And there is the greater paradox that a

---

7   Xenophanes is known only from brief quotations, paraphrases, and allusions in later writers, and there are endless controversies about many points; he was a gentleman and a poet who wrote drinking songs with conventional allusions to gods, which some determined theists would take seriously. By far the best criticism and summation of the evidence known to me is in the first volume of W.K.C. Guthrie's *History of Greek Philosophy* (Cambridge University, 1962).

doctrine which inspired the subversive agitations and revolutionary outbreaks that Robert von Pöhlmann identified as ancient Communism should have become the philosophy of the most conservative Romans. The first paradox may be explained by the fact that when Zeno went to Athens in the second half of the fourth century BC, Greece was in the midst of a prolonged economic crisis and culturally demoralized, and many of the citizens felt the morbid fascination with the exotic and alien that in our time gave prominence to "soulful" Russians and Hindu swamis. As for the second paradox, Zeno's successors so modified his doctrine that Panaetius, a Greek from Rhodes, was able to transform it into a philosophy that was attractive to Roman minds.[8]

Stoicism became for several centuries the dominant philosophy of educated men in the Graeco-Roman world for four principal reasons.

1. It claimed to be based exclusively on the observed realities of the physical world and to "follow nature," and to reject all superstitions about the supernatural. This claim was reinforced by studies of natural phenomena, such as the causes of the tides, undertaken by a few of the prominent Stoics.

2. A claim to be based strictly on reason, with no concessions to religious mysticism, and this claim was supported by a very elaborate system of logic and dialectics by which every proposition could infallibly be deduced from observed phenomena, thus providing complete certainty and satisfying minds that could not be content with a high degree of probability, which is all that epistemological limitations permit us to attain.

3. It provided social stability by guaranteeing the essentials of the accepted code of morality and stigmatizing all derogations from that code as irrational and unnatural.

4. What was most important to the Roman mind, Stoicism (as revised by Panaetius) was the one philosophy which encouraged and even enjoined men to take an active part in political life and devote themselves to service of the state and nation. Patriotism and the morality that makes great statesmen and generals were dispar-

---

8   I need not say that I am making generalizations, which I believe valid, about a doctrine that had a long and complicated history and was represented by a great many writers and teachers, who introduced various modifications of the doctrine with, of course, endless controversies. The most systematic and complete study of Stoicism is in German: Max Pohlenz, *Die Stoa* (Göttingen, 2 vols., 1948). The modest little book by Professor Edwyn Bevan, *Stoics and Sceptics* (London, 1913), can be read with enjoyment as well as profit.

aged by some other philosophical systems, especially the Cyrenaic, Cynic, and Epicurean, and virtually disregarded by the New Academy, which anticipated the methodology of modern science and represents the intellectual high tide of of Graeco-Roman civilization, but demanded a rationalism and cool objectivity of which only the best minds are capable. Everyone who has read Cicero's *De natura deorum* will remember how he was taken by surprise when Cicero, in the very last paragraph, pronounces in favor of the Stoic position, although Cicero was himself an Academic and, furthermore, cannot have failed to see which of the arguments he has summarized was the most reasonable. In that last sentence the statesman silenced the philosopher with a *raison d'état*. Stoicism, which was embraced by the majority of educated and influential men to the time of Marcus Aurelius and the twilight of human reason, was a philosophy, not a religion: It had no mysteries, no revelations, no gospels, no temples, no priests, no rituals, no ceremonies, no worship. But nevertheless, this eminently "respectable" doctrine, which extended its influence deep into the masses, was a monotheism.

The Stoics claimed that the Universe (which, remember, was for them the Earth with its appurtenances, the sun, moon, and stars that circled about it) was a single living organism of which God was the brain, the *animus mundi*. This cosmic mind ordained and controlled all that happened, so that Fate, the nexus of cause and effect (*heimarmene*), was actually the same as divine Providence (*pronoia*). This *animus mundi*, which they usually called Zeus and which some of them located in the sun, was conscious and had thoughts and purposes incomprehensible to men, who could only conform to them. Their Zeus, who, of course, was not anthropomorphic, was the supreme god, perhaps the only god. Few, however, were willing to spurn a compromise with the prevalent religions, and they accordingly admitted the probable existence of the popular gods as subordinates of Zeus, an order of living beings superior to men and more or less anthropomorphic, who were parts of the Divine Plan. They accordingly explained the popular beliefs and myths as allegories by twisting words and manipulating ideas with a sophistic ingenuity that made them expert theologians. Having made this concession to the state cults and popular superstitions, the Stoics insist that a wise man will perceive that the various gods which seem real to the populace are all really aspects of the *animus mundi*, and that there really is only One God.

Cleanthes, Zeno's disciple and successor at Athens, is best known for the eloquent prayer, commonly called a hymn, addressed to the One God, which begins "Lead me on, O Zeus!" After speaking of the majesty of the Universal Mind, he assures Zeus that he will follow willingly whithersoever the god leads him, but adds that if he were unwilling, it would make no difference, for he would be compelled to follow. This, of course, is simply Seneca's oft-quoted line, *Ducunt volentem fata, nolentem trahunt* with which, by the way, Spengler appropriately concluded his *Untergang des Abendlandes*. It makes excellent sense because we recognize in *fata* the inexorable nexus of cause and effect in the real world. We are taken aback when we find it addressed to a god, who presumably can hear the prayer, and are then assured that Divine Providence has so unalterably arranged the sequence of events that what is destined will occur anyway. A sensible man will immediately ask, *Why pray, if the prayer can make no difference?*

The Stoics have an answer. Good and evil, pain and pleasure, are only in the mind, and what makes the difference is your attitude toward events: It would be wrong as well as futile to resist the Divine Plan, no matter what it ordains for you. The only important thing is the maintenance of your moral integrity, and so long as you do that, events have no power over you. They even insist that a wise man, conscious of his moral integrity, would be perfectly happy, even if he were being boiled in oil. So far as I know, this proposition was never tested empirically, although intelligent men must often have thought that it would be an interesting experiment to put Chrysippus or some other prominent Stoic in the pot to ascertain whether the boiling oil would alter his opinion.

The Stoics insisted that since all things happen "according to Nature," i.e., Providence, there can be no evil or injustice in the world. To maintain this paradox, they had to devise various arguments, usually packed into a long sequence of apparently logical propositions, spiced with endlessly intricate definitions, some of which were mere verbal trickery that passed unnoticed in the harangue. The most plausible proposition was a claim that whatever seems unjust or wrong to us is only part of a whole which we do not see. It may be simplified by the analogy that lungs or livers considered by themselves are ugly, but may form necessary parts of a beautiful woman.

The Stoics thus constructed a theodicy that was satisfactory to them. They were, of course, intellectuals busy, as usual, with excogitating arguments to override common sense.

What we have said will suffice to show how the Stoics made

monotheism an eminently respectable creed. It became the hallmark of Big Brains.

There is much truth in an observation made by Professor Gilbert Murray in his well-known *Five Stages of Greek Religion*. Reporting the anecdote that an impressionable Greek, who had attended lectures by the Aristotelians and then heard the Stoics, said that his experience was like turning from men to gods, Murray remarks: "It was really turning from Greeks to Semites, from philosophy to religion." It is true that we know that Zeno and a few other Stoics were Semites and we suspect that quite a few others were, or perhaps were hybrids, half-Greek and half from some one of the pullulent peoples of Asia Minor that Alexander's conquests had Hellenized, but the fact is that their doctrine did enlist Aryans (there is no reason to suppose that Panaetius was not of our race) and was unsuspiciously accepted by a majority of the Greeks and Romans of the educated classes. That is what gave it prestige.

Stoicism, furthermore, was not merely an alien ideology foisted on credulous Aryans. It contained elements congenial to our racial psyche. Professor Günther has observed that Aryans "have always tended to raise the power of destiny above that of the gods," and cites the belief in an impersonal, inexorable *Moros, Fatum, Wyrd*, to which we referred above. This was approximated by the Stoics' *animus mundi* with its immutable Providence. Aryans accept the reality of the visible, tangible world of nature and instinctively reject the festering Semitic hatred of this world. "Never," says Günther, "have Indo-Europeans [= Aryans] imagined to become more religious when a 'beyond' claimed to release them from 'this world,' which was devalued to a place of sorrow, persecution, and salvation." Here again the Stoic belief that this world is the only one and that all things happen "according to nature" was consonant with our race's mentality. The Aryan belief in the unalterable nexus of cause and effect does not lead to the passive slavish fatalism, *kismet*, of Islam, but fate is, instead, a reality that the Aryan accepts manfully: "The very fact of being bound to destiny has from the beginning proved to be the source of his spiritual existence." Thus the healthy Aryan "cannot even wish to be redeemed from the tension of his destiny-bound life," and Günther quotes Schopenhauer: "A happy life is impossible; the highest to which man can attain is an heroic course of life." The Aryan ideal, Günther continues, is the hero who "loftily understands the fate meeting him as his destiny, remains upright in the midst of it, and, is thus true to himself." Compare the Stoic insistence that the maintenance of one's moral integrity is the highest good. The fatalism may seem passive, but Stoicism was in practice the creed of Cato of Utica and many another Roman aristocrat who lived heroically and died proudly, meeting his fate with unflinching resolution.

Stoicism was founded and to a considerable extent promoted by Semites, and although it included, by chance or design, much that was in conformity with the Aryan spirit and mentality, it was hybrid, a bastard philosophy, for it also contained much that was Semitic and alien to our race. As Gilbert Murray remarked, it had a latent fanaticism in its religiosity and it professed to offer a kind of salvation to unhappy mankind; despite its ostentatious appeal to nature and reason, it was a kind of evangelism "whose professions dazzled the reason." It professed to deduce from biology an asceticism that was in fact fundamentally inhuman and therefore irrational, e.g., the limitation of sexual intercourse to the begetting of offspring. Although it was the creed of heroes, we cannot but feel that there was in it something sickly and deformed.

Stoicism, furthermore, was an intellectual disaster. It carried with it the poisonous cosmopolitanism that talks about "One World" and imagines that Divine Providence has made all human beings part of the Divine Plan, so that there are no racial differences, but only differences in education and understanding of the Stoics' truth. That is why we today so often do not know the race of an individual who had learned to speak and write good Greek (or Latin) and had been given, or had adopted, a civilized name. Our sources of information were so bemused by vapid verbiage about the Brotherhood of Man that they forgot to discriminate.

Professor Murray is right in saying that Stoicism was basically a religion, but it was so wrapped in layer after layer of speciously logical and precise discourse and required so much intellectual effort to understand its complexities that it was considered a philosophy. And I think we may accept it as such on the basis of one criterion: It had no rituals or ceremonies and it had no priests. That is an important point to which we shall return later.

Chapter Four: Theodicy

THIS IS THE REEF on which founder all religions that posit a supreme and benevolent god who is interested in mankind.

The Stoics constructed for their *animus mundi* a theodicy that evidently satisfied persons who were primarily interested in ethics and desiderated a system of moral certainties to stabilize societies. The Stoic answer was like that given in the fourteenth century by William of Occam and the other Nominalists, who saw that the only escape from the impasse was to assert that whatever the Christian god ordained, was, *eo ipso*, just. The Stoic answer could not content people who wanted a god who could and, if properly appeased, would interfere with the processes of nature and make miracles for his favorites: What use was a god who couldn't do anything for you? William of Occam's answer cannot content persons who have our innate and racial sense of justice and refuse to believe that unmerited suffering, agony, and death inflicted on innocent and helpless individuals, can be right, no matter who orders it: Who can respect a god who rewards evil and punishes good?

It is the business of theologians, of course, to devise arguments and rhetoric that will confuse the issue, and the theologians of all creeds have exhibited a high degree of ingenuity, but the only way to evade the problem of theodicy successfully is to assume, as do several of the Hindu cults, that metempsychosis provides a long series of incarnations that produce a spiritual and moral evolution of the individual from the very simplest and lowest forms of organic life through ascending forms of mammalian life to mankind and then on upward to superhuman species, who reside on the moon or in some place beyond human attainment, and eventually to gods in some well-furnished heaven. On this vast scale, the suffering that comes upon any individual in any one life shrinks to insignificance and, furthermore, is condign and just punishment for the misdeeds of an earlier life and is a necessary process of spiritual purification and evolution.

If the present life is the only one we shall have on Earth it will do no good to say that divine injustice in it doesn't matter because this life will be followed by a few hundred thousand years or a few million years or even an eternity in some heaven that will be equipped to prevent its inhabitants from dying of boredom after a few dozen centuries. To our racial mind, justice does matter and furthermore it is inherently unjust to make an infinite future depend on conduct during a few years by a person who was born with certain innate tendencies and capacities and placed in situations that more or less determined how his character would respond to them.

One of the important junctures in our civilization is marked by the short treatise *De libero arbitrio*,[9] written around 1436 by Lau-

---

9   The text was well edited by Maria Anfossi (Firenze, 1934); I have not

rentius Valla, who had the most incisive critical mind of the early Renaissance. Under the transparent veil of a dialogue about Apollo's power to predict human conduct, Valla demonstrates that no god can be omniscient, omnipotent, and benevolent.

The proof is simple. Take one of the incidents, so common today, in which an obviously innocent little girl of five or six, old enough certainly to feel pain, is raped and blinded or raped and killed by one of the savages on which masochistic or sadistic British and Americans now dote. Now, if there is a god who oversees the lives of men and sparrows, did he foresee the conduct of the savage, whom he created and presumably endowed with a savage's instincts? If he did not foresee it, he is not omniscient. If he did foresee it, was he able to prevent the child's agony? If not, he is not omnipotent. If he had the power and did not use it, he willed the crime and he willed the suffering of the child, so he cannot be benevolent.

Theologians, of course, explain that if the girl had not been killed at that time, she might have grown up and become an atheist — or papa must have offended a deity who chose to take out his anger on both the innocent child and her mother (who, of course, may have done something to vex him).[10] Or we mustn't think about it, because

---

heard of a translation. Almost all scholars who concern themselves with the Humanists of the Renaissance assume that Valla could not have been so impious as to say anything that was bad for the salvation-business. It is true that at the end of the dialogue Valla says that he has proved that human reason cannot cope with the Divine Mystery, but I take that to be an anticipation of the notion of a "double truth," which enabled Pomponatius and many other philosophers of the age to affirm that they believed by faith what they had just proved to be impossible. In the fifteenth century men with inquiring minds had to take precautions to avoid being tortured to death if they annoyed the theologians. The hounds of Heaven were baying on Valla's trail often enough as it was, and once he was saved only by the intervention of King Alfonso of Naples.

10 Every such incident has repercussions on persons other than those immediately involved. Years ago, an old man, with whom I was discussing the efforts of professional holy men to attribute the coincidences that are called luck to intervention by their deity, told me that his life had been shaped by an appointment he had kept when he was a young man. He had decided to keep that crucial appointment in the metropolis by taking a train that passed through his town in the early morning. That morning his alarm clock failed to ring, and when he awoke, he threw on his clothes and ran to the station, although he knew he could not reach it in time. He was fifteen minutes late, but that morning the train, for the first time in many months, was even later: It had been delayed when it struck an automobile on a grade crossing, killing the occupants. "If I had been superstitious," he said, "I would have decided that Jesus so loved me that he killed three

thinking is bad for souls. None of these explanations will satisfy an Aryan's sense of justice.

Valla's explanation did not too greatly perturb contemporary churchmen, for Christian ditheism then attributed such things to its anti-god, who either had on this Earth a power that his celestial antagonist could not overcome or sneaked in to promote the dirty work when God wasn't looking. Everyone knew, after all, that the Devil was so powerful that he had been able to carry a third of the Christian god up to high mountains and there try to bribe him. But with the current tendency to make Christianity a monotheism, the problem has to be faced.

It is probably impossible to devise for a monotheism a theodicy that will satisfy the Aryan mind. At least, no one has done it yet.

There is one more topic that must be considered in our hurried sketch of the evolution of religions with reference to what we suppose to be the innate mentality of our race. When we speak of any religion today, we automatically think of its priests, a specialized and professional clergy. That is not a necessary connection.

Chapter Five:
Ritual and Aryan Worship

Ritual

A RELIGIOUS RITUAL is a fixed sequence of acts (often including speech) performed to make magic by influencing supernatural forces. Most rituals began at a time so remote and among men so primitive that they may antedate our race; their origins and original mean-

---

persons, a man, his wife, and their child, to enable me to keep my appointment. Or, if the train had not been late, I would have been sure that my sins had so annoyed him that he slipped into my bedroom that night and tampered with the mechanism. But that would have drastically changed the life of my wife, whom I married later, and our children would never have been born. Of course, she and I might have married other spouses, changing both their lives and our own, and each of us would have had quite different children, who would have grown up to change the lives of many others and themselves engender children. The consequences of that accident at the grade crossing are almost infinite and incalculable, for, of course, we should have to consider also the victims and the results of their death."

ings were forgotten long before the earliest written records, while the rites were perpetuated by a continuing tradition, so that even the function they were thought to serve may have changed drastically as the pattern of the ritual was handed down through innumerable generations. The process may be illustrated by a partial analogy in the development of language. As we all know, many speakers of English today, for example, will say that a man "has shot his bolt," without thinking of how long it takes to reload a crossbow; that he was "taken aback," without understanding the navigation of ships under sail; and that he "curries favor," without having ever heard of Fauvel or knowing what a *favel* is and without knowing how to curry a horse. Many persons could not think of any connection between a muscular man and a mouse, and rare indeed must be the individuals who think of the Egyptian god Amon Ra when they meet a woman named Mary.

Rituals are a common source of myths, much as one phase of the Germanic celebration of Christmas gave rise to the myth of Santa Claus, who, by the way, is a typically Aryan myth. (To anticipate a point we shall have to make later, ask yourself whether we "believe in" Santa Claus and then, would an observer come to Earth, like Voltaire's Micromégas, from a remote planet conclude that we "believed in" Santa Claus?) As everyone knows, the customs associated with Santa Claus are much older than the Christian coloring that has been given them. And finally we have an aetiological myth to explain the myth, in a story that is now having some success as an alternative to Dickens' *Christmas Carol*, a tale by an obscure writer of popular fiction who imagined that Claus was a Roman named Claudius, who was "converted" at the Crucifixion and then became the first missionary to northern countries. In a less literate age, Seabury Quinn's short story, written for a "pulp" magazine a few decades ago, would probably become an item of popular belief.

A good example of the persistence of ritual may be found in the *Thesmophoria*, the ceremony that Aristophanes so delightfully parodied in his well-known comedy. It was not an Aryan rite: It was practiced by the indigenous population of Greece when the first wave of Aryans arrived, and there are indications that for a considerable time many or most of the Greeks refused to have anything to do with the cult of the "Pelasgians" whom they had subdued. The purpose of the ritual, so far as we can determine from its performance in historical times, was to ensure that seeds planted in the autumn would germinate in the spring, but we have no idea what spirit or spirits the ritual was intended to placate or stimulate. When the Greeks took up the ritual, they decided, not unnaturally, that it must be associated with Demeter, their goddess of grain, and so they saw in the first day of the three-day ceremony a reference to her descent into the underworld. And suitable aetiological myths were produced. It is likely that the prohibition of pomegranates in the ritual contributed an important part of the myth of Persephone. The sacrifice of pigs certainly produced the myth of Eubuleus. And what was probably only a verbal similarity between the name of the secret cult objects and the Greek word for 'law and order' convinced the Greeks that the ceremony in some way commemorated the establishment of civilized society. And in our own time an anthropologist (Professor Agnes Vaughan) has elaborated a "scientific" explanation of the *Thesmophoria* that is just another aetiological myth.

Rituals are rationally inexplicable. Some, especially the cult dances of primitive tribes, may represent the "methectic collaboration with autochthonic spirits" that warms the minds of some anthropologists, but that explanation, at best, does not take us very far. When, for example, an Arval promises to sacrifice a spotless white heifer to Juno, if the goddess keeps her part of a bargain, why should Juno be interested? Oh yes, the animal is a heifer because Juno is female and her delicacy would be offended by a male offering; it is white, because she is a goddess of the world of light and a black animal would be suited only to a deity of the underworld; and it must be spotless because divinity demands what is perfect and rare. But what conceivable pleasure could Juno derive from watching her votaries banquet on *Wiener Schnitzel* while the inedible parts of the animal are burned on her altar? (The aetiological myth about Zeus's mistake is, of course, humorous and in the vein of Aristophanes' burlesque of the idea.) One can try to imagine explanations of Juno's odd tastes, but after we have discoursed about totems and theromorphic spirits and the like, we end with the conclusion that is fundamental to all religions: In this instance, the gods are pleased by the sacrifice of an animal because animal sacrifices are pleasing to the gods. Q.E.D.

Primitive rituals are comparatively simple, no more complicated than the action and pattern of a traditional Morris dance, for example. Anyone can learn the ritual by listening attentively to someone who has performed it. No technical expertise is needed to make magic in this way. Even a fairly elaborate series of rituals is no more elaborate than the ritual of a Masonic lodge, for example, which imposes so little strain on mnemonic faculties that a local barber or automobile salesman or tavern-keeper could memorize his way to exaltation as a Worshipful Grand Master or Sublime Potentate, if his finances permitted.

This is a most important point. If we restrict the word 'priest' to specialists in the supernatural, a religion of rituals requires no priests. If a priest is just a man who performs a religious rite, then, in such a religion, any person not an infant or of the wrong sex, may be a priest whenever occasion demands it.

What appears to be the native Aryan worship is therefore entirely feasible.

Aryan Worship

If we perpend the available evidence for social structure and religious practices of the Aryans when they first appear in history — the oldest hymns in the *Rig-veda*, the practices of the early Greek cults, the native religion of the Romans, what we can ascertain about the rites of the prehistoric Norse, and a scattering of corroboratory information from such sources as Tokharian and even traces in Hittite — we are driven irresistibly to the conclusion that the early and authentic Aryan religion had no place for professional holy men.

The essentials of native Aryan religious practice may be summarized in a few lines. The head of every household was its priest, who himself performed for his household such rites as the family tradition prescribed, usually or always including some *sacra* peculiar to the family line, and such other ceremonies as seemed appropriate to him. If wealthy and devoted to some particular god, he might erect an open altar or a modest temple (i.e., structure) to that deity on his own property, and the shrine would descend to his heirs in the usual way. The owner would determine whether other votaries of the god should be admitted to private property.

The tribe or the state was, in a sense, a great family and naturally had its own rites and gods to which it accorded a tribal or national worship. The rites were invariably performed by citizens, never by professionals. And, of course, the community had its own shrines and temples, which might be no more than a plot of ground in an open field or in a forest, but was usually an edifice as simple or elaborate as the community's prosperity dictated.

The rites were conducted and sacrifices performed personally by persons, selected temporarily or permanently from the citizen body, who devoted to their duties a small amount of time occasionally taken from their normal occupations, and these citizens had no assistants other than a janitor to keep the temple clean and perhaps, if inclined to luxury, a slave or temporary employee to do the more messy jobs of butchering. The *Thesmophoria* we mentioned above were rites performed by married women, and in Athens the married women, wives of Athenian citizens and necessarily also daughters of Athenian citizens, in each Attic deme selected each year two of their number, financially able to bear the modest expenses, to organize and preside over the ceremonies, in collaboration, of course, with the women elected by the other demes. At Rome, all the great priesthoods were filled by the election or co-option of men (or, where appropriate, women) from the leading families, usually Patrician families. The offices were usually held for life, but were not hereditary, and there were exceptions. For example, the priestess of the *Bona Dea* in any year was, *ex officio*, the wife of the presiding magistrate for that year. The priesthoods were high political offices and were sought as honors or for the political power they conferred.

No taint of religious professionalism appears. It is true that one of the *flaminates*, that of the *Flamen Dialis*, was hedged about with traditional taboos (the purpose of which had long been forgotten), which severely limited the political and particularly the military careers of the holder of that office: That is why the young Caesar prudently refused it. Late in the Republic some politician raised the constitutional question whether one of the other *flamens* could be prevented from taking command of an army outside Italy, but in general a Roman priest was a citizen of prominence, and no one ever imagined that he should have any religious qualification for the position, other than a suitable lineage, usually Patrician birth.

If the tribe or state had a specific ceremony for the collectivity, the priest was always, *ex officio*, the chief of the tribe, the king of the state, or a magistrate who replaced the king if the monarchy had been eliminated. In Rome under Augustus, one of the signs that the state was being gradually and almost surreptitiously converted to a monarchy was that Augustus (and his successors) became the Pontifex Maximus *ex officio*.

Aryan society doubtless included individuals who claimed some special skill in interpreting omens (one thinks of Tiresias) and religious enthusiasts. Such persons were free to communicate their opinions and might be asked for advice in perplexing situations, but they were citizens, received no emoluments, had no official standing, and could only offer advice which the king or responsible magistrate might or might not see fit to take (it was up to Agamemnon to decide whether he should pay attention to Tiresias's monitions). There were no professional holy men. No one could gain wealth or grasp power by claiming to be an expert technician of the supernatural.

In short, the evidence supports the conclusion of Professor Hans F.K. Günther: "A priesthood as a more sacred class, elevated above the rest of the people, could not develop amongst the original Indo-Europeans. The idea of priests as mediators between the deity and men would have been a contradiction of Indo-European religiosity."[11] But there are difficulties.

Georges Dumézil, a sagacious and distinguished student of Aryan religions, has identified a "tripartite" modality of thought, an instinctive grouping of concepts in units of three, as characteristic of our racial mentality; which appears in everything from our fairy stories and other fiction, in which it is always the third attempt to solve a problem that succeeds, to the grouping of gods in triads, as in the Capitoline trinity at Rome (originally, Jupiter, Mars, and Quirinus; later, Jupiter, Juno, and Minerva) and the two Norse triads (Odin, Thor, and Tyr; Niord, Freyr, and Freyja) which were reduced to the trinity worshipped in the famous temple at Uppsala (Odin, Thor, and Freyr). Dumézil finds this same tripartite pattern in a social organization consisting of warriors, priests, and commoners, thus making a priestly class a native and necessary part of early Aryan society. We may counter this theoretical objection by arguing either that the tripartite thinking did not extend to social organization or that Dumézil has wrongly identified the three elements, which could be king (or equivalent), nobility, and commoners, or even aristocracy, plebeians, and serfs. And there is the solid evidence that the earliest Aryan societies of which we have knowledge show no certain trace of a priestly caste.

The real difficulty is that no societies have been more priest-ridden than India after the Aryan conquest, where a caste of priests achieved an effective monopoly of all religious rites, and Celtic Gaul,

---

11 *Religious Attitudes of the Indo-Europeans*, translated by Vivian Bird and Roger Pearson (London, Clair Press, 1967). The question here is treated somewhat more fully in Günther's *Die Nordische Rasse bei den Indogermanen Asiens* (München, 1934) which has not been translated, so far as I know. The parts of Günther's work that are most open to question are the dating of the cult of Odin and the supposed religious toleration in Iceland, neither of which is relevant here. It may be that here and there he is not sufficiently strict in weighing data favorable to his thesis. It is true that he holds our race in high esteem, and that, I need not say, is considered very sinful today.

where the Druids had virtually unlimited power. In other Aryan societies we find a caste of professional holy men, as in ancient Persia, or a priesthood which, though not hereditary, has attained an ascendancy over the citizens and the state.

So drastic a change seems, at first sight, incredible. It seems most unlikely, *a priori*, that in India, for example, in a territory that was certainly conquered by the Aryan invaders and ruled by them, and on which they imposed their Indo-European language and presumably the culture it represented so thoroughly that all but the vaguest recollection of what had preceded them disappeared, the Aryan principalities and kingdoms should have developed a religion and a social structure that was "a contradiction" of Aryan religiosity. For this paradox, however, Professor Günther has a reasonable explanation. In all parts of the world, Aryan migrations, so far as we can discern, followed a pattern that must have been determined by our racial peculiarities. An Aryan tribe invades a desirable territory and subdues a much more numerous native population of a different race and is content to rule over them, instead of exterminating them and even their domestic animals, as the Jews claim to have done in Canaan and as the Assyrians may have done in some places. The natives, thus spared by what could be considered a biological blunder, were made subjects, but the majority of them were not enslaved or even reduced to serfdom; they and their native customs were probably treated with a measure of the toleration and protection that the Romans later accorded their subjects. The inevitable result was miscegenation, both biological and cultural. The consequence of the long and intimate association of the dominant Aryans with their subjects of a different race, Professor Günther says, was that "a spirit alien in nature," corresponding to the dilution and hybridization of the racial stock, "permeated the original religious ideas" of the Aryans and "then expressed in their language religious ideas which were no longer purely or even predominantly European [i.e., Aryan]." And he identifies certain elements in our race's mentality and especially in its religiosity, especially the lack of fanaticism, which made it particularly susceptible to the contagion of alien superstitions. What happened, in other words, was a kind of spiritual mongrelization that, in all probability, largely preceded and certainly facilitated the biological mongrelization.

We may find a small but neat example of this process in the Thesmophoria we have mentioned above. In the Peloponnesus, these rites were practiced by the native population until the Dorian invasion; thereafter, for some centuries, the ceremonies persisted only in the mountain-girt hill country of Arcadia, which the Dorians had not taken the trouble to occupy; but then the Dorian conquerors, including the notoriously conservative Spartans, begin to practice themselves the alien ritual of the Thesmophoria, giving to it a name that was at least partly Greek and associating it with their own religious concepts.[12]

The process, so clearly illustrated by the Thesmophoria, probably took place in every territory that the Aryans subdued, and the cumulative effect must have been a religious and cultural perversion that could well have produced in India, for example, even so drastic a change as the eventual subjugation of the conquerors' descendants to a caste of professional holy men. For an extreme and frightening example of what mongrelization can do to the minds of our race, we have only to consider the Guayakís of South America, who, as is conclusively shown by anthropological and especially anthropometric studies, contain a large admixture of Nordic blood and exhibit a cultural degeneracy noteworthy even among the Indian populations of that continent.[13]

These considerations, and especially our race's notorious lack of a racial consciousness and its concomitant generosity toward other races, adequately explain a corruption of its native religious tendencies, and accordingly we may accord to Professor Günther's description of our pristine religiosity a high degree of probability, although the limitations of the available data preclude certainty. We may, however, observe that it is possible to go much farther in speculations that can be no more than suggestive.

L.A. Waddell was a distinguished scholar, although his achievements and reputation have been eclipsed because his pioneer attempt to read Sumerian as an Indo-European language was as mistaken as the work of his numerous contemporaries, who were trying

---

12   There is an indubitable historical basis for this Greek tradition, first reported by Herodotus (II.171). The Greeks, naturally, had no means of knowing whence the Pelasgians (who were White, but of undetermined stock) derived the ritual or with what superstitions the Pelasgians had associated it.

13   See Jacques de Mahieu, *L'Agonie du Dieu Soleil* (Paris, Laffont, 1974); there is a German translation (which I have not seen), but none in English, so far as I know. Cf. *Nouvelle École*, #24 (mars 1974), pp. 46 sqq, Pessimists, who assume that the present direction of society in Britain and the United States will continue unchanged and have the courage to extrapolate from it, may see in the Guayakís the prototypes of what is likely to be left of our race two or three centuries hence.

to read it as a Semitic language.[14] On his misreading of Sumerian he based an elaborate reconstruction of early history that, despite the great learning shown in it, necessarily collapsed with the failure of its foundation. That does not necessarily invalidate his startling suggestion that the name of the priestly caste that worked its way to power in India, *Brāmana,* is a word derived from Semitic; that the institution of a class of professional priests in Sumeria was the work of the Semites that gradually took over Sumerian society; and that the priestly caste in India was derived from Sumeria.[15]

The etymology is probably wrong, but the suggestion is made the more impressive by the fact that Waddell in 1925 must have been prescient to anticipate that subsequent excavations would prove beyond doubt the presence in the Indus Valley of a relatively advanced civilization that flourished before the Aryan invasion and was very closely connected with the Sumerians — so closely that it is possible that the Sumerians came to Mesopotamia from the Indus Valley.[16]

---

14   We now know, of course, that Sumerian is neither Indo-European nor Semitic. The race of the Sumerians is uncertain; the possibility that they were Aryan cannot be excluded.

15   *Indo-Sumerian Seals Deciphered* (London, 1925), *passim*; *The Makers of Civilization in Race and History* (New Delhi, Chand, 1968 = London, 1929), pp. 386 sqq. If Waddell completed and published the special work promised on p. 399, I have overlooked it. I think it probable that the Sanskrit *brāhmana* is cognate to the Latin *flāmen* and is therefore Indo-European, but I need not tell anyone even casually acquainted with Indo-European philology, in which everything that is not obvious is extremely obscure, that no etymology of either of the two words is accepted by a majority of students. What is important is not the origin of the word, but of the idea that it represents. Note that there are several related words in Sanskrit that should be carefully distinguished: *brāhma* (neut.), perhaps best translated as 'divine'; *Brāhma* or *Brāhman* (neut.), the impersonal, unknowable cosmopoietic force that is regarded as the ultimate and only eternal reality; *Brāhman* (masc.), the creator god who is a member of the Hindu Trinity; *Brāhmana* (masc. with fem. *Brāhmani*), a member of the highest and most venerable caste, born holy, and first of the twice-born; *Brāhmana* (neut.), one of the commentaries on the Vedas, some of which are interesting as showing early stages of the process by which rituals were so complicated and elaborated by interpretation as to make expert assistance desirable even before the rituals were made the monopoly of experts. It is uncertain which of these words should be regarded as the one from which the others were derived.

16   Attempts to identify the civilized people of the Indus Valley as Dravidians on linguistic grounds are nugatory; on the most elaborate attempt to do so, see Arlene Zide and Kamil Zvelebil, *The Soviet Decipherment of the Indus Valley Script* (The Hague, Mouton, 1976). There are extraordinary similarities between

This suggests a question that will startle students who naïvely cling to the old notion that race is shown by geography or language.[17] What was the race of persons who contrived the establishment of priestly castes in ancient India and Persia? That the breathtaking question is not entirely idle will appear from indications that the dominant priesthoods may originally have been racial, especially the following:

The great hero of the priestly caste of Brahmans in India is Parasurāma, an incarnation of the god Vishnu and a great warrior (!), who extirpated the Ksatrias, the Aryan caste of warriors and rulers, by killing each and every member of the "kingly race" twenty-one times — a phenomenal overkill that suggests a Semitic imagination! The blessed event thus described is mythical, of course, but something did extirpate the warrior caste (unless some escaped to become the ancestors of the Rajputs (*rājaputras*) as the latter claim), and by the third century, at the latest, supposedly Aryan states were ruled by kings who were Sudras, i.e., descendants of the dark-skinned race that the Aryans, and quite possibly their predecessors in the Indus Valley, had subdued and subjected to civilization. It is probable that the ruling caste was destroyed as Aryan aristocracies always are, by miscegenation, war, internal feuds, revolution, and superstition, but the racial animus of the Brahmans' Saviour and of the Brahmans who devised and perpetuated the story is unmistakable.

The Magi, also, were an hereditary caste of holy men, who claimed lineal descent from an especially godly clan or tribe in Media. The language of the Magi and their holy books is uncertain: It may have

---

that script and the *rongo-rongo* script of Easter Island and they are too great to be coincidental; from this fact, he who wishes may evoke romantic dreams of what might have been.

17   So far as I know, not even the most advanced "Liberals" today would identify as Englishmen everyone who writes a passable English or everyone who lives in Britain, Canada, Australia, and New Zealand. Until fairly recent times, however, historians have blithely assumed that everyone who wrote in Sanskrit, at least before a comparatively late date, was an Aryan, and that everyone who lived in Rome or even in the vast territory of the Roman Empire was a Roman, unless clearly identified as of other nationality and race and this so long as the Empire lasted as a political unit and long after the Romans had become, for all practical purposes, extinct. It is true that very often — even usually — we have no means of knowing the race of an individual who has adopted a civilized name. For example, we would naturally suppose that L. Caecilius Iucundus, the wealthy banker of Pompeii, had been a Roman, if his vanity had not led him to commission the repulsive portrait that shows him to have been some intruder from Asia Minor.

been Aramaic, the Semitic tongue that was the common language of the Persian Empire (including its administration), since Persian was not widely understood by the subjects. As is well known, one of the Magi tried to grab the Persian Empire by impersonating the deceased brother of Cambyses, and when the impersonator was unmasked and killed, it was believed that he had been the leader or agent of a conspiracy of the Magi to take over the Empire, and popular indignation in the capital resulted in the famous *Magophonia*, which sounds very much like a pogrom, because the religion seems not to have been affected by it. There is no hint of a religious schism, such as that between Catholics and Protestants in Europe, and Darius himself recorded his unaltered piety in extant inscriptions. An alien caste of priests would naturally have enlisted members of the dominant race as accomplices in one way or another, and the latter could have carried on, perhaps with gratification, after their principals or superiors had been massacred. If, for example, all the Catholic priests in Italy today were massacred on religious grounds, we cannot imagine how Italy could remain a Catholic nation; but if the hierarchy and its favorites were composed of aliens — Irish, for example — and they were massacred on racial grounds, the nation's religion would not necessarily be compromised and might even be stimulated.

It is true that both the Brahmans and the Magi loudly claimed to be *ārya*, but it is not inconceivable that they began by using the word in its general meaning, 'noble, excellent,' and claiming for themselves the transcendent excellence of their holiness, extending the ambiguous word, by the verbal trickery common to theologians, to a racial signification. Nor would such a *supercherie* be impossible for clever white-skinned men of a different race dwelling among Aryans who exhibited such physical diversity, as in color of hair and eyes, as is taken for granted today. As we all know, many Jews now not only pretend to be Englishmen or Frenchmen or Americans, but, if not betrayed by too grossly alien features and if moderately discreet in their conduct, are actually accepted as such by the general populace, which exhibits the characteristically Aryan disregard of race. A comparable masquerade might not have been impossible in India and Persia.

These remarks, needless to say, are intended to suggest what speculations could be based on some neglected items in our fragmentary information about the early history of Aryan nations. If an hypothesis were based on them, it would pose some startling questions, e.g., was the caste system in India originally based, not on a distinction between Aryans and non-Aryans, but on a distinction between white and dark-skinned races? It would require a reconsideration of all the evidence for the early history of India so drastic that the very prospect would freeze the blood of a modern historian.

The speculations, furthermore, are irrelevant here. No one would contend that Aryans have not been pirates, bandits, and swindlers, exploiting their racial kinsmen; it would be absurd to ask whether they could not also have become professionals in religion!

It will suffice to have indicated the likelihood that our racial psyche, though highly susceptible to alien ideas and superstitions, is innately averse from granting power and influence to professional holy men. This may help us understand some otherwise puzzling episodes in our racial history.

Chapter Six: Shamans

WHATEVER the origin of professional priesthoods and their claim that a strange expertise is necessary to mediate between their human customers and the invisible supernatural beings that are supposed to have power over Nature, that origin was also the beginning of an interminable history of sordid chicanery, fraud, and forgery. The holy man's prosperity and even his livelihood depend on his ability, or the ability of the caste or professional organization to which he belongs, to convince ordinary mortals that he has powers they do not possess.

In the third of his *Dialogues*, Renan, speculating about the consequences of the scientific research that, even in his day, was giving governments ever-increasing power to control and coerce a populace, noted the inadequacy of religion as a means of social control. The structure of Hindu society, he observed, ultimately depended on the Brahmans' claim to have supernatural powers, including that of blasting a human being with a glance from their holy eyes. "But no human being has ever been blasted by a Brahman. He is therefore using an imaginary fear to support a mendacious creed." The Brahman's authority (and income) therefore depended on a bluff. To make his point, Renan simplified his statement by ignoring the prevalent (and non-Aryan) mentality of the masses of polyphyletic India at the time that the Brahmanic superiority was firmly established, but he has made clear by a sharp contrast the problem that confronts all professional priesthoods, whether a class of individuals without formal organization or a body of disciplined professionals directed by a person or central office that has quasi-despotic authority over them.

The Brahmans' prestige (and income) depended primarily on their theology and their supposed intimacy with, and expert knowledge of, the gods and the means of influencing them. This they augmented with stories about Brahmans, perhaps especially gifted ones (*rishis*), who, in some distant place or time, had blasted a discourteous person with a glance or impregnated a virgin by focusing his thought on her or resurrected a dead man with an incantation. Those tales edified the gullible, but there were, especially before the days of Brahmanic ascendancy, wicked individuals with materialistic tendencies who might doubt what they had not actually seen, and it was necessary to impress them. Clever and dexterous holy men found ways to do that, and thus was born the magic for which India acquired a reputation that was no doubt deserved at one time, although our own more adroit magicians regard the techniques as crude and almost childish by their more sophisticated standards. No Hindu *fakir* could compete with an ordinarily accomplished magician, to say nothing of such experts as Houdini and James Randi.

The only question is the extent of conscious fraud and deception in all religions. It is not a simple question. A well-known religious technique, which has been studied by some very competent anthropologists, is used by the Eskimo shamans. The observers have noted, by the way, that the shamans, although mentally more alert than their tribesmen, are always neurotic individuals, spiritually consumed with envy of men who are admired by the tribe for courage, skill in hunting, the virility that attracts women, or even good luck, so that the shamans are covertly malevolent toward a society that respects qualities they do not possess. They maintain their prestige by using hypnotism on the simple-minded, and by performing the less-demanding tricks of prestidigitation and illusion employed by our stage magicians. A somewhat more sophisticated stunt consists of swallowing a thin bladder that is filled with seal's blood; at the psychological moment, the shaman ruptures the bladder by contracting his abdominal muscles and vomits up a small flood of blood, thus mightily impressing with his sanctity his open-mouthed and goggle-eyed customers.

The trick is obviously a hoax and the shaman must know it, but some responsible anthropologists report that, so far as they can determine, the shaman actually believes that he is exercising a power given him by supernatural forces with which he communicates in trances. That seems incredible to us at first sight and until we remember that the shamans belong to a race that has a mentality so different from our own that we are illogical if we expect logic from them or try to set limits to what such minds may be able to believe.

Aryans, if sane, do not delude themselves when they use trickery. For example, when the little Fox girls — bored in bed and inclined to mischief — thought of a way to scare their silly mamma and their adult half-sister, shrewdly perceived the revenue-producing virtues of the spirits of the dear departed, they inaugurated one of the most successful and lucrative rackets of modern times, which kept simpletons agog for almost a century, and produced some "mediums" of really noteworthy ingenuity and dexterity — some, indeed, who imposed on such surprising suckers as Sir Arthur Conan Doyle and Sir Oliver Lodge when those otherwise intelligent gentlemen were emotionally overwrought. Now it is absolutely certain that all the successful "spiritualistic mediums," from the sub-adolescent little girls whose pranks started the craze to the individuals who are trying today to revive a discredited business, are conscious frauds who exploit the gullibility of the insatiably credulous and the sorrow of the bereaved. There have been psychopathic individuals whose hallucinations convinced them they could communicate with ghosts, but their addled minds lacked the cunning to impose on many persons.

The "mediums," however, leave us with a psychological problem of great importance, since we are dealing with Aryans. About most of the famous spook-raisers there can be no doubt: they were very adroit magicians and competent actors (or, more commonly, actresses) who cynically exploited human credulity and irrationality for profit or for the pleasure of notoriety. But the careers of some make it seem likely that they had a certain perverse sincerity. They knew that they were perpetrating hoaxes, of course, but they evidently had religious convictions and had convinced themselves that they were performing a great and pious service by so deluding others as to instill in them belief in the existence and purposes of the supernatural beings in whose reality the "medium" herself actually believed by an act of faith. Outrageous deceit may, and often does, accompany a sincere faith, paradoxical as that fact seems to a coolly rational mind. And if we do not bear that fact in mind, there is much that we will misunderstand in the history of religions.

There is another factor of very great importance that we must take into account: the hallucinatory power of many botanicals. The investigations of R. Gordon Weston have made it virtually certain that the *soma* of the Brahmans and the *homa* (*haoma*) of the Magi was the sacred mushroom (*Amanita muscaria*), which is probably the greatest single source of religious experiences, although there are, of course, many others. Incidentally, it may be worthy of note that Weston is of the opinion that the sacred mushroom was not used by the priests at Eleusis in the celebrated mysteries that gave to so many Greeks an assurance of immortality; from a cursory inspection of the records, he thinks that as many as four other hallucinatory drugs may have been used at various times.[18] Needless to say, the pious phamacopia was always a professional secret of the holy men, wherever it was used, and investigators must depend chiefly on the experiences reported by initiates, often inadvertently, since they were sworn to silence in most cults.

The hallucinations induced by such drugs partly depend on the preconceptions of the mind that experiences them; in other words, persons who have ingested the drug see, in large part, what they expect to see, usually accompanied by visual illusions of extraordinary brilliance and often beauty and perhaps auditory illusions that are in some way distorted or intensified. In other words, a person who drank an adequate quantity of *soma* for the purpose of "elevating his consciousness" to perception of a "higher world" was likely to see gods as he had imagined them, but as part of hallucinations so vivid and intense, surpassing everything in his waking experience, as to seem wonderful revelations of the supernatural. If the *soma* were administered to him without his knowledge — in a cup of ordinary wine, for example — he would probably see images drawn from his subconscious mind, accompanied, of course, by illusions so vivid that they command the credence of persons who have no knowledge of the psychagogic power of some pharmaca. Now a professional holy man who administers such a potion to his clients must (at least, if Aryan) know what he is doing, but it is quite possible that he, having himself experienced such hallucinations, is himself persuaded of their reality and believes that the sacred mushroom or whatever

---

18   See Weston's contribution to *Flesh of the Gods*, edited by Peter Furst (New York, Praeger, 1972), pp.194 *sq*. Scores of volumes and hundreds of articles have been devoted to attempts to detemine the nature of the Eleusinian Mysteries from the hints let fall by initiates who were bound by dire oaths not to disclose their experiences, but I do not recall having read one that took into account the probable use of hallucinatory drugs. Recent archaeological excavations have permitted a more accurate description of the sanctuary; see George Mylonas, *Eleusis and the Eleusinian Mysteries* (Princeton University, 1961).

other hallucinogen he is using does have the miraculous power of disclosing to mortal perception the mirific realities of a supernatural world. He may delude others, himself deluded. In the nature of things, of course, we can never be sure of the hidden thoughts and secret beliefs of any individual, and there are many circumstances in which it would be unjust to assume fraud when other explanations are not unlikely, especially when we have scientific knowledge that makes the world somewhat less mysterious to us than it was to the person whom we are judging.

Until quite recent times, the mysterious potency of the sacred mushroom and similar botanical poisons was the closely guarded secret of certain orders of holy men, who transmitted knowledge of it orally or only in enigmatic or cryptic allusions in writing.[19] Even today, we have not ascertained how hallucinations are excited in otherwise sane minds by the numerous drugs that are often designated by the offensive neologism "psychedelic."[20] We only know that they induce in the victim hallucinations that are so vivid that they seem to him as real as, or even more real than, his perceptions of quotidian reality, from which they differ so drastically as to seem supernatural.

The delusions frequently include visions of praeterhuman beings, evidently drawn from the subconsciousness of the victim.[21] In other words, the drugs induce a temporary insanity from which the victim may recover without being aware of what has happened to him, and some of the drugs, at least, if frequently ingested, bring on, by a cu-

---

19   There is thus ample justification for the method followed by John Allegro in *The Sacred Mushroom and the Cross* (New York, Doubleday, 1970), although I fear the learned and distinguished scholar sadly overworks some of his etymologies.

20   The neologism, if not an ignorant error for psychodeletic, is not only improperly formed, but even more improperly derived from *dÁloj*, 'clear, manifest,' evidently for the purpose of suggesting that fits of insanity "expand the mind's awareness" or make visible a "higher reality." This hoax naturally pleases, in one way or another, the numerous and diverse gangs that have vested interests in promoting superstitions about a "spiritual world" or in inhibiting rationality in our people.

21   In one case, a university student in his mid-twenties, having ingested a synthetic hallucinogen of great potency, lysergic acid diethylamide tartrate, fled in panic down a street until he encountered a middle-aged woman, whom he wildly implored to save him from the demons who were pursuing him. He was said not to have been superstitious when sane, but it is likely that his subconscious mind retained stories about devils and fiends he had heard in his childhood or even later.

mulative effect, a permanent mental alienation. We also know of various psychopathic conditions that involve continuous delusions, less spectacular, it is said, than those evoked by drugs, but more or less permanent, and deform only a part of the mind, so that these forms of madness do not preclude a forced rationality of conduct and are often accompanied by a very high degree of cunning. Persons suffering from these mental diseases or deformations may not seem insane to their contemporaries and may acquire prestige as prophets and the like. While they often employ fraud and deceit, the delusions from which they suffer cannot be classed as intentional.

We must often remain in doubt about prominent figures in the history of religions, even in recent times. Emanuel Swedenborg was a man of the highest intellectual ability, eminent as one of the greatest and most versatile men of the eighteenth century: he wrote Latin verse of exceptional merit; was a mathematician of note; was brilliant as a civil and military engineer; was an influential member of the Swedish House of Nobles and distinguished for his studies in political economy and mercantile theory; was an expert on metallurgy and mining; made discoveries in palaeontology, optics, physics, chemistry that anticipated discoveries made a century after his work in those fields had been obscured by his later activities; and was a pioneer in studying the structure and functioning of the human brain. There was no scientist more distinguished in the Europe of his time. It is true that he had religious interests and tried to ascertain how the brain was controlled by the soul, but this cannot explain why, in 1745, when he was fifty-seven, he was suddenly accosted by various angels, who gave him a Cook's tour of Heaven and Hell, and introduced him to "God, the Lord, Creator and Redeemer of the World," who gave him a commission to save mankind from the bloody piety of the various Christian sects then still engaged in perpetual war to extirpate heresy. Anyone who reads the nine volumes of his *Arcana coelestia* and its infernal sequel will be impressed by the ingenuity with which the author uses the theological device of allegorical interpretation no less than by the wild phantasmagoria of his hallucinations. Now Swedenborg, who had a high and evidently deserved reputation for personal integrity, was too famous to have sought notoriety, and neither sought nor obtained profit. So we remain suspended between the three possible explanations: (a) he perpetrated a calculated and brilliant hoax in the hope of ending the religious antagonisms that were still squandering the blood and energy of Europe; (b) he, perhaps inadvertently, ingested some extract of the sacred mushroom or a comparable drug that induced hallucinations he mistook for actual experiences; or (c) his mind, overheated by speculations or debilitated by premature senility, lapsed into one form of insanity.

For men such as Swedenborg, ancient or modern, one must feel sympathy and a certain respect, however we explain their activities, but there are not many of them. Throughout history, with a melancholy consistency, holy men have been imposters and swindlers, differing only, it would seem, in skill and sophistication. But our contemporaries seem to regard mention of that fact as a social impropriety, if not an obscenity.

Perhaps no archaeological find in the Western Hemisphere is more famous than the colossal heads, nine feet high, skillfully sculptured in hard basalt, that were unearthed at La Venta in Tabasco. Commonly assigned to various dates between 800 BC and 350 BC, they enter prominently into every discussion of early navigation from the Mediterranean to the Gulf of Mexico and are a prime datum in every theory concerning the race of such visitors to the Western Hemisphere and the cause of their coming; and even apart from such controversies, the heads naturally excite curiosity in themselves. Most of the references to them, however, omit the datum that in the central head a small tube was patiently bored through the basalt from the mouth to a point behind the ear as a speaking-tube for the convenience of a priest, who thus communicated the Word of God to his True Believers, whoever they were.

The promotion of holiness often demanded devices more ingenious than speaking-tubes, and inspired a great variety of mechanical, acoustical, and chemical contrivances. Even our scanty sources on thaumaturgic technology in the ancient world describe some of them. Hero of Alexandria, in his famous essay on mechanics, shows the construction of a number of miracle-making machines, but we know that even more elaborate ones were in use in various temples to show the ways of god to man. Unfortunately, we do not have a description of the apparatus that was used to make gods and other supernatural beings appear on a wide curtain of smoke or vapor, but an optical lens must have been used. Manifestations of divinity were not limited to temples. A common procedure was to take a pious person to the middle of an open field on a moonless night when some deity, such as Hecate, was scheduled to be passing by; the sucker was warned to keep his head covered and not to look on divinity, but he, of course, always risked a glance when the holy man's concealed accomplice set fire to a falcon or hawk that had been covered with tow and pitch or doused in petroleum; the anguished screaming of the blazing-bird as it flew frantically away always helped instill the fear of god and suitable generosity in the worshipper.

It would be a waste of time to multiply examples of religious techniques in the Classical world amid the first great civilization of our race, but we may mention one measure of its decline. Livy knew from his sources the secret of the miraculous torches that were carried by hysterical females during the Bacchanalian craze, excited by a Greek-speaking evangelist in 186 BC, but in the second century, Suetonius, Cassius Dio, and Pausanias mention chemically similar miracles without indicating that they did not believe them to be of supernatural origin. One hopes those authors were not so credulous, but they lived in a century in which both reason and our race were nearing their end in the mongrelized Empire that was still called Roman.

Where the skill to perform miracles is lacking, visual demonstration must be replaced by appeals to the imagination. The arts of oratory and creative writing, with rhetoric nicely adjusted to the comprehension and prejudices of the audience, can produce an effect almost as strong, and have the great advantage that they can bring forth in the mind of the hearer or reader marvels that could not be performed on even the most elaborately equipped stage. Nothing is more persuasive than narratives purportedly by eyewitnesses of miracles, preferably supported by theological pronouncements made by a divinely-inspired prophet or by the god himself.

A student of religions must carefully distinguish between myths and the kind of compositions that we may call gospels. Among Aryans, myths do not purport to be history and are not so considered by intelligent adults, whereas gospels purport to be veracious and accurate reports of events that actually happened and of words that were actually uttered.

The Homeric poems are sometimes called "the Bible" of the Greeks. The epithet is grossly misleading. The two epics were indeed the writings that every literate Greek read, but he did not imagine they were history. He knew they were poetry. He knew that the Trojan War had taken place, and he believed — more or less — in the existence of the gods Homer mentions and was willing to believe that the Greek gods had been active, some on the Greek side and some on the Trojan, for he did not have the irrational fanaticism to suppose that the war had been a contest between right and wrong or that there were evil gods. But he knew that Homer had not been present at Troy and had never known anyone who had been. The poet had worked from uncertain and often conflicting traditions, from which he had selected the ones that suited his purpose, and these he had arranged and elaborated with details that were as much his own invention as the hexameters themselves. The epics were beautiful and memorable descriptions of what might have happened, but no one was obliged to believe they were truthful. An intelligent Greek believed the *Iliad* and *Odyssey* much as we believe *Hamlet* or *King Lear* or *The Tempest*. They were literature.

The Greeks intelligently understood that all the stories about their gods were myths. No one knew — no one could know — what had actually happened. The gods probably existed, and certain traditional rituals and ceremonies were thought to propitiate or please them, and their intentions might be learned from certain oracles; furthermore, persons of extraordinary ability and achievement doubtless enjoyed divine favor and might trace their lineage to heroes, that is, to the children of gods by mortals. But no one could possibly know whether Zeus had abducted Europa or Perseus had slain the Gorgon and rescued Andromeda or Hercules had saved Alcestis from Thanatos. And since no one could know what had happened (if anything!), every poet, every story-teller was free to reshape the story in accordance with his own artistic instincts and his purpose in writing.

The same reasonable attitude appears in the Norse myths. The gods probably exist, and one should perform the traditional ceremonies in their honor, unless one is prepared to take the possible consequences of failing to do so. The *Völuspá* may well be right and it mirrors our *Weltanschauung* and essential pessimism, but, after all, no one can be sure that the sibyl was right or has been reported correctly. As for the *Rígsþula*, one would have to be feeble-minded to suppose that the story of Heimdall was intended to be believed:[22] It is, on the very face of it, a fantasy on the theme, (probably historical) that the primitive inhabitants of Scandanavia were Lapps, who were subdued by a migration of brown-haired Aryans, who were in turn forced to accept the mild overlordship of a band of blond Nordics. When the skalds recited their verses before a Norse chieftain and retinue of warriors, the listeners, who must have had a high native intelligence,[23] knew that the skald was inventing a large part of his story

---

22   Who could seriously believe that a god created mankind by visiting existing households and in some way influencing the offspring of his host and hostess?

23   The auditors, most of them illiterate, must have had both memories that

about the gods and heroes, and, what is more, many of the episodes were designedly humorous and intended to provoke laughter.[24]

To the Aryan mind, at least, myths differ *toto caelo* from gospels: the former are exercises of the imagination; the latter purport to be history.

Chapter Seven: Lying for the Lord

WHEN PROFESSIONAL PRIESTS undertake to bolster the faith of their congregations by producing historical documents to substantiate their doctrines they face obstacles that are inversely proportional to the ignorance of their customers. The production of a passable forgery demands precise and exacting labor, and what usually happens is that the holy men, whether actuated by a high-minded yearning to disseminate their own faith or by a natural wish to augment their income, do only enough work to impose on their immediate audience. It is an odd fact, however, that if they have a nucleus of fanatical followers, they can enlist their services and skills in manufacturing a hoax to spread the glad tidings. Even so, however, success will depend on the general level of intelligence in the group or community to be evangelized.

One of the most interesting illustrations of this rule may be worth a paragraph or two here.

As everyone knows, Pythagoras, who was born on the Greek island of Samos early in the sixth century BC but may not have been

---

retained an enormous oral literature and extraordinary mental agility to understand the skald's kennings, i.e., the designation of common things by elliptical allusions, many of them invented by the skald as part of his poetic technique. A modern reader, even if he has read a fair amount of Norse literature, is likely to be nonplussed by suchexpressions as "the brandisher of Gungnir" (=Odin), "the burden of the gallows" (=Odin), "Kvasir's blood" (=the art of poetry), "Ymir's blood" (=the ocean), "the speech of the giants" (=gold), "the price of the otter" (=gold), and hundreds of similar expressions, Without Sturluson's description of the art and modern commentaries based on his, we should be hopelessly at sea. But the skald's audience was delighted by his wit.

24   Occasionally we are frankly told that given sagas were "good entertainment" (*góð skemmtan*) or were recited "for amusement" (*til gamans*). The question is how many of the episodes that seem so grotesque to us in the adventures of the gods were taken seriously by the audience and how many were what we call "comic relief"?

an Aryan, was both a philosopher and the founder of a Puritanic cult, of which the doctrine may or may not have been largely derived from the religions of the Oriental lands which he was said to have visited. His sect was roughly comparable to the Masonic lodges today, since members had to undergo a fairly trying and expensive initiation before they were admitted to secret doctrines they had sworn never to reveal to outsiders, but there was the important difference that the Pythagoreans admitted women to equality with men. Everyone who has been in Rome has visited the subterranean basilica under the railroad tracks that converge on the central station, and, while express trains roared overhead, has stood in the hall in which, two thousand years ago, pious Neopythagoreans assembled for worship and earnestly contemplated the transcendental meaning of the allegorical figures sculptured in stucco on the walls. Pythagoras had, of course, been equipped long before with the usual paraphernalia of divinity, a virgin birth, a god (Apollo) as father, and an odd identification as an incarnation of his own father, who had taken on a mortal body to instruct his elite in the ways to salvation and a blissful immortality by proper conduct in their successive lives on Earth.

Almost two centuries before that basilica was constructed underground, the Neopythagoreans at Rome made a remarkable effort to increase their influence or, perhaps, disseminate their faith. Two stone chests, about eight feet long and four feet wide, were carefully made, sealed with molten lead, adorned with incised inscriptions in both Latin and Greek, and buried in a spot where a farmer, ploughing more deeply than usual, would find them. One of the chests was, according to the inscription, the coffin of Numa Pompilius, the legendary successor of Romulus and second King of Rome, who, according to tradition, had established the official religion of Rome. That chest was empty, doubtless on the theory that Numa, having been a pious prophet, had ascended to Heaven to join his divine relatives. The other chest contained seven books in Latin and seven in Greek, written by Numa to describe the true structure of the Universe, as it had been revealed to him by Pythagoras, and the true religion, which he had established at Rome and which, as everyone who read his holy books could see, differed enormously from the corrupted and perverted practices of the time at which the farmer, perhaps by divine instigation, had uncovered the chests. Precisely what Numa's precious words ordained, and what political purposes lay behind them, we do not know,[25] any more than we know to what ethnic groups

---

25 For one conjecture about the contents, see A. Delatte's article in the

most of the members of the Pythagorean lodges at Rome belonged. Numa's books, by the way, had been perfectly preserved, because he had taken the precaution of saturating the papyrus with oil of cedar to preserve them through the centuries.

In 181 BC, the Roman aristocracy was still preponderantly Aryan, rational, and hard-headed. When they learned of the providential discovery, they were not deceived by the forgeries. Discounting the chances of human bodies floating heavenward, they knew that some remains of a corpse would be left in a sealed stone casket, even after five centuries. Oil of cedar would not have preserved papyrus so well for so long a time, and there were doubtless other signs of forgery.[26] The aristocracy regarded one religion as intrinsically as good as another, but they recognized the devastating effects of religious agitation and emotionalism on the lower classes and on excitable females and "intellectuals" in their own class. The religiously incendiary books were accordingly burned. Whether copies of them were surreptitiously kept is unknown, but the faith of the Pythagoreans at Rome seems not to have been shaken, for Cicero, in the second book of his *De republica*, thought it worth while to point out, *ob iter*, that it was chronologically impossible for Numa to have been a disciple of Pythagoras.

The difficulty of providing religious documentation may be further illustrated by two of the most recent Christian gospels, each of which is instructive in its own way.

When Joseph Smith, an enterprising young man in Palmyra, New York, found that swindling farmers by claiming that his magic stone monocle enabled him to see buried treasure underground resulted in unpleasant experiences in court, he turned his fertile mind to higher things and manufactured a whole new "New Testament" with the aid of an obscure book that had been published in a small town in Vermont some years before, and (probably) the manuscript of an unpublished novel, and (certainly) his thorough knowledge of the diction and contents of the English Bible and his own lush imagination. With the aid of his stone monocle, now put to godly use, he was able to translate into Biblical English the fifteen books of his supplemental scriptures from the hieroglyphics inscribed on massive gold

---

Bulletin de l'Académie royale de Belgique, Lettres, 1936, pp.19-40.

26   Our sources (principally Livy and Seneca) do not inform us whether the devout Pythagoreans tried to reproduce the Greek and Latin scripts that were appropriate to the time of Numa or the orthography, which, especially in Latin, would have differed greatly from that with which they were familiar in their own time.

plates, which an obliging angel prudently carried off to Heaven as soon as he had completed his inspired task. Smith found a few perjurers, mostly members of his own family, who were willing to swear they had seen the gold plates before they were removed to God's city in the welkin. Later, when Smith decided to write a "Book of Abraham," he tried for greater verisimilitude, but was less cautious. He procured part of one of the cheap papyrus copies of the Egyptian *Book of the Dead* from the wrappings of the Egyptian mummies that were being used at that time for fuel on the Nile steamboats, and exhibited it to the gawking True Believers as an autograph manuscript, the crudely drawn hieroglyphic text being one in which he could recognize Abraham's own handwriting. On the basis of a drawing of the dead Osiris, which is usually found in such copies, Smith elaborated a fantasy about how the priests of the Egyptian Pharoah in Chaldaea (*sic*), after sacrificing a bevy of virgins, thought of popping young Abraham onto the altar in the posture shown by the picture with which Abraham had illustrated his holograph. This naturally called for prompt action by the Lord God, and the tale came to a happy ending. Now Smith was so reckless that he not only preserved the papyrus (which, after his death, was presented to the Metropolitan Museum as a priceless treasure by a True Believer with more faith than education) but had the tell-pictures, with only the head of Anubis crudely redrawn, copied on wood blocks and printed with the text of his latest holy book to impress the yokels. The only reasonable explanation of such astounding indiscretion is that Smith was interested only in enjoying his eminence (and other men's wives) during his lifetime, and cared not at all what would happen to his sect after his death.

Smith had a shrewd successor and thus became the founder of the most cohesive and strongest Christian church in the United States, which has survived frantic persecutions by competing holy men and their followers, and almost succeeded in establishing a country of its own in what is now Utah. The major Mormon sect has more than three million members in the United States and at least a million in other parts of the world. The three minor sects, products of various schisms, probably number no more than two hundred thousand all together. And we should note that the members of the Mormon Church in its earlier days were almost exclusively, and still are predominantly, of English ancestry.

Another recent gospel-writer is a pleasing contrast to the Prophet of the Latter-Day Saints. One cannot avoid the impression that the prime object of Joseph Smith's devotion was Joseph Smith, and it must require much Faith to like him, but the Reverend Mr. William Dennis Mahan is a sympathetic figure, a man whom we must respect for a deeply sincere Christian faith and his effort to defend it. I confess that I was prejudiced against him when I began to look into his career, but I ended by liking and pitying the man. He was an ordained Presbyterian minister, born in 1824, and in 1879 he was the poorly-paid pastor of the local church in Boonville, a little town, scarcely more than a village, in central Missouri. For years, from his scantily-furnished parsonage in the boondocks, he had watched with sorrow and dismay as infidels, especially Colonel Ingersoll, blasphemed against his god and excited doubts that caused many of Jesus's sheep to stray from their folds. And then in 1879, Ingersoll expanded one of his famous lectures, "The Mistakes of Moses," into a book of 270 soul-destroying pages and published it. For years, America's most eminent divines had screeched at the eloquent Beelzebub from their opulent pulpits and preached jeremiads about the apostasy of a nation in which it was not possible to flay Ingersoll alive or, at least, cut his tongue out — but they had appealed to god and man in vain. So poor Mahan girded up his loins to defend his faith. Mahan published *A Correct Transcript of Pilate's Court*, a precious historical document that he had obtained from the Vatican through the good offices of an itinerant German scholar, whom he had befriended when snowbound in Missouri twenty-three years before. The book created a sensation and was promptly pirated by clergymen throughout the nation. In 1883, Mahan started all over, and produced a much-improved version of the document, now called the *Acta Pilati*, and supported it in the following year with a whole passel of historical records that conclusively established the truth of the "New Testament," including "Jonathan's Interview with the Bethlehem Shepherds," "Gamaliel's Interview with Joseph and Mary," the authentic "Reports of Caiaphas to the Sanhedrim" concerning (a) "the Execution of Jesus" and (b) "the Resurrection of Jesus," the speech given by Herod before the Roman Senate when he was prosecuted for his "conduct at Bethlehem," and other equally precious documents, making a total of sixteen. And then, of course, there were letters from strangely named European scholars who had helped Mahan find these treasures in the Vatican and the "Library of St. Sophia" in Constantinople, and letters from other scholars authenticating those letters. To this collection, Mahan gave a title too long to be quoted here, but some of the later publishers brought it out under the odd, but concise title *The Archko Volume*.

This collection enjoyed a considerable success; I do not know how often it was published and have not tried to find out, but I have noticed fourteen editions between 1884 and 1942, including some by Eerdmans, one of the most prominent religious publishing houses in the United States. The report from Pontius Pilate to Tiberius has been the most popular item in the collection and frequently reprinted separately, most recently, to my knowledge, in 1974, when the clergyman who published it claimed that his "transcription" had been verified from the original by the British Museum! I should not fail to mention a remarkable edition printed on a long strip of oilcloth attached to small wooden cylinders with projecting umbilici to resemble an ancient papyrus volume.

One feels sorry for Mahan. He was a poor man, and although he made some money from his first hoax, despite the pirating by brother clergymen, he had to borrow $150 from a bank so that he could hide out in a village in Illinois called Rome to prepare his greater effort and to permit his wife to aver that he had gone to Rome, whence he was sending her letters regularly. He had so little experience of the world that his account of his voyage to Europe, his meeting with "Dr. McIntoch" and "Dr. Twyman" of the "Antiquerian (sic) Lodge, Genoa, Italy," their researches in the Vatican and St. Sophia, etc. would be ludicrous, if it were not pathetic. He was an ignorant man, knowing only what he had learned in a Presbyterian seminary and probably without even the most elementary works of reference at hand. He seems not even to have known that the early Christians had forged quite a variety of letters from Pilate to Tiberius or Claudius, reports on the Crucifixion from a Roman consul to the Senate, and letters written by Jesus and the Virgin Mary, and scores of other documents from which he could have assembled quite a bouquet of sacred blossoms, for which he could plausibly have claimed a respectable antiquity and exhibited texts in Latin or Greek. The great weakness of his imposture was that he had only English "translations" to show. The Reverend Mr. William Overton Clough, who was one of the first of the holy men to pirate Mahan's work, translated parts of it into Latin to make it seem more authentic to his readers, but Mahan evidently could not do as much. Mahan's compositions are filled with wild anachronisms and grotesque errors of every kind, which only the eye of Faith could overlook, but he did his best for his religion, and perhaps that best required hard labor. And he undoubtedly did succeed in bolstering the faith and warming the emotions of many thousands of Christians who read his books.

There is no indication that Mahan sought profit or notoriety. There is evidence that he was a sincerely devout Christian and, unlike so many of Jesus's shepherds, truly believed in the religion he professed. He tried to defend it when clergymen more learned and more prosperous than he failed to confute the infidels. And given his attachment to his faith, I see something tragic in his declaration in his edition of 1887: "I have as much reason for believing the genuineness of the contents of this book, as I have to believe the genuineness of the Scriptures, looking at the question from a human standpoint."

The way of the forger is hard, and poor Mahan attempted the impossible. A book recently published in England purveys a revised Christian doctrine, including the claim that St. Paul, instead of wasting much time in the Mediterranean, hot-footed it to London to announce the glad tidings to his fellow Anglo-Saxons on the site of St. Paul's Cathedral, which, however, he is not credited with building. This is doubtless a doctrine that will be attractive to many Christians, but to be really effective, it would require the corroboration of a suitable gospel or, at least, an 'Epistle to the Britons' opportunely discovered. But that can't be done. There are probably a score of scholars in the world (I am not one) who could compose to specifications a gospel or epistle in the somewhat peculiar dialect used by the writers of the letters now attributed to Paul. I hope that none could be hired to do it, but if a linguistically sound forgery were produced, it would be impossible to manufacture papyrus that could pass for ancient, and while a case could perhaps be made for a use of parchment in remote Britain, I doubt that it would be possible to prepare and chemically age parchment that would not betray its modernity, if subjected to rigorous tests. Ancient ink could probably be duplicated, but then we would face the enormous task of finding an expert palaeographer who could, after months of practice, simulate a script appropriate to the supposed date. Then we should have to manufacture an hermetically sealed container, indistinguishable from an ancient one, in which the document would have been preserved. And if that were done, it would still be necessary to plant the container somewhere — in the ground or in the wall of a building — and the techniques of archaeology are now so refined that there is no chance of a planting that would not immediately be identified as a hoax. And even if all these obstacles were overcome — and that would be the greatest of miracles — there would remain the radioactive isotope of carbon that would betray the date of the very best forgery!

Lying for the Lord is a normal exercise of piety, but it is becoming harder and harder.

Chapter Eight: Theoktony and Belief

Theoktony

IN CONCLUDING this highly, and perhaps excessively, condensed prolegomenon, we must notice a fact of the utmost importance in the history of religions. There is a relatively high mortality rate among the immortals.

The basis of all religions is a belief that there are gods who control natural phenomena and can be persuaded to use their power for the benefit of their votaries when placated by rituals and prayers. But what happens when the approved methods prove inefficacious?

Some tribes of American aborigines end periods of drought by performing methectic dances to stimulate the rain-spirits to action. Observers report that the dances frequently produce the desired effect, since, in well-run tribes, they are performed when the old men sense an impending change in weather. Christians, by the way, are less circumspect and often pray for such benefits unseasonably. One remembers the *bon mot* of the young Duke of Clarence who later became King William IV. At a church service at which the clergymen were exhorting Jesus to make rain, he remarked *sotto voce* to his entourage, "Egad, it won't work while the wind's in the southwest."

Any respectable theologian can produce offhand a dozen explanations why gods remain obdurate in any given case, and worshippers, like gamblers, are not discouraged by a few failures, since they hope they will hit the divine jackpot the next time. Constant disappointment, however, leads polytheist worshippers to transfer their supplications from an obdurate god to one untried, and when accumulated experience engenders doubts about the goodwill of several gods, they welcome new ones, who may be more amenable to persuasion. This undoubtedly accounts in large part for the loss of popularity suffered by many gods and eventual changes in a people's pantheon. One is reminded of the Norse who, when the northern peoples were being solicited by Christian missionaries, remarked that since Odin had done nothing for them, they would try the new god. Some students believe that at an earlier date Odin had supplanted Tyr for the same reason.

A powerless god is a contradiction in terms, and when a god's impotence is spectacularly demonstrated, he ceases to inspire awe and worship. When the Christian sect headed by the Fathers of the Church shrewdly acquired influence over the despots of the decaying empire that had once been Roman, Christian mobs began to plunder the homes of wealthy citizens in some cities and to pillage and destroy the shrines of the gods whom the Christians hated. That was by far the most effective Christian propaganda. The "pagans," as the clever Fathers of the Church called them,[27] naturally reasoned that if their gods were unable to protect the stately and beautiful temples that had been built in their honor and adorned with the irreplaceable masterpieces of the world's greatest artists, those gods must be less powerful than the god of the religion that was so steadily taking over the government of the state. As temple after temple throughout the world was defiled and destroyed by the rioting mobs, it required great faith in Symmachus and the other members of the "pagan aristocracy" to remain true to their ancestral creed, and perhaps they could not have done so, had not some of them thought of attributing to the impiety of the Christians the disasters that were accumulating upon the dying empire as it yielded ever more and more to the virile barbarians from the north, who must be the instruments of the outraged gods. It will be remembered that since the Fathers of the Church had not yet gained control of the state's police powers and army to begin persecuting in earnest, Augustine had to try to answer that argument with his famous *De civitate Dei* and to prod one of his followers, Orosius, into compiling a distortion of history, now remembered because it contains some fragments of ancient historians whose works were lost. And when the Fathers finally could use the army for ruthless persecution, they not only stamped out the worship of the discredited gods but acquired a theological argument that was irrefragable and even more effective than the terrorism of fire and sword in destroying the competing Christian sects. The congregations of those sects naturally reasoned that the Christian god must have approved the theology of the Fathers to grant them such power. There is truth in the American proverb that nothing succeeds like success.

The converse phenomenon may be seen in Christian Europe during the sixteenth and seventeenth centuries. The schism that fractured forever the unity of Christendom was essentially religious and appeared to both sides as the work of the anti-god, although

---

27   On this ingenious device in propaganda, see below.

opinion was naturally divided as to whether the Devil had inspired Luther and the other heresiarchs or had been put on the defensive by attacks on the Church which he had thus far controlled. The result was the long series of Wars of Religion, as the True Believers on each side rallied to the support of their beleaguered god and enthusiastically butchered millions of their fellow Aryans, sacked great cities, and made waste lands of rich provinces *ad maiorem gloriam Dei*. But after two centuries of godly slaughter and destruction, the zealots on both sides had to stop in sheer exhaustion, and each had to concede that God had been either unable or unwilling to help them exterminate the servants of Satan. That admission necessarily undermined their faith, and the agnosticism and atheism that had theretofore been the secret belief of a very few learned men gradually spread to ever wider circles. We are reminded of the Icelandic chieftain who, as the *Hrafnkels Saga* tells us, was specially devoted to Freyr, to whom he built a temple and consecrated the prized stud-stallion that, by the god's power, was engendering a superior breed of horses. When his enemies destroyed the temple and cast the stallion into the sea, the chieftain concluded that there were no gods and religion was only a grand hoax. The Wars of Religion, even more than the steady advance of scientific knowledge in the eighteenth century, accounted for the mounting wave of scepticism and incredulity that was checked only when the ferocity and horrors of the French Revolution demonstrated, as Gibbon said, "the danger of exposing an old superstition to the contempt of the blind and fanatic multitude."

There is another factor, however, that must not be overlooked when we are dealing with our race, of which a major characteristic is the capacity for objective thought, which Professor Haas terms the philosophical mentality and which has made possible what we call science, which is simply the systematic investigation of natural phenomena to ascertain their natural causes. It begins, as everyone knows, with the earliest Greek philosophers and especially with Thales, although some scholars now question the tradition that he, at so early a date, not only understood the cause of eclipses but had sufficient data to predict them accurately. However that may be, when the physical causes of natural phenomena are ascertained, the power of the gods is thereby contracted.

In 168 BC, L. Aemilius Paullus ordered an assembly of his army to listen to a lecture in which C. Sulpicius Galus explained the causes of eclipses and why he knew that an eclipse of the moon would occur at a stated hour on the following night. Thus did Aemilius, a sagacious general, avert the panic or dismay that would have destroyed the efficiency of the legions with which, two or three days later at Pydna, he broke a Macedonian phalanx in an open field and thus assured the supremacy of Rome in the civilized world. Aemilius, a sagacious Roman aristocrat, had no wish to impair the religiosity which he deemed the irreplaceable basis of an ordered society, but, of course, he did so. In the minds of the common soldiers, one large and important province was taken from the gods and restored to the nexus of cause and effect that governs the real world and with which no god can tamper.

From Thales to the present, interrupted only by a long relapse during the Dark Ages, the growth of scientific knowledge has steadily forced the gods to retreat from the real world into an invisible world of the supernatural, out of time and space, with consequent loss of their powers of imminence. In 1902, when the eruption of Mt. Pelée, so vividly described by Edward Dieckmann Jr., in his *Volcano Mondo* (Los Angeles, Pinnacle, 1977), devastated a tenth of the island of Martinique, including the capital city, the clergy, whose colleagues in St. Pierre had been praying diligently ever since the volcano showed signs of activity, were much embarrassed. They did not dare to claim that Jesus had incinerated more than fifty thousand persons, including the pious who had taken refuge in his cathedral, so they had to concede that the phenomenal firestorm had been due to natural causes, and the best they could do was exploit the coincidence that in the ruins of the totally destroyed cathedral one sacred image was found unbroken. That, they claimed, proved that Jesus had belatedly intervened to save the garish statue while he obviously paid no attention to his most pious votaries and even made no effort to save his own consecrated priests. But with persons capable of even a modicum of reflective thought, that extemporized proof of divine activity did more harm than good to their faith.

We must not forget that the retreat of the supernatural is in accord with the innate propensities of the Aryan mind, shown by the universal Aryan belief in a destiny — *Moros, Fatum, Wyrd* — inherent in the nature of the physical world and beyond the power of whatever gods there be. So strong was this racial instinct that it eventually produced the Anglo-Saxon proverb, "Christ is powerful, but more powerful is destiny."[28]

Destiny is simply the Greek *heimarmene*, the nexus of cause and effect that unalterably governs the physical world. It is not remark-

---

28   Quoted by Gunther, *op. cit.*, p. 33.

able that atheism appears very early in the thought of our race.

The outlines, at least, of Greek philosophy are too well known to justify a description here. We have already mentioned Xenophanes and Critias, and the common noun, 'Euhemerism,' will remind everyone of Euhemerus, whose ironically entitled *Sacred Scripture* was translated into Latin as the *Sacra Historia* by Ennius when Rome was still predominantly Aryan. We should note that Critias was so frank in his play, performed for the whole body of Athenian citizens, as to impair the social utility of religion.[29] Aristotle was content to remark in his *Metaphysica* that since society depended on a moral order, religion was necessary "to convince the masses." This view was held by a large part of the Roman aristocracy in the great days of the Republic. The elder Cato said that he wondered how an *haruspex* could avoid grinning when he met a colleague: He could speak freely about foreigners;[30] it would have been bad taste to speak so crudely about members of a Roman religious collegium and, in any case, a well-bred Roman was supposed to maintain his *gravitas* in public. Cicero, who had attained the coveted honor of co-option to the college of augurs, had no illusions about the religious efficacy of an office which was prized for the political power it gave as a constitutional check on the actions of certain magistrates.

We are here in the presence of a very important factor in religious history: the belief, possibly correct, in the necessity of religion to perform the function Critias had attributed to it. This, of course, has had great weight, not only with sagacious students of politics, such as Machiavelli, but with many churchmen, although few have been so candid as the celebrated Cardinal Dubois, whose opinion we mentioned above. One thinks, for example, of the Protestant minister, Allamand, whom Gibbon knew in his youth and who adroitly fostered the young man's intellectual development, but, since Gibbon was still a Christian, "had some measures to keep" and never showed him "the true colors of his secret scepticism." Allamand, like

---

29　We do not know in what part of his *Sisyphus* the preserved passage occurred, nor are we informed about the plot. The character who spoke those pregnant lines may have been punished for his rationalism, thus satisfying the religious.

30　The official *haruspices* were noble Etruscans and were summoned from Etruria when it was thought necessary to consult them about the wishes of the gods. On one famous occasion, in 162 BC, when they returned a politically inexpedient opinion, Tib. Sempronius Gracchus (father of the noted "idealists"), then consul, denounced them as foreign barbarians and had them thrown out, but he had eventually to yield to the superstitions of the populace.

the famous Father Jean Meslier, who left, disguised as a last will and testament, an avowal of his own atheism, was a man of high moral principles, and in antiquity, as in our own time, the description *est sacrificulus in pago et rusticos decipit* may sometimes correspond to a high sense of social responsibility, although, of course, it more often describes only a cynical exploitation of the credulity of the masses.

Atheism, furthermore, is by no means restricted to the main stream of our civilization. Among the Norse there were many 'godless' (*goðlauss*) men, and although we can be absolutely certain only about those who said specifically that they believed only in their own strength and courage (*á mátt sinn ok megin*) and destiny (*auðna*), it is highly unlikely that any of them retained any superstitions about the supernatural, although some scholars of Norse antiquities would like to salvage by conjecture some vestiges of religiosity.

What may astonish some readers is the fact that atheism also appeared among the Aryans of India. In the great uncertainty that besets all attempts to fix a chronology of the early history of India, one cannot be certain of anything, but I feel confident that the strict materialism and atheism called *Lokāyaka* accompanied the breakdown of the Vedic religion and was a pre-condition to the rise of Buddhism; I therefore place it at least as early as the beginning of the sixth century BC, the date favored by Paul Masson-Oursel. It is certainly older than the *Maitri-upanisad* (whatever its date!), which mentions (iii.5) atheism (specifically *nāstikya*) among human afflictions. It is certainly older than the oldest parts of the *Mahābhārata*, which mention atheism. Some passages, probably interpolated, threaten persons who do not believe in a "spiritual world" with condign punishments, and one amusing episode (XII.clxxx.47) introduces us to a jackal who laments that in his previous life he was an "infidel" (*pāsanda*) and so wicked that he was a rationalist (*haituka*), devoted to the "useless art of reasoning" and so perverse as to doubt what he was told by the professional priests. It is uncertain how long the Aryan (philosophical) mentality persisted in India after it was finally mongrelized by Buddhism and the dominant mentality became what Haas termed philousian, which is capable, by some mental operation incomprehensible to us, of seeing itself in the clouds, the Sun, and the whole living Universe, of which it feels itself a part.[31] As late as the fourteenth century (AD), Mādhava, in his *Sarva-sar-*

---

31   Günther, who believes that a pantheistic mysticism is also native to our minds, would take exception to my implication that the "philousian" mind is entirely alien. One can argue the question both ways.

gana-samgraha,[32] included a chapter on the materialists (*carvakas*), who deny the existence of gods, souls, and other spooks, and assert that religion "was made by Nature for the livelihood of persons who are destitute of both learning and manhood," and is therefore a racket that provides professional priests with an assured income. It is doubtful whether Mādhava, at so late a date, actually knew persons who held such opinions; he could have derived his information about such sinful ideas from written sources.

All of the three independent Aryan cultures of which we have good records early developed atheism as a *Weltanschauung* of some men. As was only to be expected, professional holy men, understandably alarmed by the threat to their incomes, clamorously assert that atheists are dreadfully wicked and immoral. They seem not to stop to reflect that an atheist who had no moral principles would naturally become an evangelist himself, and obtain a handsome income and flattering prominence by hawking salvation to the masses or otherwise exploiting their credulity. In our society, the avowed atheist clearly places his devotion to intellectual integrity above the material rewards that he, as a materialist, should primarily seek! Explain that paradox as you will. Given the innate propensity of the Aryan mind, we are left with the uncomfortable fact that in general we cannot tell how many holy men are atheists at heart, and how many atheists profess conformity to the established religion to avert damage to the social structure.

Belief

Psychologists have speculated endlessly about the true nature of the human psyche[33] and hence about its susceptibility to systematic

---

32   There is a generally good translation by E.B. Cowell and A.E. Gough (London, Kegan Paul, 1904), who, however, translate as "demons" etc. (i.e., supernatural beings) words which really mean "savages," i.e., the dark-skinned aboriginal races of India in their native habitat, creatures whom the Aryans regarded as evil and so described by words (*paisaci*, etc.) which also mean 'demon.' There is an odd tradition that Gunādhya wrote his *Brhatkathā* (the source of the well-known *Ocean of Story*, elegantly translated by C.H. Tawney and commented by N.M. Penzer, 10 vols., London, 1924-1928), in the "Paisaci language," which is absurd unless the word there means some adulterated dialect comparable to modern Urdu; cf. ancient Hittite.

33   We should remember that, properly speaking, psyche is the vital principle, the life-force that distinguishes a living organism from an inanimate one. As Aristotle defines it in the *De anima*, all living things necessarily have a psyche of

superstition, commonly called religiosity. Into that pathless labyrinth we need not venture, and we cannot take the time even to outline what is the most cogent of the innumerable theories. It may be that, as Carl Jung claims, religiosity is an inherent and inherited tendency of our nature, determined by the archetypal symbols that are latent in our subconscious minds as our inheritance from the collective unconscious of the race to which we belong — a psychic substratum that was formed by our race's collective experience during all the millennia since it became a human species. But although Jung's arguments are plausible, his theory is, at the limit, no more demonstrable than the many that are more superficial.

There are, however, two indubitable factors that we may mention, since they are sometimes so obvious they are overlooked, being simply taken for granted.

Although all of the higher mammals have certain rudimentary powers of reason and communication, the several species that are distinguished as human possess, in varying degrees, the ability to form a language, by which certain arbitrary sounds are given specific meanings and may be assembled into the sentences of a statement that becomes a substitute for visual, auditory, or tactile perception. The word 'spear' causes the hearer's imagination to form a picture of a specific instrument, and the statement 'I hurled a spear at the tiger' makes the hearer visualize in his consciousness not only the weapon, the tiger, and me, but also the act in which I am said to have engaged. There is nothing in the statement or in the hearer's imaginative reaction to it that indicates the truth or the falsity of the statement. Language, in other words, confers the power to lie, and the validity of

---

an appropriate degree of complexity. The simple psyche of plants enables them to absorb nourishment, grow, and reproduce. Animals have a more complex psyche, which gives them also the power of movement and of perception through the five senses. The human psyche has, in addition, the kind of consciousness that embraces the cognitive and ratiocinative faculties. When death supervenes, the psyche (including, of course, the human personality) ceases to exist, since it was inherent in the functioning of the organism, from which it can have no separate existence. The energy that produces such faculties is, of course, a part of the structure of the Universe; a modern reader will most readily understand the disputed passage at the end of III.5 by an analogy with Schopenhauer's doctrine of the survival of the will as an impersonal force. Aristotle logically denies the possibility of a personal immortality, such as is so beautifully set forth in the poetry of Pindar, who is believed to have been the first to use psyche (in a famous passage quoted by Plato, *Meno*, 81a) to designate a personal entity that is supposed to survive death and be capable of reincarnation.

any statement, if it possesses internal consistency, can be determined only by external criteria, the common-sense test of plausibility in the light of our own experience of reality, and, if that test is passed, the availability of independent corroboration of the statement. If I tell you that I was in London this morning, you will know that I lie, because I could not conceivably have returned thence in the elapsed time. If I tell you that I *thought* of London this morning, you will never be able to determine whether or not I have told the truth.

If we read Sir Walter Scott's *Life of Swift* and his *Waverley*, there is nothing in either narrative that permits us to distinguish between biography and fiction. We know, however, from our basic education that there was a distinguished writer named Swift who lived at the time mentioned in the first of these books, and what we know of his writings and the circumstances of his life agrees with what Scott tells us; we therefore accept the *Life of Swift* as a statement of facts, truthful and accurate, except insofar as Scott may have overlooked or misunderstood data that we can ascertain from other and reliable sources.[34] When we read the second of these books, however, we have no means of knowing offhand whether a man named Edward Waverley lived at the time indicated and we could not find out, except by a prolonged and laborious search through the vast mass of relevant records that might contain mention of him and confirm at least some of the acts attributed to him; but Sir Walter has informed us in his preface that Waverley is merely a creation of his own imagination.

If we read Hervey Allen's *Anthony Adverse*, we know that it is a novel, for so the author has told us. If it were labelled a biography, we might wonder how some of the incidents and personal sentiments recorded became known to the writer, and we might be sceptical about parts of the narrative, but an enormous amount of research would be necessary before we would dare affirm that the protagonist never lived. Kenneth Roberts' *Oliver Wiswell* would present an even more difficult problem, since almost all of the leading characters except the protagonist are historical figures who did participate in the events that are described in the book with historical accuracy, as can be determined from some or many authentic sources, and the protagonist is essentially an observer, so that we should have to prove

---

34   We may remark in passing that we normally do not make a search for verification of all details, especially if the work is a recent one and so presumably is based on all relevant knowledge now available. We are thus vulnerable to the sophisticated technique of mental poisoning now practiced by professional liars, who produce a generally accurate and verifiable narrative and artfully imbed in it the one crucial lie that they wish to implant in the minds of their victims.

that he could not have witnessed those events.

If now we turn to the famous works of J.R.R. Tolkien, we find a narrative that is, *per se*, as circumstantial and seemingly realistic, as convincing, as any of the books mentioned above. We know at once, however, that we are reading fiction — and we should know it, no matter how positively the author asseverated that it was a veracious account of actual happenings — because we know, from our basic education, that no such beings as hobbits, elves, and wizards ever existed and that many of the incidents described violate the ascertained and indubitable laws of Nature. We know, beyond possible doubt, that Tolkien's books are grandiose tissues of falsehood, of what would be impudent falsehood, if the author pretended otherwise. They are, however, works of brilliant and almost poetic fantasy and so serve a spiritual need that is an essential part of our nature and cannot be denied with impunity.

For our aesthetic satisfaction, therefore, we practice what is called the "poetic suspension of doubt," that is to say, we, by an act of will, assume that the narrative is a factual and veracious account while we are reading it and in our minds, so to speak, we temporarily suspend the laws of Nature and our own rationality, so that we may enjoy a delightful illusion and satisfy our emotional need to escape for a time from the grim limitations of reality. *Dulce et decorum est desipere in loco*. At the end of the reading, as though at the end of a symphony, having experienced the spiritual and emotional release that our psyche needed, we return to reality and the dire world from which we escaped for a time in imagination. We return to painful sanity in a world in which, alas, there is no magic.

If we were propense to superstition and could not bear to surrender the dulcet illusion, if we were willing to believe what is manifestly impossible, only the author's explicit statement that he wrote fiction would save us from taking Tolkien's books as the veracious gospels of a religion more plausible and internally consistent than any other. Tolkien's books are the work of a single and singularly lucid mind, not a mere congeries of myths elaborated at widely different times for widely different purposes by many obscure authors and never given competent editorial revision, which would have eliminated internal inconsistencies in each tale and gross contradictions between tales, such as have to be explained away by the theologians of all religions that have sacred scriptures. When Tolkien wrote his trilogy, he revised *The Hobbit* to make it agree with what he said in the later work; his *Silmarillion* was published posthumously from many shorter narratives, written at various times, mere tentative drafts that the author would have revised and harmonized with the published volumes, had he lived to combine them into a continuous narrative.

There are some inconsistencies, therefore, but far fewer and far less troublesome than the flagrant self-contradictions found in the holy books of every revealed religion.[35] It is possible, indeed, to pre-

---

35 Bibles that are the work of a single author are likely to show fewer inconsistencies. An obvious exception is the Koran (*Qu'rán*), which I have read through only in the English translations by J.M. Rodwell (Everyman's, 1909) and R. Bell (Edinburgh, 1937-39). God's Word appears to be almost entirely the composition of Mahomet (Muhammad), but its chapters have been lumped together without the slightest regard for either logical or chronological order, and each *sura* seems to preserve the form in which it was dictated by God's Prophet at some point in his long and adventurous career, which was marked by many vicissitudes and drastic changes of circumstances. He frequently found it expedient to have God change his mind, but while he sometimes remembered what he had had God say months or years before, he never attempted to revise or reconcile pronouncements made over a period of about twenty-two years. The result, of course, is an indigestible mass of grotesque internal contradictions, which, however, pious Moslems read in a trance, much as Christians read their Bible, such powers of reflective thought as the reader may possibly possess by nature having been congealed and anaesthetized by religious awe. Moslem theologians, whose ambitions naturally thaw out their brains, use the technique of *násikh* and *mansúkh*, determining what passages were abrogated by what other passages, with an ingenuity and effrontery worthy of the most eminent Christian theologians. Needless to say, Mahomet's innumerable *hadíth* were invented by many theologians, each trying to sharpen his own axe.

There are, of course, very many other bibles composed by a single *halluciné* or charlatan. I read Joseph Smith's *Book of Mormon* rather cursorily many years ago; I do not recall having noticed conspicuous inconsistencies. At about the same time, I read Swedenborg's *Arcana coelestia* with somewhat greater attention and, given the wild imaginings of the author, did not notice internal contradictions, although I did remark passages in which I thought the author's Latin designedly ambiguous. Mary Baker Eddy's *Science and Health*, while not attributed to God as author, is really the gospel of a sect which deserves attention as one of the two major religions invented in the United States; the book appears internally consistent, doubtless because its authoress gave it a careful revision before publishing it. Lodowicke Muggleton (1609-1698) and his cousin, reputedly the Prophets of God whose coming was foretold in the Apocalypse, produced *The Divine Looking-Glass*, at which I have glanced (in the edition of 1846), but without attempting to determine whether the divine ravings have any coherence. It was with reference to this book that Hervey Allen, in his best-known novel, succinctly described the reaction of a pious reader of revelations: He could not understand the words and was, therefore, profoundly moved by them. The quantity of divine-

dict a collapse of our civilization and a new Dark Ages, and to imagine that the text of the *Silmarillion* and perhaps the other books will survive the destruction of most of our culture and come into the hands of ignorant survivors of our race or barbarians of a race to which our modalities of thought and feeling are congenial, with the result that Tolkien's fantasies will be taken as the Sacred Bible of a new religion.

Tolkien's work has both coherence and a noble morality, but neither is requisite for sacred writings. The late Clark Ashton Smith wrote a series of short stories about a continent named Zothique that will appear in the far distant future, and the late Robert E. Howard published a large number of short stories about a continent that vanished in the remote past; neither author aimed at more than a superficial similarity between the various short stories' imaginary setting, and each story was composed for its own dramatic and romantic effectiveness in exciting horror and wonder in the readers of the popular periodicals in which the various stories were published over a period of many years. Nevertheless, the admirers of each writer have drawn maps of the imaginary continents, arranged the tales in a chronological order, and compiled biographies of the principal characters, explaining away inconsistencies with only a modicum of the ingenuity that theologians have to put into concealing the irremediable conflicts within their chosen body of myths. And the same admirers could, if they wished, read into the stories a religious significance. We may be quite certain that any moderately competent theologian could take the diverse tales thrown together in Andrew Lang's varicolored *Fairy Books* and, with the usual techniques of sophistry and mendacity, make of them an apparently coherent doctrine and a religion that many of our contemporaries would be prone to accept.

Language, in other words, can be used to portray what never happened and never could have happened in terms so vivid that

---

ly inspired trash is simply enormous in all literate parts of the world. A man who took the time to read the *Bāni*, composed by Dadu, a Hindu Representative of God, (1544-1603), for his 152 disciples, informs me that it is an unusually intelligible revelation of a religion tbat is essentially an odd mixture of Euhemerism and monotheism. All of the scriptures mentioned above depend on affirmations purportedly made by a god, and it may be worthy of note, as illustrative of the innate mentality of our race, that when educated Aryans intoxicate themselves with mysticism, they characteristically do so with the methods of scholarship; a good example is Godfrey Higgins' *Anacalypsis* (London, 1833-1836; republished, New York, 1927).

they will induce belief subject only to the vigilance of the reader's common sense and knowledge of reality, his critical faculties, which will enable him to test the story's consistency, and, if necessary, his knowledge of the relevant facts of history and science. We know that no man can walk on water, that an omniscient god could not be surprised by an unforeseen event, and that the Sun cannot be stopped above a town on Earth. If such events were narrated in fiction written with a very high degree of literary skill and imaginative art, we could, for a brief time, feign belief in them for the sake of aesthetic satisfaction, but if we permit emotional cravings to put our rational faculties permanently into cold storage, there is absolutely no limit whatsoever to what we can believe, and even the crudest tale will induce chronic delusions. Oddly enough, however, the paralysis of the intellect can be limited somehow to certain *idées fixes*. thus permitting the mind to reason from its own delusions, as in the well-known story about Dr. Abernethy's insane patient: The man was convinced that he was dead, and when the physician lanced his arm, the patient congratulated him on having made an epochal medical discovery, to wit, that dead men can bleed.

Obviously, an individual's credulity is relative to two quite different factors, first, the quality and vigor of his intellect, which is genetically detemined,[36] and second, the amount of factual knowledge at his disposal, which depends on his education and, above all, on the extent of the accurate information that has been accumulated by his society in the time at which he lives. He cannot avoid erroneous

---

36   It must be noted that two distinct factors are here combined, the intelligence of an individual relative to the average for his race, and the racial determinant of his mental processes. The latter was identified for our race by Professor William S. Haas in his fundamental *Destiny of the Mind* (New York, 1956), to which we may add the sociological data adduced by Géryke Young in her *Two Worlds, Not One* (London, 1969). Ours is what Haas terms the philosophical mentality, and, to use his example, an Aryan who thought that he saw himself in the clouds would be rightly adjudged insane, but, as he shows, persons who have been born with a philousian mentality can do so and are sane in terms of the innate conformation of their racial mind, which is basically beyond our comprehension, although we may observe its effects in their conduct. When we deal with Mongolians, Jews, and other intelligent races (including many hybrids), it is only fair and prudent to remember that they do not perceive reality as we do and cannot think about what they perceive with our logic. At the limit, of course, this poses one of the epistemological problems that are abstractly insoluble and to which, as Hume proved, we can only give the summary answer demanded by our will to live.

suppositions about phenomena that have not yet been explained or correctly observed, and it is only natural that whenever an increase in knowledge destroys a false belief that is emotionally comforting to human weakness, many individuals will suffer a psychic perturbation that is strictly comparable to the "withdrawal symptoms" experienced by addicts who have been deprived of their drugs. What concerns us here is the persistence of belief in what is known to be impossible.

We must first of all remark that such an irrational belief satisfies a craving of our subliminal psyche, which is certainly shaped by our genetic inheritance and, most probably, by the collective unconscious of our race as formed by the evolution of our species for a hundred thousand years or more. It is a craving only a little less imperative than sexual desire, which is partly physical,[37] and which, as Hippolytus discovered, men cannot deny with impunity. A yearning to transcend the cruel reality of a world in which we are ephemerae is born in us and is today made only the more imperative by our knowledge that our twenty thousand days under the Sun are but a moment, no more than the dance of a midge that is born in the morning to die at evening, in the infinite time of a Universe in which we, and our race, and all mammals, and our peculiar planet itself are infinitesimally unimportant epiphenomena in a Universe that is

---

37 Only partly physical in our race, at least, since there is often the spiritual component of a need for permanent companionship and reciprocal trust to assuage an individual's terrible loneliness and bolster his weakness. It is only fair to add that a comparable need appears to be felt instinctively by the many species of animals that mate for life, i.e., numerous species of birds and mammals, including (contrary to vulgar belief) most wolves (as distinct from dogs). The intensive effort in our schools to force members of our race to believe that sex is a strictly physical function, like defecation, represents, of course, a concerted and planned assault on our racial survival. I do not know whether or not the female professors who proclaim that "we must destroy love," that "we have to abolish marriage," and that "we must encourage women not to live individually with men" are Jewesses obeying their race's animus against ours; if they are Aryans, they are a terrifying illustration of the extent to which the racial psyche of our women can be poisoned by systematically induced delusions. In any case, although the proclaimed "liberation" of our women from their biological nature is accompanied by a theoretical presumption that children will continue to be engendered and will be raised, like chickens, in pens provided by the government and explicitly designed to enforce equality with the lowest species of human life, it is obvious that the necessary result will be that women of an intelligence above the animal level will refuse to bear offspring, and our race, or at least the valuable part of it, will become extinct, as is, of course, tacitly desired by the promoters.

vast beyond our comprehension and actuated by the blind forces of an inexorable and insentient Nature from which there is no appeal. Cultured men and women can satisfy this yearning with great literature, both poetry and highly imaginative prose, and, less directly, by music and the aesthetic satisfactions afforded by mimetic arts that correspond to our racial conceptions of beauty.[38] Such rational indulgence of a psychic need is not available to the unfortunate individuals who have been denied participation in our cultural heritage by their schools, their private circumstances, or their own abilities, and it is not remarkable that the sabotage of our civilization by "educators" is currently producing a frightening increment of voluntary belief in the impossible, thus more and more levelling our population to a peneplane on which it will be impossible for our race to retain the intelligence requisite for survival.

The fact that religiosity does correspond to a psychic need accounts, of course, for its persistence in otherwise intelligent individuals who were in their early years subjected by clever teachers to a process of conditioning that implanted a habit before the development of rational faculties in the child's mind. A maxim frequently repeated in the schools of several religious corporations states the principle quite bluntly: "If we have them until they are seven, we've got them for life." This, of course, is an exaggeration: The technique often fails, either because the pedagogues who apply it are inefficient or because they encounter a firm resistance in the minds of precocious children. The method is not infallible, but it is often successful. We have all encountered from time to time men who have attained distinction in historical scholarship or technology (including the methodology of the genuine sciences), but have never been able to break the religious habits formed by the mold in which their infan-

---

38   Here again we cannot determine whether the obscenely disgusting malformations that are so successfully peddled as "art" by Picasso, Epstein, *et alii quam multi*, really correspond to some way in which Jews perceive reality or are an expression of racial hatred or are merely devices to profit contemptuously from the gullibility of barbarized Aryans. Picasso once declared, seemingly with candor, that he was just exploiting the suckers. The question cannot be resolved by the well-known fact that identical "art" is produced by hopelessly schizophrenic children in asylums for the feeble-minded. Much "art" of this sort is also produced by Aryans for profit and the pleasure of thumbing their noses at boobs. As an "artist," who collected junk from the city dump and piled it up in front of a hotel to collect a handsome fee for "sculpture" from the proprietor, remarked to one of his friends, "If the jackass will pay twenty dollars a pound for scrap metal, why not?"

tile minds were forced to grow. This is the psychic equivalent of the physical deformation of the skull practiced by many savage and barbarous tribes, possibly for the subconscious purpose of concealing some racial diversity in the components of the tribe, at least at the time that it came together. Our children are born with the psychic need for transcending reality and instinctively take pleasure in fairy stories, tales of the marvellous and impossible, but naturally outgrow serious belief in such things as they grow up; but if childish belief in a given set of fairy tales is enforced by an imposed routine of acts of worship, thus implanting a habit that is both physical and mental, the sapling thus bent may become a tree that retains the inclination thus forced upon it. The efficacy of this psychological device was first discovered by religious organizations, but, as we all know, it is now intensively used by the revolutionaries who have made of the public schools in the United States a monstrous tool for the sabotage of our civilization and liquidation of our race. Their deformation of children's minds and characters does not concern us here, since it does not at present induce religiosity,[39] except insofar as the stunting of

---

39   Unlike religious schools, our public schools, devoted to the revolutionary implementation of "democracy," are naturally most concerned with blighting the character of our children by destroying the racial psyche. For example, as we all know, the schools work intensively to incite indiscriminate copulation in children at the earliest possible age, preferably before puberty, to destroy their capacity for sexual love and thus render them incapable of ever experiencing the greatest of all the psychic satisfactions demanded by our racial instincts. The very institution of public schools in which children of greatly differing intelligence are lumped together has, of course, the effect of aborting innately superior minds and that purpose is even openly admitted to the accompaniment of mawkish snivelling about the "underprivileged" (if we may use one of the most disgusting nonsense-words coined by the con men). Forcing Aryan children into close association with savages is obviously a device to destroy their self-respect and their capacity for culture. A remarkable statistical proof of the efficiency of American schools is given by Professor Raymond B. Cattell in his *New Morality from Science* (New York, 1972), p. 378: "In the early part of this century the classical studies of Burt (1917, 1925), Chassell (1935), and Terman (1926), clearly showed a decided tendency of delinquents to be below average in intelligence, and of highly intelligent children to be on an average of superior character and emotional stability. In some [recent] studies the correlation *now approaches zero.*" (My italics.) The distinguished author goes on to point out that it is imperative for us (assuming that we do not acquiesce in our liquidation) to train our citizens "in defenses against psychological warfare." He does not explain, however, how this is to be done without abolishing the publicly financed boob-hatcheries and crime-breeding centers.

native intelligence so debilitates the mind that it becomes susceptible to uncontrolled emotions and induced hallucinations.

Aside from conditioning in infancy, the emotional fixation requisite for belief in the impossible depends on two factors, if we exclude cases of patent insanity, temporary or permanent. As the promoters of "democracy" well know and vociferously deny, human beings, from both mental indolence and fear of the unknown, try to shirk responsibility for decisions that will affect their own future. The sentimental idealization of childhood springs, not so much from oblivion of the tears shed and pain felt in early years, as from recollection of the happy state in which all important decisions were made by parents, who sheltered, clothed, fed, and educated the child without requiring him to make any decision of real moment. When those happy years are past, the adult yearns for a replacement of the lost parent whenever he is confronted by a need to make a decision in circumstances in which it is not obvious to him which of the alternatives will be the more advantageous. He wishes to transfer the responsibility to the stars, oracles, or soothsayers, and if he cannot believe in such frauds, he can at least tell himself that a Big Daddy in the clouds is watching over him and, if he is a good boy, will save him from serious harm. Political theorists,, especially if "conservative," like to forget that for the masses, as for children, "liberty" is merely freedom to indulge whims and appetites, at present most commonly in a bar room, where alcohol will give them a happy hour and a female can be picked up for nocturnal exercise, but *alia aliis*, for there is a variety in such tastes. Given the "liberty" they prize, they will welcome any dictation not physically painful that will spare them the unpleasant exertion of thought about decisions of which the consequences on their own lives may be problematical. They can be stirred from the most supine acquiescence in decisions made for them only by a prospect of more money, i.e., of indulgence in more whims and sensual appetites. The liberty about which "conservatives" so constantly and vainly orate is desired only by an aristocracy, and, in cold fact, can in any society be fully enjoyed only by a privileged minority, which may be either an aristocracy or the masters of an ochlocracy. Given this fact, it is easy to see why individuals, especially if, as at present, they feel the terrible loneliness of men without status or secure social ties, feel a need for reliance on some supernatural being, *faute de mieux*.

As we remarked earlier, the survival of the anthropoids that evolved into the several human species was made possible only by their association in packs for hunting and self-protection. The very function of a pack requires that its members feel the unanimity without which it would be merely a chance collection of helpless individuals, and this law of the pack was bred into our subliminal psyche through a hundred millennia or more before we became recognizably human. It is so deeply embedded in our being that everyone knows packs, mobs, crowds are collectively capable of a unanimous action that few or possibly none of the individuals in it would consciously undertake. We need not explore *la psychologie des foules*[40] to perceive that obvious fact, nor need we question the report of competent observers that a unanimity of emotion or purpose in a large crowd may produce in an observer and even more in the leader who is temporarily the crowd's master a distinctly perceptible sensation that has been compared to an electrical charge in the atmosphere.[41] However that may be, it is also a matter of common knowledge that a crowd, however strong its collective emotion, is incapable of action without some initiative, some modicum of leadership at least, on the part of some individual. A crowd strongly charged with emotion is like a supersaturated solution (of sodium thiosulphate, for example) that will remain liquid until a small shock, no more than a light tap with a pencil on the exterior of the flask, causes it to crystallize instantly. Here again we have the law of the pack, which always follows a leader, the individual whom social biologists now call the alpha male or, in some circumstances, the alpha female. When wolves, for example, assemble for a hunt, the dominant individual (who, incidentally, takes the greatest risk) leads and the rest of the pack fol-

---

40   I allude, of course, to the magisterial work by Gustave Le Bon (Paris, 1895), one of the truly great men who undertook an objective study of human society. His work is denounced by the professors who are working the "social science" rackets, since it negates many of the myths they propagate for profit — and often, no doubt, to compensate for a dim awareness of their own inferiority. There is an English translation, which I have not seen.

41   So far as I know, there has been no investigation of this phenomenon. It probably has no relation to the now fashionable fraud called "Extra Sensory Perception." There may be some relation to the ability of a dog to sense the mood of his master when the latter, so far as he knows, has given no indication of it by word or gesture. The ability of many animals to sense fear in a human being is usually explained by reference to their olfactory sense, and anger stimulates glandular reactions that a dog may perceive in the same way. Such perception seems most unlikely in human beings. Speculation about brain waves would be gratuitous in the absence of a scientific study of a phenomenon which could be illusory.

lows him with a spontaneous unanimity. After the common purpose has been served, the pack disperses, but within the territory which it has taken for itself and which its leader patrols. The members of the pack retain a sense of their unity, however, and are aware of it when they encounter one of their fellows.[42] In human packs, unanimity in a common purpose or belief satisfies an immemorial instinct of the species and is doubtless pleasant in itself. For that emotional satisfaction, men in general are quite willing to believe what their fellows in the pack believe.

This human tropism can be distinguished from the use of religion as a force for social cohesion, which we discussed above. The cohesion is requisite for large societies, which do, indeed, generate an emotional unanimity for an urgent common purpose, most commonly that of defending the state or of looting another state. When the larger cohesion is not imposed by some stress, the emotional satisfaction of belonging to the pack is normally felt only by comparatively small groups, a few score or hundred at the most, probably the limiting size of the packs or small tribes of our prehistoric ancestors. This probably explains the disintegration of all religions into small sects when no external force compels a formal cohesion for a common purpose that transcends or constrains the tendency to give allegiance to a comparatively small pack, which usually persists in the formation of factions within the large sect. For our purposes here, we need only note the psychological fact that assent to, and even belief in, a given superstition is a price that most individuals are willing to pay for the comforting sense of belonging to a pack, a sense that is some vestige of the instinct implanted in our remote ancestors when belonging to the pack was a matter of life or death.

I have tried to account, in the simplest possible psychological terms, for the persistence of belief in religious dogmas that demonstrably demand belief in what is impossible. The analysis is applicable only to laymen, votaries, congregations, and the like. Professional holy men, who have made religion their business, necessarily represent a quite different mentality.

---

42   The many similarities between wolves and men make a study of their social organization particularly interesting; see the recent work by Barry Holstun Lopez, *Of Wolves and Men* (New York, 1978). It is, incidentally, odd and perhaps significant that wolves are now generally regarded with hostility and aversion, whereas our Aryan ancestors regarded them with a just admiration, as is obvious from the number of men today who bear such names as Ralph, Raoul, Rudolph, Adolph, Randal, Randolph, Rolf, Ulric, Wolfram, Pandulf, Bardolf, and doubtless others that I do not call to mind at the moment.

Chapter Nine: Zoroaster

WITH SO MUCH of a prolegomenon, and with an iteration of the proviso that we are trying only to summarize the bare essentials of a subject that is almost infinitely complex, we may turn to Christianity, which, as everyone should know, was not an Aryan religion. It may be succinctly described as a Judaized form of Zoroastrianism. That relationship, indeed, is acknowledged in the Christian gospels which state that Zoroastrian priests (*Magi*) were present at the nativity of Jesus, some of which specifically ascribe their coming to a prophecy made by Zoroaster.[43] As we shall show below, however, there was a third major source of Christian doctrine, which we may identify as

---

43   Zoroaster was doubtless named in all versions of the story about Herod and the *Magi*, but the reference was attenuated in the version of the Gospel of Matthew that the Fathers of the Church decided to include in their anthology when they put their "New Testament" together near the end of the fourth century. In the present version, the *Magi* are made to say (2.5) that the christ they are seeking will be born "in Bethlehem of Judaea, for thus it is written by the prophet." The Prophet, of course, is Zoroaster, whose name is retained in other gospels, e.g., in an *Euangelium Infantiae* which says (6), "*Magi* came from the East to Jerusalem in conformity with the prophecy of Zoroaster, and they had with them gifts, gold, frankincense, and myrrh, and they worshiped him [the infant Jesus]." The intention, of course, was to represent Jesus as the Saviour (*Saošyant*) whom Zoroaster expected to be his eventual successor. The Christian form of the prophecy is doubtless preserved in the writings of Salomon, Bishop of Basra, and Theodore bar Konai: Zoroaster said to his favorite disciples "At the end of time and at the final dissolution, a child shall be conceived in the womb of a virgin… They will take him and crucify him upon a tree, and heaven and earth shall sit in mourning for his sake… He will come [again] with the armies of light, and be borne aloft on white clouds…. He shall descend from my family, for I am he and he is I: he is in me and I am in him." The prophecy thus put into the mouth of Zoroaster originally referred to his son, to be born of a virgin in the miraculous way I shall mention below, which could not be fitted to a story that placed the birth in Judaea. The text of the *Euangelium Infantiae* I mentioned above may be found in the *Codex Apocryphus Novi Testamenti* edited by Ioannes Carolus Tbilo (Lipsiae, 1832), vol. I, p. 71. This is one of the gospels that records the first miracle (omitting the famous one listed in the Gospels of James) of Jesus: When a mad youth tried to steal one of Jesus's diapers, which had been washed and were hanging on a clothesline, contact with the cloth, which was, of course, imbued with *mana*, drove the demons from his body and he became sane. An 'apocryphal' gospel is one that the Fathers of the Church excluded from their collection when they finally agreed on the contents of the "New Testament."

Buddhism. We shall therefore notice, as concisely as possible, the three principal constituents of the religious amalgam.

Since the term 'Magian' is best reserved for a group of related religions and the culture they represent, I shall use 'Zoroastrianism' to designate the specific religion, also called Mazdaism, that was traditionally founded by a Saviour, to whom I shall refer by the familiar form of his name, derived from Greek references to him, Zoroaster, although his name in Persian was something like Zarathustra (*Zaraüstra, Zaratüstra, Zaratost, Zaradost, Zarahust, Zardust,* etc.).[44] The name may not be Indo-European; scholars who think it must be have proposed various etymologies, most of which posit that the man's name had something to do with camels.

Some scholars have held that no such man ever existed, that he is merely a mythical figure to whose name were attached religious pronouncements and marvellous tales invented by successive generations of holy men.[45] They are right in that no individual could ever have done and said a tenth of what tradition ascribes to Zoroaster, but the same could be said of Gautama, Vaddhamana, Jesus, Mahomet, and other founders of new religions who, it is generally agreed, were historical figures, although their personalities and careers have been all but totally obliterated by the jungles of myth and superstition that have grown over their graves. Furthermore, as many scholars have judiciously remarked, the existence of Zoroaster is virtually guaranteed by the *gathas*, crude hymns and purportedly inspired utterances, attributed to him in the extant *Avesta*.[46] As the case was neatly

---

44   In what follows, I shall give the exact form of proper names at their first occurrence and thereafter dispense with diacritics, which I necessarily retain on words printed in italics. In transliterating Old Persian, Avestan, and Pahlavi, I use the old system that was once standard. The more modern transliterations, found in recent studies (e.g., the ones by Mary Boyce and Marijan Molé that I cite below), are more accurate but involve the use of special types that would needlessly exasperate the printer of this book.

45   For a convenient conspectus of conjectures about Zoroaster and the time at which he lived, see the relevant chapters in A. Christensen's *Die Iranier* (München, 1933 = *Handbuch der Altertumswissenschaft*, Abteilung III, Teil 1, Band 3, Abschnitt 3, Leiferung 1). Naturally, it does not cover more recent studies, notably the ones by Molé and Miss Boyce that I shall have to mention below.

46   The *gathas* form twenty-seven (Nos. 28-54) of the seventy-two chapters or sections of the *Yasna*, which is the first of the five parts into which the extant *Avesta* is divided. The language of most of the *gathas* differs markedly from, and is presumably more archaic than, the language, now called Avestan, of the rest of *Avesta*, which does not even purport to be the work of Zoroaster and is obvi-

stated by Professor K.F. Geldner, the Zoroaster who speaks in the *gathas* "is the exact opposite of the miraculous personage of later legend… He …had to face, not merely all forms of outward opposition and the unbelief and lukewarmness of his adherents, but also the inward misgivings of his own heart as to the truth and final victory of his cause. At one time hope, at another despair… here a firm faith in the speedy coming of the kingdom of heaven, there the thought of taking refuge by flight — such is the range of the emotions which find their immediate expression in these hymns." It is inconceivable that theologians would or could forge such a document as a proof of the glorious triumph of a Son of God who delivered the world from

---

ously the work of generations of theologians who were industriously entrenching themselves in a monopoly of the new religion. Since Zoroaster betrays his emotions in some of the *gathas* but alludes to very few facts, we have to depend on the rest of the *Avesta* for the traditions about his life. Avestan became a dead language long before the final recension of the text in the time of Chosroes I, so the meaning of the Avestan text was expounded in commentaries written in Pahlavi, and an enormous bulk of theological writing was produced thereafter in that language. Most of it was destroyed by the Moslems when they conquered Persia, but what remains is enough to daunt any man by both its bulk and the theological unreason it naturally displays. Selections from it are quoted by Molé. I do not pretend to have read more than samplings of this trash. The translation of the *Avesta* that I have used is by James Darmesteter, *Le Zend-Avesta* (3 vols., Paris, 1892-93).

Avestan (to say nothing of Pahlavi!) is a crude language in comparison with Sanskrit or even Old Persian. It may be significant that the Zoroastrian scriptures known to the Greeks were written in Aramaic, which was then the sacred language of the *Magi*, although they used Greek in intercourse with more civilized people. Aramaic must also have been the language of the *Magi* in the time of the Persian Empire, since Old Persian, the native language of the ruling Aryans, was not widely understood, while the Persians themselves used as the language of administration, Aramaic, the Semitic dialect that was generally known throughout their empire and used internationally beyond their borders. Aramaic could have been the language of the *Magi*'s ceremonies and sermons even to Persians. The *Avesta* (the title may not be Indo-European) may therefore have been translated from Aramaic into a decadent form of Persian, so that Avestan, which does resemble in many ways the corrupt Persian of the last days of the Empire, may be a late, not an early, dialect. I should consider the evidence for a Semitic original conclusive but for the apparent authenticity of the *gathas*, which seem to represent what Zoroaster said. That is an obstacle, but not an insurmountable one. It is quite likely that many of the statements attributed to Jesus in the "New Testament" were actually made by a man of that name, but no one would believe that he spoke in Greek to the Jewish rabble. For our purposes here, I am content to leave the question open.

infinite evil and whose divinely contrived nativity had been attended by all the miracles that Saviours customarily perform at birth. The *gathas* must represent, at least approximately, texts that were already fairly well known before the holy men undertook to elaborate the religion for the stupefaction of their customers.

We need not hesitate therefore to believe that there was a man whose name was something like Zarathustra, that he propounded a drastically new religion, which he claimed had been divinely revealed to him, and that most of the *gathas* bear a fairly close relation to what he actually said. He was therefore the inventor of the basic structure of Zoroastrianism, which is all that will concern us here, and naturally was not responsible for the innumerable surcharges and embellishments that were added by the theological ingenuity of the *Magi*.

There is doubt about the date at which the founder of the religion lived. The priestly traditions that credit him with a fantastic antiquity are, of course, to be disregarded. A recent scholar, Dr. Mary Boyce, following Eduard Meyer and others, would place him between 1300 and 1000 BC on the basis of tenuously hypothetical determinations of the probable date of the pastoral society that seems implied in some of the *gathas*, the putative date of a conjectural schism in the Vedic cults, and a late genealogy of Zoroaster that need mean no more than the genealogies in the "New Testament." The only secure historical evidence shows only that Zoroaster began to propagate his religion at some time before Cyrus the Great conquered Media in 550 BC or soon thereafter. A much earlier date would make it extremely unlikely that the utterances of Zoroaster could have been committed to writing and would have been preserved with some approximation to accuracy. In all probability, the dates for Zoroaster's life, c. 628 to c. 551 BC, accepted by a majority of modern scholars, are at least approximately correct.

With the exception of the Jews' claim that Zoroaster was a Jew,[47]

---

47   The Jews claimed that Zoroaster was a Jew and wrote in Hebrew; see the texts cited and quoted by J. Bidez and F. Cumont, *Les Mages Hellenisés* (Paris, 1973 = 1938), Vol. I, p. 50, nn. 3,4, and Vol. II, pp. 103-104, 129, 131. It is entirely conceivable that Zoroaster really was a Jew, whose true name was Baruch; that he was born in the colony of Jews which, according to Jewish tradition (Reg. IV [= Kings II], 17.6 & 18.1), had been planted in Media; and that, as Jews so often do, he masqueraded as a White man to start a disruptive religious agitation and exploit the credulity of the *goyim*. Furthermore, as we remarked earlier, the *Magi* claimed to be a tribe of incomparably holy people in Media, and there are some indications that they were racially distinct from the Persians, i.e., were not

all traditions agree that he was an Aryan. His mother is most commonly described as a Mede, and her husband is sometimes said to have been of the same nationality; but an extraordinary number of places are identified as the site of his birth and childhood. Almost all of them are cities or districts in ancient Media, Atropatene, or Bactria (approximately the parts of modern Iran that lie south and west of the Caspian Sea or the northeast corner of Afghanistan with the Soviet territory immediately north of it).

Needless to say, Zoroaster, as is *de rigeur* for all Saviours, was born of a virgin who had been fecundated by a supreme god, who sent an emanation of himself (*hvareno*) to impregnate her, much as Yahweh despatched the Holy Ghost to carry out his philoprogenitive wishes in the "New Testament." His wondrous nativity was preceded, accompanied, and followed by the miracles that are customary in such cases.[48] He did, however, distinguish himself from other Saviours by

---

Aryans. The racial arrogance, even greater than that of the Hindu Brahmans, also sounds Jewish in their insistence that their godly ichor was transmitted through females (hence their famous dogma of *xvaetvadatha*, which I shall mention later), but chronology favors the view that the Jews took over and adapted devices which had been so successful and lucrative for the *Magi*. The *Magi* could have been Jews, and that would explain a great deal! But there is no substantive proof that they were, and since deceit and forgery are simply normal racial habits of the Jews, it is safest to assume that their claim that Zoroaster belonged to their race was just another example of their policy of filching any esteemed historical or mythical figure that would enhance their own claims to racial superiority. There are innumerable instances of this Jewish custom, but one of the most impudent may be found in *Maccab.*, I.12.19-23, a forged letter, purportedly from a King of Sparta, who had consulted his historical archives and discovered — oh, joy! — that the Spartans were descendants of Abraham and therefore blood brothers of the sacred race of Jews in Jerusalem. The first two of the four books of "Maccabees" are included in many Christian Bibles as "apocrypha," as though they could be more apocryphal (in the common sense of that word) than the rest of the collection.

48   Most of the miracles were taken over by the Christians in one or another of their many gospels, although not necessarily all in gospels that were included in the Fathers' anthology. One that has some slight theological significance appears in most of the versions of the Gospel of James (who was Jesus's brother and should have known!): When Jesus was born, time stopped for a while and everything on Earth was temporarily petrified, as in many fairy stories, such as the one of the Sleeping Beauty; the Sun was motionless and birds flying high in the air were frozen in place and did not move; the hands of men who were carrying food to their mouths or raising a staff to strike stopped midway in the intended act, etc. Then time started again. Given the Zoroastrian doctrine

one act: As soon as he emerged from his mother's body and dazzled bystanders with the effulgent light of his divine ancestry, he laughed loudly, thus signifying that life is good and should be enjoyed.

According to tradition, Zoroaster, despite numerous and various persecutions and temptations by the indefatigable powers of evil, remained at home, wherever that was, until he was twenty, when he bade farewell to his parents and either became a vagabond or retired into a desert to think things over for ten years. One morning, when he was thirty, he went at dawn into a river to bathe and fetch fresh water for a matutinal cup of *haoma*. As he emerged, he was accosted by the archangel Vohu Manah ("Good Intentions"), who conducted his soul into the presence of Ahura Mazda, the supreme god. Enthroned in glory and attended by the six archangels who are his principal lieutenants, Ahura Mazda revealed to Zoroaster the True Religion and ordered him to save mankind from perdition by preaching it to all the world.

The foregoing, which is supported by references in the *gathas*, must be the account of his Revelation and Ministry that Zoroaster gave to his converts, and there are obviously only three possible explanations, *viz.*:

1. He did in fact converse with Ahura Mazda, by whom he was instructed in the True Religion, which you and I must profess, if we are not to be damned to eternal torment.

2. He had delusions, either from an overheated imagination or after imbibing *haoma*, i.e., an hallucinatory drug prepared by crushing and dissolving in water the active ingredients of the sacred mushroom, *Amanita muscaria*.[49]

3. He deliberately devised a fiction to impose on the credulous — an odd procedure for a man who professed that his mission in life was to combat deceit. Whether he contrived the fraud to dignify a moral code that had caught his fancy or to exalt himself above ordinary men, is a secondary question of no great importance.

The first of these explanations will seem cogent only to Parsees, so we are left with the other two. Whichever of the alternatives we choose, Zoroastrianism is equally spurious. Whether it was the product of temporary insanity or of cunning artifice, the religion, no

---

of time, which the Christians echoed only in a few phrases they did not try to understand, the borrowing of the idea in that popular gospel is significant. A common version of the Gospel of James is translated into English in *Excluded Books of the New Testament*, translated by Lord Bishop J.B. Lightfoot et al., (London, s.a., 1927).

49   See above, p. 52.

matter how numerous its adherents and great its influence, can have been nothing more than an epidemic delusion and another example of human credulity.

It is a distressing fact, however, that many of our contemporaries, including some who have learned the techniques of scholarship, have been so habituated by Christianity and its derivatives to the kind of irrationality that George Orwell calls "doublethink" that they will argue that what is false is true. Persons in whom religiosity is stronger than reason will opt for the theory that Zoroaster was "sincere," i.e., that he was a madman who could not distinguish between his hallucinations and reality, and they will then assure you that the crazy man proclaimed "spiritual truths" of "surpassingly great value" for the "salvation" of the whole world or, at least, "all mankind." This strange but common phenomenon is a fact with which all students of religion or society today must reckon, however the aberration may be explained in terms of psychology or psychopathology.

Zoroaster, after receiving his revelation and commission from God, wandered from place to place throughout the Middle East, preaching the Gospel to whomsoever he could induce to listen to him, for ten years, naturally encountering the persecutions and temptations that are obligatory of all first-class Saviours; but although he was advised on six separate occasions by one of the six archangels in turn, he did not succeed in making a single convert. At the end of the ten years, however, he, having apparently wandered back to his homeland, wherever that was, met his first cousin in a forest wilderness and persuaded that man to become his first disciple and the "leader of all mankind" to the Truth.

Encouraged by his first success and a fresh consultation with Ahura Mazda, Zoroaster, now accompanied by his faithful acolyte, preached the Gospel fruitlessly for two more years, roaming from place to place, until they came into Bactria. There his sermons incensed the local "pagans," servants of the Evil One, whom he floored in a debate, whereupon they slandered him, accusing him of the thirty-three mortal sins and planting proofs of his iniquity that were discovered when his luggage was searched. He was accordingly arrested and thrown into prison, where he suffered hunger, thirst, and assorted torments for a long time, until he performed a miracle, healing the king's favorite horse of a supernatural disease. Released and accorded royal favor, he set to work to save the soul of the legendary or unidentifiable king of Bactria, Vistaspa, and after two years of persuasion brought the king to the point at which he admitted the truth of Zoroaster's revelation but insisted that his sins were too numerous to be forgiven by God. Zoroaster then performed a miracle that sounds authentic: He gave the king a big slug of *haoma* and put him into a trance during which the monarch beheld the glory of God and all the wonders of Heaven.[50] When he recovered consciousness, Vistaspa had Faith.

According to one version, Vistaspa, having seen the Light, proceeded to save the souls of his subjects by giving them a choice between becoming righteous and becoming corpses. He then mobilized his army and embarked on a Holy War to give neighboring peoples the same freedom of choice.

In the meantime, it would seem, Zoroaster performed another miracle. He ascended to the summit of a mountain, where the powers of Evil, in a last desperate effort, rained down fire that enveloped the peak in flames and liquefied the rocks, but naturally left the Saviour unscathed, so that he strolled down from the burning mountain and taught the True Religion to the assembled tribe of *Magi*, who thenceforth became its apostles and priests.[51] Thus launched at last,

---

50   Zoroaster is commonly said to have spiked the *haoma* with *mang*, which was probably hashish. It would have prolonged the intoxication and further stimulated the imagination of the drugged man. Of such are the wonders of Heaven.

51   It is noteworthy that the word for *Magus* (*magu*),was never used by Zoroaster and is said not to occur in any part of the *Avesta*. He does use the word *maga*, which has flustered linguists who want to identify it, but was, in all probability, a neologism that Zoroaster coined to express the holiness of his new religion. (If he had in mind the Vedic term *maghá*, 'gift,' he intended his coinage to express something like the Christian 'gift of the Holy Spirit' or 'gift of God,' i.e., Salvation.) What is clear is that a man or woman who has been Saved is a *magavan*, and since Zoroaster invented a religion of spiritual egalitarianism, every *magavan*, regardless of race, sex, or social status, is the religious equal of every other. The term, therefore, cannot possibly be the equivalent of *Magus*, a professional holy man with hereditary superiority to ordinary mortals. The only terms for persons with religious function are (1) *zaotar*, which is usually held to be the equivalent of the Vedic *hótr*, who, as we observed in the first part of this essay, must originally have been the head of a household in his capacity as the family's priest; and (2) *athravan*, a word which was probably thought of as meaning 'fire-kindler,' even though linguists assure us that it could not be derived from *atar*, 'fire.' (Although linguists assure us it hadn't ought to, the Vedic word *átharvan*, however perversely, did designate the man who had care of the fire on the altar and, perhaps, the *soma*.) Zoroaster (assuming *gatha* 42 is his) uses the word *athravan* to designate the missionaries who are to carry his Gospel to all the world. It could be argued, therefore, that he did not envisage a professional priesthood, but, whether he intended it or not, his religion inevitably required

the new religion spread quickly throughout the territories that were to become the Persian Empire.

It is a general rule that Saviours should disdain females,[52] but Zoroaster was an exception, as befits one who, by his laughter at birth, affirmed that life is worth living. As soon as he had established himself at the court of King Vistaspa, he married, but, being given to moderation, he contented himself with three wives, of whom the third, Hvovi, was the daughter of the King's Prime Minister.[53] By his

---

the services of specialists, experts in righteousness, who knew exactly what Ahura Mazda wanted of every individual in every circumstance of his mortal life.

52   Jesus cannot be considered an exception, for the Gospel of Peter, which represents him as travelling with Mary Magdalene as one of his disciples, and the Gospel of Philip, which says that his male disciples were jealous of his passion for her, were rejected by the Christian sect that the Fathers of the Church made victorious over all the others. If we now had the whole of the Gospel of Philip, we would probably find that it followed the tradition that Mary Magdalene was the concubine (or, with Salome, one of the concubines) who accompanied him on his evangelical peregrinations and whom he was wont to kiss and fondle in public. That tradition sent the Fathers into a tizzy at the thought of it, and they also excised, at a fairly early date, the homosexual episode in the Gospel of Mark that they did include in their anthology. They made of their Jesus an ascetic who condemns sex and despises women, even his Virgin Mother, whom he contemptuously addresses as "woman" and informs that he will have nothing to do with her.

53   This is undoubtedly the original story and could even be authentic insofar as it describes Zoroaster's marriages. I insist on its significance: The later tradition credits him with having married his seven sisters and the sister-daughter that his mother conceived by him. That was undoubtedly invented by the *Magi* to support their dogma of *xvaetvadatha* and their own peculiar tastes. The legitimacy of marriage between brother and sister is necessarily recognized by all religions which, like the Zoroastrian and Christian, teach that all human beings are the descendants of an original man and woman. Christian theologians worm their way out of the obvious implications of the myth of Adam and Eve, but Zoroastrian theologians logically accept the myth that the first pair were *Masi* and *Masanl*, who were twins. (Feminists should note that the First Lady of the world was not an afterthought, hurriedly manufactured from a spare rib, but, as is proper in an egalitarian religion, was her husband's twin sister and came into the world, at the same instant, as his equal.) Whether Zoroaster thought of the logic of that myth (or even knew of it), I do not know. It is possible, of course, that he did not marry a sister because all of his were back home (wherever that was), but the point is, that, according to the early tradition, he did not. What seems peculiar in the theology of the *Magi* is the doctrine that a man acquires a big hunk of religious merit by having sexual intercourse with his mother. They undoubtedly invented the dogma of *xvaetvadatha* to justify the marriages with

several wives, he had sons and daughters, whose careers are reported at length in the legends. What is even more unusual, he, by an odd relationship with Hvovi, engendered a son who has not yet been born, but whose birth, according to one chronology, may be expected around AD 2341.[54] Most Saviours, after they have ascended to Heaven, either personally return to Earth in glory to complete their work or have themselves reincarnated in a new body, but here also Zoroaster showed a certain originality. Having fulfilled his mission on Earth and attained eternal beatitude, he will have no need to interrupt his celestial bliss and undertake a new mission, since he, so to speak, presciently planted while on Earth the seed from which, in the fullness of time, will come his son and successor, the *Saosyant* (*Sosan*), who will definitively deliver the world from evil, resurrect

---

sisters, mothers, and daughters by which they preserved the divine ichor of their holy race from all danger of genetic pollution. And I am quite sure that they also, and for the same reason, amplified the cosmological myth by inventing Gayomart, whose elder sister conceived him by her father and in turn conceived by him the twins, who then peopled the world. I therefore regard strophes 3 to 6 of *gatha* 73 as a priestly forgery. I am not in the least interested in vindicating Zoroaster's morality; I merely call attention to a neat example of the methods by which Salvation-hucksters manipulate their customers.

54   When Zoroaster was engaged in coitus with Hvovi, he had an orgasm *extra vaginam*, and his semen was taken by waiting angels (*fravasis*) to Lake Kayansih, where it is being guarded by angels (according to one count, 99,999 of them) until the appointed day, still far in the future, when an unsuspecting virgin will bathe in the lake, be impregnated by the semen, and (to her astonishment) bear the new Saviour. If you doubt this fact, you have only to go to Lake Kayansih (if you can locate it), and you will see the fecundating essence glowing in the depths of the lake like three lamps. It is like three lamps because it is divine, but the Magian theologians later elaborated the myth to give Zoroaster three sons (by as many virgin baigneuses); they will successively be Saviours at intervals of ten thousand or eleven thousand years. When one reads the *gathas*, one has the impression that Zoroaster expected the Last Judgement in the near future, though not necessarily in the lifetime of his disciples, but, unlike the Jesus in the "New Testament," he was not so rash as to set a time limit for the occurrence of the eschatological Big Bang and thus leave to his professional successors the embarrassing task of inventing an explanation for the untoward delay of the scheduled event. The only plausible explanation, of course, was the well-known myth of the Wandering Jew, who, it should be noted, considerately appeared in Europe to reassure True Believers eighteen times between 1575 and 1830 and even visited Salt Lake City in 1868. The legend was much improved by the invention of a Wandering Jewess, which, I believe, is to be credited to Eugene Suë in his *Le Juif errant*, of which the prologue is worth reading.

the dead, preside at the Last Judgement, and then abolish space and time to inaugurate an era of perfect, unchanging happiness for his True Believers. As Zoroaster is the son of Ahura Mazda, so will his son become the last Saviour.

Zoroaster flourished until he attained the age of seventy-seven years and forty days, when he was slain by one of the votaries of the false religion he had come to supplant. When dying, he forgave his assassin, as etiquette requires Saviours to do.

So much for the legends. Historically, Cyrus the Great probably became a Zoroastrian at some time in his career, for at his death Zoroastrianism was the official religion of his capital city and, probably, of his empire, and the *Magi* had attained the monopoly of religion that is always the first goal of godly ambition. If the dates I have accepted for Zoroaster are correct, the new religion, once launched, must have spread with the rapidity of a pestilence, but that is not astonishing, if one perpends the novelty of Zoroaster's invention and the various elements in it, which we shall examine later, that aroused enthusiasm in very large segments of the subject population of the multiracial Persian Empire. What is more remarkable is the anomalous but indubitable fact that the innovation, although alien to the native tendencies of the Aryan mentality, became, as did Christianity much later, an Aryan religion in the sense that it was accepted by Aryans.[55] It was considered to be, and probably was, the characteristic and only proper religion of the Persians and other Aryans of the ruling race.

It is at this stage that we begin to receive independent information from the Greek writers whose interest in, and observations of, Zoroastrian cults extended over seven centuries.[56] Information from sources earlier than the third century BC is especially valuable as confirming or supplementing what we can infer from Zoroastrian sources about the religion under the Persian Empire. It must be used with discretion, however, for the Greeks were confronted by a kind of religion that the Aryan mind does not find congenial and has dif-

---

55 In this sense, of course, Buddhism could be called a Mongolian religion since it was accepted by the Chinese and Tibetans and indeed flourished among them after it had vanished from the land of its birth.

56 The sources besides Herodotus were partly collected by A.V. Williams Jackson in his *Zoroaster* (New York, 1901), which is still useful, and more thoroughly by Bidez and Cumont in *Les Mages hellenisés*, which I cited above, and in which texts are accompanied by invaluable critical notes. I need not remark that what counts is not the date of a given writer but the date of his source, assuming that we can rely on him to have reported it accurately.

ficulty in understanding, although it evidently can accept such alien beliefs when they are imposed on it by circumstances.[57] Further-

---

57   For example, Greek sources as early as Aristotle and probably as early as Xanthus, who was not much later than Herodotus, report a Magian claim that Zoroaster lived six thousand years or more before their time. We may be virtually certain that what the Magi claimed was the doctrine, of which we know from late Zoroastrian books, that the soul of Zoroaster was created by Ahura Mazda in heaven at a date equivalent to 6630 BC, but was, so to speak, kept in storage in heaven for six thousand years before it was sent to Earth and became incarnate in the body of Zoroaster, the Saviour of mankind. To the Greek mind, the notion of souls created by gods and kept in cold storage for millennia was absurd, so the Greeks naturally interpreted the Magi's pronouncements as meaning that Zoroaster had been born on Earth at the specified time, for a claim to such enormous antiquity seemed less incredible. The well-known Egyptologist, E.A. Wallis Budge, in *The Gods of the Egyptians* (London, 1904; available in a Dover reprint), observes, in his preface to Volume I:

> The only beliefs of the Egyptian religion which the educated Greek or Roman truly understood were those which characterized the various forms of Aryan religion, namely the polytheistic and solar... For all the religious ceremonies and observances which presupposed a belief in the resurrection of the dead and in everlasting life... he had no regard whatsoever. The evidence on the subject now available indicates that he was *racially* incapable of appreciating the importance of such beliefs to those who held them, and that although... he was ready to tolerate, and even, for state purposes, to adopt them, it was impossible for him to absorb them into his life.

Budge italicized the crucial word in a statement that I regard as unexceptionable insofar as it describes the innate quality of what is, in Haas's terminology, the philosophical mentality. Our minds can contemplate the existence of several supernatural beings as the causes of unexplained phenomena, but they instinctively reject the irrational mysticism that one god controls elements that are at war among themselves, or can perform miracles, such as the resurrection of a putrified body, that are patently impossible. Ours, however, is also a mentality that accepts facts, however unpleasant, and it must be remembered that our ancestors accepted Christianity because they had been made to believe that its holy books were records of historical facts, of events that had actually occurred and which therefore proved the existence of a god, a terrible god, in whom they were obliged to believe, despite their instinctive aversion. And it may be doubted whether any Aryan understood that Magian religion in the way its founders intended: He read into it terms that were comprehensible to him. At the limit, Christians always had recourse to the theologians' favorite gambit — that what was unreasonable and incomprehensible was therefore too profound for the weak minds of mortals, whom their creator did not intend to be rational anyway. That notion is always manna from heaven to persons who have not learned to control their emotions or are averse to exercising brain tissue unnecessarily.

more, when the Greeks report matters beyond their own observation of the cult's ceremonies, they were largely dependent on what the *Magi* told them or translated for them from their sacred books in Aramaic. And the *Magi* with whom a Greek was most likely to come into contact were missionaries who were peddling their Gospel in and near the Greek cities in Ionia and elsewhere that were subject to Persian dominion or on the borders of the Empire.

Perhaps the most important single datum from Greek sources is the proof that in the time of the Persian Empire the Magian theologians were already at variance with each other and engaged in doctrinal disputes as each tried to twist the cult's dogmas into the form most agreeable to his tastes and ambitions. This, to be sure, is only what we should expect, for first-rate theologians are always eager, each to sharpen his own axe and make himself a leader instead of a mere follower, a rank that only humbler and duller holy men are willing to accept. But it is good to have historical proof that everything was normal in Zoroastrianism and the doctrines known to the Greeks were diverse and disparate. We hear of a board or commission of seven Magi who were the supreme religious authorities and located in the Persian capital; it was doubtless their function to consecrate a Persian king when he succeeded to the throne and to suppress heresy. As we all know, a heresy is a theological doctrine that is denounced by theologians who call themselves 'orthodox,' especially when the orthodoxy of the latter is guaranteed by the police and hangmen. We do not know to what extent the credentials of orthodoxy were made available to the Zoroastrian substitute for a Papacy, and it is even possible that the power of the supreme Magi was broken when they overreached themselves.[58] It is certain, however, that heresies did flourish, possibly including some important ones that we shall have to mention in a later section. It would be vain, however, and for our purposes otiose to try to reconstruct from the exiguous data the views of Zoroastrian heresiarchs, especially since we cannot be certain what dogmas had come to be accepted as orthodox.[59]

---

58 I do not know what weight should be given to Ammianus Marcellinus who, reporting earlier sources that he unfortunately does not name, says that the power of the priestly oligarchy was broken by Darius after their *coup d'état*, by which they usurped the Persian throne, having a Magus impersonate the dead brother of Cambyses. If that is so, the heads of the priesthood could have been replaced by seven or eight more cautious holy men, or, on the other hand, the religion could have been left without authorized managers. In the absence of more information, it would be foolish even to guess.

59 For example, the dogma of the pre-existence of Zoroaster that I men-

There is one point of some passing interest. Although it falls short of proof, the evidence strongly suggests that during the Persian Empire the *Magi* who were in contact with the Greeks had already deformed the name of their Saviour from something like Zarathustra to Zoroaster.[60] If we could be certain of that, we could then try to

---

tioned above flatly contradicts the *gathas*, which were accepted as Zoroaster's own words, and contradicts the assumptions underlying most of the *Avesta*, according to which Zoroaster (even if born of a virgin, etc.) was a mortal man and discovered the Truth only when it was revealed to him by Ahura Mazda, with whom he presumably had no previous acquaintance. We may think it highly improbable that "orthodox" Zoroastrian theologians would have promulgated a doctrine so obviously contradicted by their own holy book, but we must remember that Christians, who believe all the tales about their Jesus in their "New Testament," which clearly state that, although he was a bright youngster, he didn't get his inspiration until after he was baptized by a John "the Baptist," and that thereafter he behaved in most situations as a mortal man, are also able to believe in his pre-existence and that he was 33⅓% of their god. If they think at all, they must assume that part of their god forgot the rest of himself and everything he had known from all eternity in heaven when he decided to have his conjoined Holy Ghost insert him into Mary's womb. If orthodox Christianity can accept such a dogma without laughter, it is certainly possible that orthodox Zoroastrians had accepted a comparable negation of their own scriptures. There is simply no limit to the effrontery of theologians or to the gullibility of their sheep.

60   Linguists try hard to imagine how a Persian word like *Zarathustra* could have been so mispronounced or misunderstood. The question arises only from an odd fixation among our contemporaries, who assume that holy men always mean well, despite all the evidence to the contrary. A little common sense will show us that since the *Magi*, probably before the fall of the Persian Empire and certainly soon thereafter, made astrology a very lucrative part of their holy business, it was obviously advantageous to them to give their Saviour a name which would suggest to persons who knew Greek that he had been a prophet of astral phenomena. A verbal change so helpful in their trade could hardly have come about by chance. According to a record preserved by Diogenes Laërtius (*Pro.* 6.8), the *Magi* claimed that Zoroaster's name meant 'priest of the stars' or 'diviner by the stars,' evidently assuming with wonted impudence that he had been named in Greek at birth. (A scholion on the pseudo-Platonic *Alcibiades I* (*ad* 121E) says they claimed 'Zoroaster' was the Greek translation of his Persian name.) A better explanation devised by some of the *Magi* is preserved in two of the earliest Christian gospels, both purportedly written by Clement, a close friend and companion of Peter, the apostle of Jesus. In the *Recognitiones* (4.28) Zoroaster's name is said to mean 'living star.' Clement is more explicit in one of the *Homilies* (9-5), memoirs preserved in his correspondence with Jesus's brother James, which is further authenticated by a prefatory letter from Peter himself; in this text, he says that the name represents "the living influence of the star." According to Diogenes Laërtius

estimate to what extent these missionaries (possibly heretics at the time) were already peddling astrology as a useful adjunct to their evangelism, thus anticipating their successors in the Hellenistic Age.

The scanty information that we derive from the inscriptions by Persian kings is by far our best: There can be no doubt about either its authenticity or its dates.[61] We may use it to trace summarily the evolution of official Zoroastrianism in the Persian Empire, and, incidentally, to check the claim of a learned Parsee who has recently argued that "the wars of expansion waged by the Persians under the Achaemenids" should be compared to the early wars of Islam, for the Persian kings "had a divine mission to offer mankind," so that their wars "were dominated by a religious fervor that must be taken into account."[62] It is quite true that the teachings of Zoroaster enjoined on

---

(*ibid.*, 2.2), two or more great *Magi* who flourished before the time of Alexander the Great bore the name Astrampsychos, which was probably intended to mean 'the living star' or 'incarnate star.' This could have been originally just a variation or explanation of 'Zoroaster.' There is extant under this name a curious art of fortune-telling, commonly called the *Sortes Astrampsychi*, which should be read in the edition by Professor Gerald M. Browne, which is forthcoming from Teubner at Leipzig. The 'oracles' are elicited by a kind of arithmetical trickery, and I think it likely that the method goes back to the Persian *Magi*, although the extant versions, as Professor Browne has shown, are late and were probably concocted in Egypt, where, by the way, the name of Zoroaster was still potent in the early centuries of the present era. One of the gospels found at Chenoboskion is so arranged that the holy man using it can attribute the divine revelation to either Thoth or Zoroaster or Jesus, depending on his estimate of which is the most likely to impress his clientele. I believe this neat device was first identified by Jean Doresse in *Les livres secrets des Gnostiques d'Égypt* (Paris, 1958). The association of Zoroaster with the 'living stars' explains, of course, the tale in the "New Testament" about the star which, floating through the atmosphere, led the *Magi* to the marvellous Nativity at Bethlehem. Oddly enough, none of the gospels, so far as I can recall at the moment, tells us whether the obliging star returned to heaven when its mission was accomplished or simply vanished.

61   The text of the relevant inscriptions may most conveniently be consulted in Roland G. Kent's *Old Persian* (Yale University, 1950).

62   Ruhi Muhsen Afnan, *Zoroaster's Influence on Anaxagoras, the Greek Tragedians, and Socrates* (New York, 1969). The book is valuable as a reminder that Zoroastrianism, which is still a living faith, had the qualities that attract the masses and are requisite for a "universal" religion, but the influence of which the author speaks is largely illusory. The Greeks were naturally interested in the religion of the vast Persian Empire, with which they came into conflict many times, but 'Medism' is a strictly political term, which came into use when the Greek cities of Ionia tried to defend themselves diplomatically by maneuvering between

the Persian monarchs an enthusiasm for Holy Wars, but they were also Aryans and not without political intelligence, so it will be well to look at the record.

Cyrus was a Zoroastrian himself and made the new faith the official religion, but he was not a fanatic. He was a statesman and not only paid off the Jews for their work of sabotage in undermining the Babylonian Empire and their treachery in opening the gates of Babylon to him, but also placated the Babylonians by honoring their god, Marduk, and probably constructing a new temple for him, and he authorized or himself founded other temples for the local gods of the many and diverse nations that he had subjected to his tolerant rule. He probably encouraged the Zoroastrian missionaries to spread the Gospel by haranguing such audiences as they could attract, but he must have thwarted the holy men's professional eagerness to start persecuting.

He was succeeded in 530 by his son, Cambyses, whose major exploit was the conquest of Egypt. We are entitled to surmise that he was a godly man and that his piety motivated the contempt or hatred of the Egyptians' religion that he exhibited by violating sepulchres, ordering priests to be beaten for speaking on behalf of their cult, and slaying the sacred Apis bull, which was the incarnation of the soul (or part of the soul) of Osiris. We know, however, that he did not exhibit this fanaticism throughout his rule in Egypt.[63]

While Cambyses was in Egypt and just before his death in 522, the *Magi* carried out a *coup d'état* by having one of their number impersonate Smerdis, the brother of Cambyses and next heir to the throne, and installing him in power. They were thus able to coöperate with Ahura Mazda and to gratify their pious itch to persecute. They destroyed the "pagan" temples that Darius, in his famous inscription at Behistan, said he had to restore, and, knowing holy men,

---

the proximately dangerous power of Lydia and the more remote power of the Median kingdom. During the Persian invasions of the Greek mainland, it was applied to the Greeks who thought the might of Persia irresistible and believed that it would be prudent to come to terms with it. Even the Delphic Oracle, whose priests, like all 'psychics,' had to base their predictions on the best information available to them, made that mistake.

63   There is evidence, collected by Georges Posener, *La première domination perse en Égypte* (Cairo, 1936), that Cambyses during part of his reign conciliated the Egyptians by treating their deities respectfully, but it is uncertain whether he concealed his fanaticism until after his conquest was completed or abated it after he began to suffer military reverses in his efforts to conquer adjacent lands that were defended by natural barriers.

we may assume that they also enjoyed some exhilarating killing *ad maiorem gloriam Dei*. It is likely that their overweening fanaticism touched off the many revolutions in the provinces that Darius says he had to suppress. In 521, the false Smerdis was assassinated by a band of conspirators led by Darius, and there followed the pogrom of Magi we mentioned earlier.

Darius was the greatest of the Persian kings, and his reorganization of the Persian Empire still commands admiration. We may be sure that he did not try to combine fanaticism with government, and he undoubtedly kept a tight rein on the holy men. We have also the confession of his personal faith in documents of signal importance since they undoubtedly show the official doctrines of Zoroastrianism in his day. He attributes his victories and power to the One True God, Ahura Mazda (*Aüramazda*), who bestowed the kingdom on him, and of whom he says: "He created the Earth, he created the heavens, he created mankind, and he established *siyatis* for mortals." (There is no precise equivalent of the Persian word, which, from its basic meaning, 'welfare,' had come to imply security on Earth and happiness after death; 'salvation' or 'way of salvation' would do, provided we understood it to apply to both this world and heaven.) We thus have assurance that Darius put his trust in the one good god of Zoroaster's revelation.[64]

---

64   Some scholars are misled by the fact that Darius refers to Ahura Mazda as *mathista baganam* in several inscriptions and late in the long one at Behistan (§62) acknowledges help from *aniyaha bagaha*; they assume that *baga* means 'god,' so that Ahura Mazda is merely the greatest among many. Old Persian *baga*, Sanskrit *bhaga*, seems originally to have meant 'giver of gifts, lord,' and in both languages it was a title of respect that could be applied to a human, as well as a supernatural, superior. Given Darius's confession of faith in Ahura Mazda as the unique creator, the most reasonable explanation is that he intended *baga* to be the equivalent of the Avestan word *spenta*, which Zoroaster used as an adjective to describe Ahura Mazda (to whom he also referred as the *spenta mainyu*, meaning something like 'the bounteous lord' or 'the power of goodness') and also as a designation of the six *amesa spentas*, the six great archangels who are emanations of Ahura Mazda, representing abstract virtues ("Truth," "Good Will," etc.).; they are really aspects of the Good God, but are also thought of as his lieutenants; it will be remembered that after Ahura Mazda revealed himself to Zoroaster, he, from time to time, sent one of his *amesa spentas* to advise him in the course of his missionary efforts. The word 'archangel' is a convenient English term for an emanation of the Zoroastrian god, although the *spentas* differ from the Christian archangels in that they have no will (and hence no personality) of their own, it being explicitly stated that their will is always Ahura Mazda's, so that while *spenta* and *baga* (in my understanding of Darius's meaning) may be used in the plural,

Xerxes, who succeeded his father in 486, was a king more to the liking of the holy men. We do not hear of persecutions in his own realm, but we may conjecture that religion played some part in the revolts that broke out soon after his accession. He desecrated the great temple of Marduk in Babylon, slaying at least one of the priests, and carried off the huge statue of the god, which was said to be of solid gold. Historians believe that his purpose was political, to destroy the god who was traditionally the protector of Babylon and would serve as the focus of a separatist movement and revolt, but at the very least Xerxes must have had such confidence in Ahura Mazda that he feared no reprisals from the Marduk whom he contemptuously outraged and whom, as a good Zoroastrian, he should have regarded as the diabolical enemy of his own Good God. Piety could have moved him as much as political expediency, especially since the *Magi* at his court would have constantly reminded him of the duties of righteousness. And Xerxes has left us one eloquent witness to his religious fanaticism, the now famous inscription at Persepolis in which he prematurely boasts of his conquest of Greece and particularly of his godliness in destroying the temples on the Athenian acropolis in which the Greeks had worshipped devils, and in commanding them to worship such beings no longer. He presumably purified the polluted place, for he consecrated it to his one god, Ahura Mazda, whom he worships reverently in the confidence that the god will grant him felicity on Earth and beatitude in heaven.[65]

Xerxes' untimely vaunt must have seemed ironic after the suppos-

---

the plural does not detract from the unity of Zoroaster's one Good God. So far as we know, the Old Persian word may have been in general use among Zoroastrians in Darius's time with the meaning I have suggested, and Darius, as a prudent monarch, would not have been concerned if the "Pagans" misunderstood it.

65   Xerxes does not name Athens, but his meaning is unmistakable. The Persians also piously destroyed the Greek temples at Branchidae, Naxos, Abae, and doubtless other places of which we hear nothing; and we may be sure that they spared Delphi only because the priests there had made a poor guess and had their god advise the Greeks to yield to Persian might. It is slightly amusing that before the discovery of the inscription at Persepolis, quite a few historians discounted as "probably untrue" the statements of Herodotus and Cicero that Xerxes had destroyed the temples on the Acropolis; some still question Herodotus's report that the holy men at Xerxes' court egged him on to the invasion, promising him the conquest and annexation of all Europe. After Xerxes had to run back to Persia, he must have wondered why his *Magi* had sold him such a bill of spurious goods, and he probably asked questions, but holy men can usually think of an explanation to satisfy the customer.

edly subjugated Greeks inflicted two disastrous defeats on him, and the collapse of his great plan to conquer all Europe must have shaken his faith as well as that of many other Persians. Ahura Mazda hadn't helped the righteous! Nevertheless the theology of Darius and Xerxes seems to have undergone no significant change before the death of Darius II (the king who shrewdly intervened in the Peloponnesian War) in 405,[66] but his son, Artaxerxes II (the king of the Anabasis, once known to every schoolboy), attests a remarkable change in theology: He worships a Trinity. The tendency to tripartite thinking that Dumézil identifies as distinctively Aryan may have had some influence, but it is clear that at least two of the pre-Zoroastrian gods refused to be permanently suppressed in the minds of their "converted" votaries. Artaxerxes prays to Ahura Mazda, Anahita (the Virgin, *an-ahita*, 'undefiled'), and Mithra. The exact relationship of Ahura Mazda to his virginal consort is uncertain; it is not inconceivable that she was regarded as the Virgin Mother of Mithra at this time, having conceived miraculously, as mothers of gods usually do, and moreover, having like Mary in the Christian tale, given birth to a child even more miraculously and without rupture of her hymen,[67]

---

66   In one of his inscriptions at Susa, Darius II asks Ahura Mazda to protect him *hada bagaibis*; the noun is in the instrumental case, so the passage may be interpreted in conformity with what I said about the great Darius in note 64 above.

67   This is stated in all the versions of the Gospel of James, which describe more or less explicitly the proof of it in connection with the first miracle performed by the Saviour, when he was only a few minutes old. The most explicit account that I have seen is in the *Genesis Mariae* preserved in a third century papyrus now in the Bibliotheca Bodmeriana. Salome refuses to believe the midwife's assertion that the mother is still a virgin; she thrusts her finger into Mary's vagina and finds the hymen intact, but the vaginal membranes are so charged with divinity that her finger is set on fire and she is in great distress until she thinks of praying to Jesus's celestial father, who obligingly sends an angel to tell her to touch the divine infant; she does so and is instantly healed. Then the *Magi* come in, etc. It is hard to see why the Fathers did not include this gospel or, at least, some version of the Gospel of James, of which the authority was certainly guaranteed (since the author was the younger brother of Jesus), in their "New Testament." It is one of the earliest of the gospels and was accepted by many of the Fathers before the contents of the anthology were more or less settled by Athanasius in 369 or by Damasus in 382 (whose list of the contents is probably reproduced in the Decree that was forged in the name of Gelasius sometime after 495). Although the gospels that contained the proof of Mary's virginity *post partum* were excluded from the final compilation, many of the early Fathers of the Church, e.g., Didymus the Blind, Jerome, Ambrose, maintained the perpetual

or, alternatively and more plausibly, having the power to renew her virginity by bathing in magical water.[68] According to Berosus, Artaxerxes II not only introduced the worship of Anahita but also, by an equally daring innovation, set up statues of his gods, obviously in defiance of Zoroaster's explicit command that God was to be thought of aniconically and represented only by the flames of a sacred fire. The king's theology was unquestionably orthodox during his lifetime, since his army remained loyal, but it must have dismayed many, perhaps a majority, of the True Believers, and have excited furious controversies and intrigues among the *Magi*, but of those religious tempests we have, so far as I know, no record at all. It is doubtless significant that the king's son, Artaxerxes III, expelled Anahita and worshipped only Ahura Mazda and Mithra,[69] but we have no means of knowing exactly what it signifies.

The innovations of Artaxerxes II foreshadow the later evolution of the Zoroastrian cults. Poor Anahita was paradoxically identified with a Babylonian goddess and became Anaitis, whose attributes

---

virginity of Mary, belief in which became an orthodox dogma in the fifth century. No one ever tried to explain in detail how she remained a virgin after Joseph began to have sexual intercourse with her, as is explicitly stated in Matth. 1.25, and she bore him four sons, but theologians like to have things both ways. It is astonishing that no one thought of taking a Gospel of James in which Simon appears as Mary's stepson and her attendant at the time of the Nativity, interpolating it to make James *et al.* younger stepsons left at home, and then attributing the authorship to Simon, who would have had more opportunity to observe than a younger son of Mary. It would have been only reasonable to delete the line in the Gospel of Matthew and replace it with a few words stating that Joseph had the decency to respect the Wife of God. That would have settled everything nicely; but the sheer carelessness of the Fathers, evinced by so many contradictions they could have edited out of God's Word, constantly astonishes us as we read the texts they approved.

68 This oddly anatomical conception of virginity was doubtless of Oriental origin, but there was a Greek myth, mentioned by Pausanias (II.38.2), that Juno regularly renewed her virginity by bathing in a magical fountain, and, more to the point, Aelian (N.H., XII.30) mentions a goddess who restored her virginity after every coitus by bathing in a fountain located between the upper Tigris and Euphrates in the very territory in which contemporary Zoroastrians located some of their holy places. I need not remind the reader that my suggestion about Anahita is sheer speculation.

69 An ambiguity in the cuneiform script of an inscription of Artaxerxes III at Persepolis would make it possible to argue that he regarded Father and Son as one person, thus anticipating the paradox in one of the later Christian ideas about the constitution of a Trinity, but I think this highly improbable.

were the very antithesis of virginity. Mithra, a solar deity, is the son of Ahura Mazda, however he was engendered, and, as the Sun moves between the Earth and the vault of the sky, so was he the intermediary between mortals and his more inaccessible Father; he, moreover, had been born on Earth with a miraculous nativity first witnessed by the shepherds who reappear in the Christian legend, and on the day that the Christians, after long debate, finally selected as the birthday of their Saviour. And, as happened in Christianity, the Son eventually, for all practical purposes, replaced his aloof Father, producing the late derivative of Zoroastrianism that long competed with Christianity in the dying Roman Empire.

Chapter Ten: Zoroaster's Creation

ZOROASTER'S RELIGION, often called Mazdaism, is the greatest religion ever created by one man. It is the religion that had the greatest influence on our race, although most of that influence was exerted through its derivatives. And its invention was one of the crucial events in the history of the world.

It does not greatly matter whether Zoroaster was deranged and suffered from continual hallucinations or consciously manufactured his doctrine for some altruistic or egotistic purpose of his own. He so altered the subsequent course of civilization on this planet that we become dazed when we try to conjecture what we would be today, had Zoroastrianism never been invented. We cannot name another man whose effect on human history was as profound and as permanent as Zoroaster's. And it would be a mere quibble to argue that if he had not lived, some other revolutionary would have done as much.

Zoroastrianism was a spiritual catastrophe. It was the archetype of all the "universal religions," of which only Toynbee seems to have perceived the crucial importance as forces that constrict and deform a people's native culture and mentality. Toynbee, however, did not see, or thought it expedient not to notice, how lethal are religions that induce delusions about "all mankind" and propagate the idiotic notion that "all men are created equal." Zoroaster's doctrine of Salvation introduced some very peculiar and epochal superstitions that have been profoundly deleterious to all the races influenced by them, perhaps including even the Jews, although they profited most by exploiting them.

Zoroaster created a supreme god of good, whom he called Ahura Mazda, and a supreme god of evil, whom he called Angra Mainyu.[70] In the beginning, only these two great gods existed,[71] but they were antagonists from the first, each striving to his utmost to destroy the other and all of the other's works. Each created for himself subordinate generals and legions of supernatural troops to fight for him in the Cosmic War. Either of the two gods would be omnipotent if the other were conquered; and they and their vast armies are now locked in a desperate struggle for supremacy and mastery of the whole Universe, a perpetual war between pure Good and pure Evil. Since it posits the existence of two great and hostile gods, neither of whom can now overcome the other, Zoroastrianism is obviously a ditheism, a religious dualism. And so, of course, is the Christian *rifacimento* of it. It must be remembered that the word 'monotheism' is a neologism formed from Greek roots and introduced into English around the middle of the seventeenth century; and it can mean only one thing: belief in the existence of only one supreme god. Such a god, by definition, must have a power that is not limited by the power of any other supernatural being. Now it is true that during the past three centuries an increasing number of Christian theologians have wanted to make their religion a monotheism, but they can do this only by junking their Bible, and that would leave them without any basis for a belief in the existence of Jesus & Co. Their "New Testament" explicitly states that Satan is the mighty "prince of this world" and had such power that he was able to kidnap one-third of their God, carry him off to a mountain top, and there offer him wealth and dominion

---

70 My account of the Zoroastrian religion conforms to what would have been found in standard reference works (e.g., the Eleventh and Twelfth Editions of the *Encyclopaedia Britannica*) in the first third of this century and no further comment would have been needed. Subsequent research and study has produced no fact which would call for a significant modification in the essentials (with which we are alone concerned here), but it has produced a great proliferation of theoretical reconstructions of what Zoroaster supposedly believed but never said. This has caused a great deal of confusion, and I feel obliged to consider summarily, in Appendix I below, the cardinal point in all such reconstructions, although I consider it too nebulous and hypothetical to be of practical (historical) value.

71 Zoroaster is not sufficiently explicit in the *gathas* to enable us to be certain how he explained the origin of two antagonists, but his reference to them as "twins" suggests that he thought of both as existing from the very beginning of time. The alternative explanation, which is quite early, is that the Good God inadvertently created the Evil God by having a moment of doubt, i.e., stopping to think, which, as any theologian will tell you, is very bad business indeed.

that Jesus was obviously unable to obtain for himself; and the gospels in the collection are full of stories about activities of Satan and his lieutenants that God was obviously unable to prevent. It is clear, therefore, that the Christian god's power is limited by the power of a rival god, who is as strong and sometimes even stronger than he, and that the Earth must be regarded as a kind of No Man's Land between two opposing armies. That is precisely the Zoroastrian doctrine.

Some Christians try to twist their way out of the dilemma by claiming that their god is the only one that True Believers should worship, but that is simply monolatry, a phenomenon which, as we have already said, appears in many polytheistic religions. Another favorite evasion is resort to the Zoroastrian prediction that the good god will at some time in the future conquer the bad god, but that ploy will not work in talking about the present: If there is a war going on, it is necessarily a combat between two opposing forces, and it would be lunacy to pretend that there is only one force, and therefore no war, because one will in the end be victorious over the other. Modern theologians cannot improve on the old sophistry that Satan is not a god, although a god is, by definition, a powerful supernatural being, and Satan's right to that title is obvious from almost every page of the Christians' holy book. This device is one of the most ingenious tricks of early Christian propaganda.

In all of our languages, the word 'god' is a common noun designating a class of beings, specifically powerful supernatural beings, just as 'woman' is a common noun designating a class of human beings, and the individuals in a class must be identified by a personal name, such as Zeus or Helen. Now the early Christians took to calling their god *deus* (we can distinguish by writing *Deus*, but, of course, that use of capital letters is a modern innovation, unknown in Antiquity), and by baptizing their god "God" they could claim that all other supernatural powers were non-gods, just as you could baptize your daughter "Woman" and thus claim that all other females are non-women. A very few among the early Christians, especially Lactantius (*Institutiones*, II.9.13) were honest enough to call Satan an *antitheus*,[72] but the purloining of the common noun *deus* was commonly covered by imitating Zoroaster and inverting the meaning of

---

72   Readers of Homer will not need to be told that the word is here used in a sense that has nothing to do with the familiar Homeric epithet. In Lactantius, who died around 320, the word has come to mean 'anti-god,' i.e. a god who is the adversary of another god or gods, as the Titans were of the Olympians in the well-known myth. Lactantius, of course, says that Satan is a *pravus antitheus*, but in this passage, at least, he shows him a decent respect.

another common noun, *daemon*, which designated a larger class of supernatural beings that included not only gods but less powerful spirits. The Christians called all the other gods (in whose existence, of course, orthodox Christians must firmly believe) *daemones*, which was strictly correct, but then they claimed that all *daemones* were the subordinates of Satan, just as Zoroaster had audaciously claimed that all of the *devas* were the subordinates of his Angra Mainyu. Thus did Christians create the word 'demon' in its current sense of 'devil.' Their propaganda was certainly adroit, and we must give them credit for having improved a little on Zoroaster. But the verbal trick should impose on no one.

So much had to be said at this point to make it clear that both Zoroastrianism and its late derivative, Christianity, are equally ditheisms — and that if, by some sophistry, the term 'monotheism' is to be perverted and applied to one, the other has an equal title to it. Both posit the existence of only two great gods, each of whom is supreme in his own territory and neither of whom can now overcome the other. And this has the strange consequence that although the good god (Ahura Mazda, Yahweh) had the power to create the whole Universe and is now supported by angelic legions commanded by his trusty and doughty archangels, and the evil god can marshal legions of mighty and valiant devils, including all the gods previously worshipped by men, both antagonists need to recruit reinforcements from the puny race of mortals and strive to enlist every one of the weaklings they can persuade.[73] The cosmic conflict between the two gods and their supernatural and human armies is now a desperate one, waged with all their resources and causing infinite devastation and suffering on Earth, although, bizarrely enough, the result is a foregone conclusion and everyone knows that the good god will triumph in the end and spend eternity in joyously tormenting his defeated adversary and all of the fallen monarch's wickedly loyal and luckless followers.

One can only marvel that so preposterous a fiction could have imposed on Aryan minds. It is not only illogical, but one of its basic premises is alien to our racial mentality. The Aryans' gods are never evil. They may, of course, punish mortals who have insolently offended them, and they may act, as do all the forces of Nature, with complete disregard of the convenience or safety of individuals

---

73 If we use the Zoroastrianism of Artaxerxes II for comparison, the congruency will be perfect, since the good gods of the two religions will also have the support of their mighty sons (Jesus, Mithra).

or nations, but they are never malevolent. Pan (the model for Satan in Christian iconography) does indeed excite panics, but every man who has found himself utterly alone in a desert, pathless mountains, or a great forest has experienced the god's power. You and I know, of course, that the reaction of our nerves, the subconscious fear of helplessness that it requires an effort of reason to overcome, is atavistic and represents a flaw that lies deep in the human psyche, but it can be thought of as some power that abides in the place, a *numen* that is hostile in the sense in which other great forces of Nature, such as a hurricane or an angry ocean (note the pathetic fallacy), are hostile because they reck nothing of us; but they are not malevolent, they do not have a conscious purpose to destroy us. The Great God Pan is the spirit of the wild, of the Nature on which we can intrude only at our own peril.[74] He does not really differ from, say, Poseidon or Aphrodite, gods who also have purposes that are not ours.

The Norse religion is likewise true to Nature. There are beings that are hostile to gods and men in the sense that they injure and destroy, but they are essentially natural powers and without malevolence. Fenrir is not malicious: He is a celestial wolf, the counterpart of terrestrial wolves, who pursue and pull down deer because it is their nature to do so, not because they wish to inflict pain on their victims. Nigg gnaws at the roots of Yggdrasill as cut-worms destroy plants

---

74   Since verbal misunderstandings play a large part in the evolution of religious beliefs, I note that Pan is a pastoral deity whose name, of uncertain derivation (one possibility is that it comes from the Indo-European root represented by the Sanskrit verb *pus* 'to nourish, to cause to grow'), has nothing whatsoever to do with another word of identical spelling and almost identical pronunciation in Greek, *pan*, which is the neuter of the adjective meaning 'all,' so that the god's name could be, and was, misunderstood to mean 'everything,' i.e., the whole Universe. The mistake was compounded by the tendency of pious persons enthusiastically to exaggerate the attributes and powers of a god to whom they are particularly devoted (see above). Since no one seems to have noticed it before, I recommend to students of religion a doxology that they can also enjoy as poetry, unless their canons of Latinity are so strict that they cannot appreciate the *Pervigilium Veneris*, which comes from about the same time. I refer to a hymn to Priapus ("*pater rerum*" and so identified with the universal Pan) that will be found in the *Corpus inscriptionum Latinarum*, XIV. 3565. The author of these genial stanzas (they are stanzas, with a refrain) is unknown; it is most unlikely that they were composed by the freedman who had them engraved on the marble base of the statue that he, at the behest of his god, commissioned and had set up at Tibur, where I was told by a local antiquary that the beautiful statue was destroyed by Christian fanatics around the end of the eighteenth century, a late, though not impossible, date.

by feeding on their roots. The relation between the Norse gods and the Giants is a general hostility moderated by visits and occasional alliances that seem odd and even perplexing to modern readers until they understand that a *Jötunn* is not a devil in the Christian sense but a supernatural being of a race that is fundamentally incompatible with the race of the *Esir* and *Vannir*. The relationship is analogous to that between the aborigines and our race when we invaded North America: The two races were necessarily enemies and each had to try to destroy the other, but in the meantime, some individuals of different race could meet and associate on terms of neutrality or temporary friendship.

Loki often appears evil to minds that have been imbued with Christian notions, and even scholars, who should know better, try to decide whether he is a 'good' god or an 'evil' one. The answer is that he is simply a supernatural human being. He exhibits the feckless mischievousness that is natural in children and accounts for their more vexing pranks on Guy Fawkes Day or Hallowe'en, and is often found in adults who humorously perpetrate "practical jokes" or "initiations" into "fraternal societies" that sometimes result in the unintended death of one or more victims. At the worst, he is like so many of our contemporary "intellectuals," who take a perverse pleasure in siding with our enemies, but, if put to the test, would not murder us in cold blood. Loki exists as a supernatural being like the gods, but no one worships him, because it would be folly to expect help from so irresponsible an individual. The Aryan mind instinctively rejects the notion of divine malevolence. When forced to accept the unpalatable notion by an alien religion, however, the racial mind can interpret it in terms of our feeling for the dramatic and heroic.[75]

---

[75] It is instructive to compare Tolkien's three romances. Some of the praeternatural beings we encounter in *The Hobbit* are noxious (Goblins, Trolls, Dragons), but that is because it is their nature to prey on us: they are like cannibals and dinosaurs, creatures that we would exterminate in any region we inhabit. That is one of the several reasons why the book is an entertaining and absorbing tale, but not one that moves us deeply. The Lord of the Rings, however, takes up the Zoroastrian idea and is dominated by the equivalent of Angra Mainyu, a mighty supernatural being who is supernaturally malevolent and exerts all of his vast powers to inflict degradation and suffering on our race and its allies; and that is one of the factors that make the book a story of high emprise and heroism that often rises to the level of epic poetry, and assure it of a place among the great literature of our race. The *Silmarillion* is, so to speak, a new Bible, a combination of cosmological and pseudo-historical myth that is free from the gross immorality, disgusting vulgarity, and patent absurdities of that holy book and vastly supe-

And the idea does acquire some plausibility because we always imagine our gods as anthropomorphic and malevolence is an exclusively human trait. Whereas all other mammals kill only because they are hungry or have to defend themselves, and never inflict pain for the satisfaction of seeing suffering, the several species called human kill and torture for the sheer joy of inflicting death and pain and take an even more disgusting pleasure in watching others inflict agony and death, especially when the victims have offended them in some way or merely refused to listen to them, as did the persons whom Jesus wanted to have murdered where he could enjoy the spectacle of their death-agonies.[76] Sadism and kindred passions are exclusively human, and when we call the more repulsive human beings, savages or the degenerates of our species, brutal and bestial, we are traducing the innumerable species of morally superior animals.

It is an identifiable characteristic of our race, which distinguishes it from all others, that while we, if we have not become effete, kill with exemplary efficiency the enemies who are a danger to us, we are averse from inflicting unnecessary suffering even on them and, what is more, if they are enemies whom we can respect in terms of our standards, even feel compassion and regret that we must slay them.[77]

---

rior from every standpoint, but it inevitably fails to give a convincing account of the origin of supernatural evil and resembles a panoramic painting of the Dutch school that depends for its total effect on our observation of a large number of small figures crowded, with distracting detail, into every square inch of the large canvas. Hence the disappointment of many readers; poetic suspension of doubt has its limits and cannot approximate a religious faith.

76   Our holy men try to ignore the significant pronouncement at Luke 19.27, although it is an essential part of their creed.

77   The reader may be interested in an example from a source from which he would scarcely expect it, one which will incidentally show that although India became a multiracial jungle, something of the Aryan mentality survived as late as the seventh century. Many years ago l essayed a verse version of a stanza by Mayura that is preserved in the *Saduktikanamrta* (I.xv.3). It is based on the story that the Asuras had three great cities, of silver, gold, and steel respectively, and made war upon the old Aryan gods. The Thirty-three Gods were unable to resist the Asuras, and so appealed to the great Trinity. In answer to their prayer, Siva, the dread and ruthless god of destruction, destroyed the three cities of the Asuras with his arrows of unquenchable fire.

> I sing the god of world-destroying might,
> Siva, who smote with bolts of quenchless flame
> The triple city of the anti-gods:
> For when he saw the molten walls decay
> And fall, the thund'ring bow fell from his hands

Unlike all other races, we find the gratuitous infliction of pain on any mammal repulsive and disgusting. And when members of our race violate our racial instinct, we consider them degenerate or insane, except in the rare instances when an individual has himself suffered, in his own person or in that of persons dear to him, such enormous outrage that a frenzied passion to inflict the utmost retribution is understandable, though scarcely laudable.

Malevolence is human. That is why it is so commonly attributed to the spirits of the dead, who, in the popular superstitions of many races, are supposed to be invidious and to envy the living and therefore seek to harm them. A striking example is the Ciupipiltin of the Aztecs: The ghosts of women who died in childbirth hover about the living and strive incessantly to injure women who have been more fortunate than they and especially to cripple those women's children. Our race is more apt to attribute malignity to the ghosts of the wicked or, sometimes, to mindless entities that lurk in the corruption of the grave.[78] From this it is a small step to belief in demons — but let us always remember that, as we have already remarked, the Christian

> And his immortal eyes were touched with tears.
> In inner rooms the demon-women stood;
> He saw the fire cut away the hems
> Of their embroidered robes and lave their hair.
> He saw the flame upon their bodiced gowns
> He saw its fingers stroke their girdled loins
> And pluck the silver apples of their breasts.

Siva felt compassionate admiration for the noble enemies whom he had to destroy. That is what it means to be an Aryan. When Philip of Macedon, in all the pride of his great victory, saw the men of the Hieros Lochos of Thebes, who lay dead in their ranks on the field at Chaeronea, he wept. A Jew would have spat and urinated on them.

78   In modern literatures, the ghost of a murdered man may justly seek vengeance on his murderer, but the ghosts of murderers are sometimes thought of as lamenting or expiating their crimes, and sometimes as bent on multiplying from beyond the tomb the crimes they committed while alive. There is, of course, a large Christian element in these superstitions. Literary critics have often remarked that Classical ghost stories are comparatively tame; Sherwin-White, for example, thinks that is because Graeco-Roman society did not have Mediaeval castles or isolated manor houses for ghosts to haunt, but that is to miss the point. In the Classical tales, such as the well-known ghost story told by the younger Pliny (VII.27) or the yarns collected by Lucian in his *Philopseudes*, the ghost clanks chains or makes terrifying gestures, but all that he wants is decent burial for his corpse or bones. What is lacking is the element of actual or potential malevolence that spices so many of our tales of the supernatural.

word is a typical perversion of the Classical *daemon*, which designated a supernatural being that was often benevolent and, at worst, uninterested in human beings who do not offend it.[79] Zoroaster's great invention was his dichotomy of the whole world, natural and supernatural, by a moral division between perfect goodness and perfect evil. Each of these fictions logically implied its antithesis, and they may have been simply the spontaneous product of his imagination. If, however, we seek a source for the un-Aryan notion of an evil god, we may find it in the Semitic religions, of which Zoroaster is likely to have had some knowledge. As is generally known, the predominantly Semitic Babylonians[80] thought themselves encompassed by

---

79   *Daemon* is a word of very wide meaning and also serves in Classical psychology to explain the operations of the subconscious mind, including instincts and intuition, which we ourselves do not fully understand and commonly regard as separable from conscious personality, for we generally attribute the excellence of a poet, musician, or other artist to his genius rather than to the man himself, and we do so correctly, for he usually explains his achievement as the result of inspiration rather than conscious thought; and we commonly understand and accept such explanations of peculiar conduct as "something made me do it." Every man has his genius or *daemon* that accounts for the intuitive and sub-rational part of his personality, which often determines his success or failure in a given undertaking or in his life as a whole. One thinks of the *daemon* of Socrates, for example, and I note that William G. Simpson, in his admirable book, *Which Way, Western Man?* [Cosmotheist Books; cosmotheistchurch.org — Ed.], posits a virtually identical force in the human mind. I emphasize the psychological application of the word in ancient literature because I have noticed a deplorable blunder in our standard Greek-English lexicon (Liddell-Scott-Jones), in which the Greek *kakodaimon* is defined as "possession by an evil genius" and *kakodaimonao* is actually defined as "to be possessed by an evil spirit," definitions which will certainly mislead persons who have not read much Greek and may imagine some connection with Christian notions about persons "possessed of the devil," etc. Nothing could be more erroneous. There is no idea whatsoever of a malevolent spirit. A man is *kakodaimon* because his own character (or sometimes, chance) has made him, unfortunate; he is "cross-grained" or "a blunderer" or "unlucky," and his conduct is of the kind that we often describe by saying "he won't listen to reason" or "he has an unattractive personality" or "his instincts are all wrong" or "he is his own worst enemy." A misunderstanding of the Greek words is a measure of the extent to which our Aryan mentality has been distorted by Semitic ideas.

80   The Babylonians were the dominant power at the time Zoroaster began to preach his gospel, and he may have been influenced by their culture and religion. Most scholars agree that the Assyrian-Babylonian demonology had no precedent in the religion of the Sumerians, from whom the Semites derived the greater part of their culture. In the time of Zoroaster, the Babylonians were

swarms of maleficent demons who, inspired by an abiding malignity, ceaselessly strove to injure men by every means, from diseases to hurricanes, under the command of the Seven Evil Gods, Namtaru, Rabisu, Pazuzu, *et al.* These demons would destroy mankind but for the precarious protection that might be won from the more placable gods, especially Marduk, the solar deity, and his purifying agent, fire, which significantly reappears in Zoroastrianism as the power that wards off evil.

The Evil Gods hated mankind and their devices were subtle and endlessly varied. In one of the tales about Naram-Sin[81] (grandson of Sargon of Agade), which probably grew from a germ of fact, we are told that his realm was invaded by an enormous horde of beings who had the faces, and apparently also the bodies, of ravens. The urgent question whether they were demons or mortals was settled by the discovery that they bled when wounded, but nevertheless they,

---

predominantly Semitic, but it is a mistake to infer from their language that the population belonged entirely to that race. There was a large admixture of other races, almost certainly including descendants (perhaps more or less mongrelized) of the Cassites, who conquered Babylonia near the end of the seventeenth century BC and ruled it for about five centuries. The Cassites spoke an Indo-European language and seem to have been Aryans, although they, like the Mitanni, who conquered Assyria in that period, may have been a nation composed of an Aryan aristocracy and subject masses belonging to one or more other races. In Zoroaster's time, the Jews were well established in Babylon, which they would betray to Cyrus the Great in return for rights of occupation in Palestine, to which they despatched a contingent from their wealthy colony in Babylon. It is not remarkable that most of their mythology is Babylonian in origin.

81   Naram-Sin, like his grandfather, was the hero of a cycle of tales composed many centuries after his death. This tale probably represents a folk-memory of events of which we know from Sumerian historical sources, an invasion by the Gutians, a wild and barbarous people (who may have had Armenoid features that suggested birds' beaks), and other disasters that ended the empire of Agade soon after Naram-Sin was succeeded by his ill-fated son. There followed a period of anarchy which the Sumerian king list neatly summarizes in the words, "Who was king? Who was not king?" A Sumerian religious text informs us that the invasions and disasters fell upon Naram-Sin because his troops had looted the temple of Enlil in Nippur. In requital of that outrage, a curse was put upon Naram-Sin's capital, Agade. The curse served as a model for the cursing attributed to Isaiah (13.19-22) in the "Old-Testament," with the difference that Agade was totally destroyed, whereas the city of Babylon (and its wealthy Jewish parasites) flourished for centuries after the futile raving in that chapter, which was probably composed as propaganda to demoralize the Babylonians at the time of the Persian invasion of their territory in 540.

zealously assisted by the Evil Gods, brought manifold disasters upon the kingdom until the god Enlil was persuaded to take some action against them that was described on a missing part of the clay tablet. Enlil was a deity taken over from the Sumerians and eventually supplanted by Marduk, the 'Son of the Sun,' who was thoroughly Semitized.

Although his influence on Zoroaster is more problematical, we should mention another contemporary god of evil. In the overgrown and incoherent theology of the Egyptians,[82] Set (Seth) was originally a companion of the beneficent Horus, but later regarded less favorably, and after 1570 BC he was execrated as the very incarnation of evil and the enemy of mankind for two reasons between which the connection is not entirely clear.

1. Osiris was the Egyptian version of the god whose death and resurrection made it possible for righteous men to attain immortality. According to an account that seems relatively early, while Osiris was on Earth, he was murdered by Set, who first concealed the body and later dismembered it, scattering its various organs throughout Egypt to prevent the Resurrection, which was eventually brought about through the devotion of Isis, sister and wife of Osiris. Set was therefore the implacable enemy of the beneficent gods and consequently of mortals, and his malignant hatred was manifested, even after the Resurrection, in many ways, including, for example, an attempted homosexual rape of the divine child, son of Isis and Osiris.

2. Egypt long suffered from a steady infiltration of Semites, a con-

---

[82] E.A. Wallis Budge's *The Gods of the Egyptians*, available in Dover reprint (2 vols., New.York, 1969 = 1904), is the most convenient survey of Egyptian theology, although three-quarters of a century of intensive archaeological exploration and scholarship have naturally produced many additions and corrections, of which only one is really crucial. Egypt was a union of many regions that were strung out along the Nile from its mouths to the First Cataract, and its religion was necessarily a theocracy, which was never made coherent. Our minds boggle, for example, when we discover that Horus was the brother of his father and the son of his aunt, and that he mourned at his father's bier although he was not conceived until after his father rose from the dead. Confronted by this *fatras* of absurdities, Sir Wallis, who was impressed by the fact that Christians could believe a Trinitarian doctrine, which made an "only begotten son" as old as the father who begat him, tried to read a monotheistic basis into the incoherent polytheism, as though the many gods had been aspects of a single divinity. This view, set forth in his short introductory volume, *Egyptian Religion* (New York, 1959 = 1900), only slightly contaminated the major work I cited above. Egyptologists now emphatically reject a notion for which there is no evidence whatsoever.

tinuous trickle of covertly enemy aliens across the Sinai peninsula, who, after they became sufficiently numerous, gnawed away the foundations of Egyptian society by the usual techniques of political subversion, inflicted on the nation all the horrors of a proletarian revolution, and finally took it over, ruling it, with the aid of native traitors, from about 1780 BC until they were finally expelled by an Egyptian revolt in 1570 BC. The Semites had a tribal god, comparable to the Jews' Yahweh, whom they identified with Set and whose worship they tried, whenever it was not politically inexpedient, to impose on all the Egyptians. The insidious aliens were cordially hated by the Egyptians (including, no doubt, the opportunists who served the enemy as front men and collaborators), and after the expulsion of the Semites, their god, Set, was abominated as the patron of the foul race that had brought on Egypt innumerable disasters and two centuries of ill-disguised servitude.

Both of these considerations made Set an analogue of the Christian Satan, an anti-god whom the Egyptians execrated — most of the time, for we cannot expect logical consistency from their religiously muddled minds.[83]

It is possible, though not demonstrable, that Zoroaster was influenced by what he had heard of the Babylonian and perhaps Egyptian polytheisms when he formulated his revolutionary dualism.

---

83   Set was loathed as the god of all evil, but, incredible as it seems to us, he was at times simultaneously worshipped as a benefactor and shown special honor by the kings of the Nineteenth Dynasty (1320-1200), two of whom even took the name Seti (*Sethos*) to identify themselves as his special protégés. That is as though some kings of Christian Europe consecrated cathedrals to Judas and Satan! Racial decay probably set in fairly early in Egyptian history, but as late as the Twelfth Dynasty we find an intelligent understanding of racial differences; under the rule of the Hyksos, the country was rather thoroughly mongrelized and its religion became a chaos of confused superstitions. So far as I know, there is no evidence that would authorize a conjecture that the Setis' worship of Set had racial implications, nor need there have been in a religion in which a goddess can become the mother of her father. Egyptian religion is a case of national schizophrenia.

Chapter Eleven:
The Great Überwertung, Psychic Magic, God's House, Buddhism, and Tapas

The Great *Überwertung*

WHEN WE CONSIDER Zoroaster with historical objectivity, we are awed by the enormity of his religious revolution.

He invented a perfectly good god, Ahura Mazda, whom he identified as the Creator and unique source of all moral probity; and since it is hard to imagine a hermit god, he had his god create for himself a court of divine satraps, so to speak, the six Amesa Spentas, who are simply personified abstractions. They are Volu Manah ("Good Will"), Asa Vahista ("Truth" = What is Right, both physically and morally), Xsathra Vairya ("Righteous Goverment"), Spenta Armaiti ("Piety"), Haurvatat ("Perfection" = Health of all parts), and Ameretat ("Immortality"). These celestial noblemen naturally have their retinues of angelic servants and warriors, but obviously our devotion must be to the one good god. To be saved, we must enlist in his army.

As the antithesis of his good god, Zoroaster invented a god of pure evil, Angra Mainyu, the unique author of all sin and wickedness and of all the suffering of all human beings. This implacable enemy of the good god created his legions of devils to seduce and afflict mankind, and these malignant spirits are simply all the gods of all the peoples on Earth who haven't been taught to worship Ahura Mazda. And the votaries of those gods are therefore the mortal soldiers of the immortal enemy of Righteousness.

It follows, therefore, that it is the duty of all who have been Saved by Zoroaster's Revelation to "convert" or annihilate all the peoples of the Earth who worship other gods and thus serve Angra Mainyu in his Cosmic War against the Good.

Zoroaster would doubtless have been distressed had he been able to foresee that no lieutenant of Angra Mainyu could have done a better job than he, for his Revelation brought upon mankind the calamitous epidemic of religious mania that characterizes all "revealed" religions,[84] the anaeretic fanaticism that dares confidently to say "*Gott mit uns!*" The more rational polytheism of the Aryans and of other races prevented men from taking leave of their senses in that way. You could never be sure of the favor of any god or of the limits of his power. The Athenians honored Poseidon, but that did not avert the squall that spoiled their naval victory at Arginusae. Athena was doubtless pleased by her temple on the Acropolis, but she was not able to save the city that had taken her as patroness, or even her own temple, from Xerxes. And if some gods favored you, you could be sure that the enemy also had gods on his side. In the Trojan war, some of the Olympian gods favored the Greeks and some favored the Trojans, but the most that a god could do was give a little help to his favorites in a struggle that was decided by human courage and strategy and by the impersonal power of the Destiny that is greater than the gods. A polytheist might venerate his chosen gods, but he knew that he would nevertheless have to reckon with reality. But a man who has been Saved by a glorious Revelation, achieving solidarity with an omnipotent (well, almost omnipotent) god, can run berserk with Righteousness.

By inverting the Aryan religion and turning its gods into demons, Zoroaster invented the arrogant zealotry that reappeared so often and so terribly in all of subsequent history. Thence came, for example, the poisonous fanaticism of the Christians, who never doubted the existence or even the power of Jupiter, Mars, Venus, Apollo, and the other gods of the Classical world, but regarded those august, handsome, and often gracious beings as foul fiends,[85] who could not be slaughtered themselves, but whose beautiful temples could be defiled and destroyed, whose votaries could be terrorized or butch-

---

84 The reader may also profitably contrast *revealed* religions (in which the founder of the religion somehow receives a divine message from a god, and this "word of god" becomes the basis of the religion),with a *natural* religion such as William Luther Pierce's Cosmotheism, more akin to a Nature-based philosophy, based on evident or scientifically demonstrable facts, and reasonable extrapolations from those facts. — Ed. (see *Cosmotheism: Religion of the Future*; Pierce, William, *et al.* Cosmotheist Books, Mountain City, Tennessee; cosmotheistchurch.org.)

85 Orthodox Christian doctrine is stated concisely by Augustine, *De civitate Dei*, IV.I: "The false gods, whom they (the 'pagans') once worshipped openly and even now worship secretly, are the most filthy spirits and devils, so extremely malignant and deceitful that they rejoice in whatever crimes are, whether truly or falsely, imputed to them …so that human weakness …may not be restrained from the perpetration of damnable deeds."

ered while their elegant homes were profitably looted, and whose supposed patronage of the arts and sciences gave a welcome pretext for sanctifying ignorance, boorishness, and misology. And when the Christians began at last to doubt the existence of the "pagan" gods, we see an ominous fissure in the wall of their Faith.[86]

Zoroaster and his spiritual descendants, Jesus, Mahomet, and many less successful Saviours, made of the world a vast battleground on which Ahura Mazda and Angra Mainyu (under these or other names) are waging a perpetual war for dominion, over the whole world, and since the two almost omnipotent deities somehow need men to fight for them, every human being must necessarily take part in the desperate war for the world, and if he does not fight for the good god, he is serving the evil one.

It becomes the duty of every "righteous" man to preach the new gospel to all the world, as was done by Zoroaster and his disciples, but when the evil god's troops are so perversely obdurate to rhetoric that they will not desert their commander, they must be destroyed. Zoroaster, in other words, invented the *jihad*, the Holy War, and his invention must be regarded as one of the greatest calamities that has fallen upon our race and even upon mankind. When the Zoroastrian cult is described by scholars who have retained the lees of Christianity in their minds, they expatiate unctuously about "spiritual values" and "lofty morality," but they never think of counting the corpses.

According to the Zoroastrian tradition — and it does not really matter whether that tradition records actual events or holds up an ideal for True Believers — when Zoroaster succeeded at last in bringing the Gospel and Salvation to a king, Vistaspa, that monarch naturally wanted to save the souls of his subjects and he piously gave them the option of being Saved or having their throats cut. Having thus consolidated the Church Militant (with the aid of his courtiers and officers, who, of course, had immediately perceived the Truth of the new religion on the "conversion" of the king, who was the

---

[86] Few have perpended the profound significance of the revival of Classical mythology in the Renaissance. The Humanists, who responded to the true beauty of the ancient myths and the noble literature that enshrined them, were able to claim that those gods were only lovely fictions and did not, in fact, exist. That was a drastic weakening of Christian orthodoxy, as was justly perceived by some contemporary Christian misologists, e.g., Giovanni da Sanminiato, whose uncouth *Lucula noctis* was first edited and published by Edmund Hunt (University of Notre Dame, 1950). Coluccio Salutati ridiculed his Latinity, which, while not so painfully barbarous as much Mediaeval stuff, was syntactically and lexically defective. In an age of reviving learning, that was enough to shut up the holy man.

fount from whom all revenues flowed), he was ready to turn his pious thoughts to the neighboring nations, and we are treated to a long chronicle of extremely sanguinary conquests, which are actually called the "Wars of Religion" in the Pahlavi annals. The wars and battles are described in considerable detail. In the first great battle, for example, Vistaspa lost 38 of his sons, 1,163 noblemen, and 30,000 common soldiers, but the wicked "pagans" lost more than 100,000 men. The result is an armistice, but the war is renewed and, after many peripeties and vicissitudes, the True Faith triumphs and the righteous have learned to grant no quarter and to spare the lives of no "infidels." Glorious are the heroes who are the Sword of God and do what they can to expunge sin with blood![87]

When we turn from legend to history, the monarchs of the Persian Empire were, as we have seen, pious Zoroastrians and attributed their power to the supposed benefactions of Ahura Mazda, but such religious zeal as they may have felt was more or less moderated by political prudence until we come to Xerxes. He has left us proof of his fanaticism in the inscription in which he proudly records his devastation of the Athenian Acropolis: "there was a place in which devils (*daiva*) were formerly worshipped. There, by the help of Ahura Mazda, I demolished that lair of the devils and I issued an edict, 'You shall not worship devils.' And in the very place in which devils had once been worshipped, I piously and with Righteousness worshipped Ahura Mazda."

At Salamis and Plataea the Greeks saved Europe (for a few centuries) from a spiritual pestilence.

Psychic Magic

The godly tribe of Ahura Mazda's clever priests gave us the word 'Magic,' but none of their feats of prestidigitation was half so marvelous as the magic Zoroaster says he performed at the very beginning of his ministry. In one of his *gathas*, he lavishly praises a Turanian named Fryana, and according to the uniform tradition, this man and his family were among the very first converts to Zoroaster's religion.[88] They were among the first Apostles and they and their de-

---

[87] For an attempt to extract some history from the tales, see Professor A.V. William Jackson's *Zoroaster* (New York, 1901). There have been later speculations, of course, but when we go beyond the probability that there was a king of Bactria who believed Zoroaster we are lost in a fog, without a single item of historical evidence to guide us.

[88] There is an even stranger tradition (not supported by the *gathas*) that

scendants were revered as such. In other words, Turko-Mongolians were transformed into Aryans (or the equivalent) by believing, or saying they believed, Zoroaster's tall tales about his newly created god. Zoroaster seems to have been the inventor of the notion of a "spiritual transformation" effected by a religious "conversion," which is, of course, much more marvelous than the conversion of a princess into a white cat or a frog, of which we are so often told in fairy tales. The tales suppose that the princess remains herself, with her mind and character unchanged by confinement to a feline or batrachian body, whereas the miracle of a religious "conversion" is said to change character and thus transform the individual into a different person.[89]

The Turanians were transmuted into more than Aryans. By believing Zoroaster, they enlisted in the army of the good God, and they thus became vastly superior to all the Aryans who refused Salvation at the hands of God's salesman. They acquired a right, nay, a duty to help smite all those Aryans, whom they must regard as agents of the evil god and therefore their deadly enemies. And the Aryans who

---

the very first person whom Zoroaster tried to "convert" after his conference with Ahura Mazda was not an Aryan! He was a Turanian named Urvaitadeng, a just and honorable man, who would have accepted the Gospel, had he not drawn the line at the theological doctrine of *xvaetvadatha*, which recommends as especially pious and meritorious sexual unions between mother and son and between brother and sister (see above). That idea shocked the Turko-Mongolian, so he rejected Salvation and he and his progeny were damned forever and forever. Let that be a lesson to all doubters, who let their own feeble minds interfere with obedience to the Will of God, which is a mystery beyond all human understanding!

89   Miss Boyce believes that in the time of Zoroaster the Turanians (*Tuirya*) were one of five related tribes of the same race; that when they are described as the foes of the Aryans (*Airya*), the reference is not to the race but to one of the five tribes; and that the name 'Turanian' was transferred to the Turko-Mongolians when they displaced the Aryan tribe and occupied the territory we know they held in the time of the Persian Empire. This, which seems unlikely in itself, depends on the very early date she assigns to Zoroaster and on her claim that he had no association at all with Medes, Persians, and *Magi*, so that the traditions about his parentage, travels, ministry, and enlistment of the *Magi* are all late and baseless inventions. If that is true, we must resign ourselves to knowing nothing about Zoroaster, and it becomes likely that the *gathas*, which purport to record his pronouncements, are only very clever forgeries, and that the religion was concocted *ab ovo* by the *Magi*. This seems to me extremely improbable in the light of what we know about the genesis of "revealed" religions and the tenor of the *gathas*.

took to the new religion must accept the equally sanctified aliens as their brothers-in-arms, while the other Aryans, including perhaps those who were a man's nearest and dearest, have become their enemies, evil beings who, if they do not yield to exhortation and harassment, must be destroyed to help make a Better World. Zoroaster could have exulted, as did Jesus much later, that he had "come to set a man at variance against his father, and the daughter against her mother, and ...a man's foes shall be they of his own household." Religion has become a corrosive acid that dissolves all the natural bonds of society, kinship, family, social status, race, and even government, and replaces them with the factitious and unnatural bond of unanimity in superstition.

A recent writer does not greatly exaggerate when, thinking to praise Zoroastrianism, he describes it as "a universalist religion, advocating spiritual equality between all races, nations, and classes, even between man and woman.... The state was not considered to be the supreme reality.... It was to constitute an atmosphere [!] wherein all individuals, irrespective of their sex, or class, or race could achieve perfection [!]."[90]

The Zoroastrian cult and all the cults derived from it can be summarized in one sentence. They replace race with a church. They are a deadly racial poison. They are a bubonic plague of the mind and spirit, which has sapped the vitality of our race for centuries and has now brought it to the point of death.

It is true that we have little information about the racial application of the religion in its early stages.[91] Zoroaster tells us that he

---

90   Ruhi Afnan, *op. cit.*, p. 30.
91   We must not exaggerate. Miscegenation long antedates Zoroaster, and the religions merely sanctified an inveterate vice and eroded an already feeble racial consciousness. Wherever our race has established itself, our men have been unable to keep their hands off the women of other races. Viking expeditions were necessarily small bands of warriors, and when they occupied territory far from home, as in the Western Hemisphere, miscegenation was inevitable, though deplorable, especially in its effect on the resulting mongrels. In tribal migrations, such as that of the Aryans into India, there was no valid reason for such feckless indulgence in lust, which can be excused only by their ignorance of genetics. The crucial importance of racial heredity, indeed, is a recent discovery, abhorred, of course, by our enemies and by all of our people who profit from ignorance and superstition. It is true that until our race finally succumbed to the "one world" poisons and became crazed with a suicidal mania, we did try to keep our women uncontaminated and there were, from time to time, in various societies some efforts to restrict legal marriages to women of our race, leaving the males free to

hated everyone who did not accept his "revelation," and a probably authentic tradition adds that Ahura Mazda commanded him to curse all who did not embrace the Gospel and that Zoroaster commanded that in every land persons who reject Salvation must be slain at once. Obviously, there was no thought of sparing Aryans. And on the other hand, Zoroaster rejoices over Turko-Mongolian converts and sends his missionaries into "far lands," presumably regardless of the race inhabiting them. The sense of racial integrity was not quickly destroyed, however, for when Darius boasts that he is "an Aryan of the Aryans," he is obviously speaking of race, and, no doubt, he understood in the same way the Zoroastrian dogma, which probably dates from his time, that only Aryans should rule. What is odd, however, is that the only early term for the adherents of the new religion seems to have been *Airyavo danghavo*, which identifies them as the "Aryan people," but must include converts of other races to the "universal" religion. And there are instances in which the meaning of the noun is ambiguous before we come to the late writings in Pahlavi in which 'Aryan' (*Eran*) and 'non-Aryan' (*Aneran*) simply mean 'Zoroastrian' and 'infidel.' As I indicated in an early section of this book, I suspect, but cannot prove, that the *Magi* resorted to a verbal trick, more *theologorum*. The word *arya* means 'noble, honorable,' and since the people of the good god must be excellent people and superior to the wicked, they could be described as *aryas*, 'respectable persons, the better folk,' even if they were not Aryan by race. The studied ambiguity would then be comparable to the verbal tricks employed by the early Christian Fathers.

Unfortunately, we do not know just how the replacement of race by church was treated theologically, or even politically, in the Persian Empire, and we must, as always, lament the destruction of virtually all of the copious writings of the *Magi* when Persia was conquered by the Moslems in the seventh century, and, of course, the earlier loss of the extensive translations of the principal Zoroastrian scriptures and theological works into Greek, which had been made to satisfy the enlightened curiosity of Alexandrian scholars in the time of the Ptolemies and certainly did not survive the final destruction of the great library at Alexandria by mobs of ignorant and viciously misologic

---

engender mongrel bastards who could not inherit property or citizenship. Such prudent regulations, however, were not long maintained in practice, even when they were not destroyed by the egalitarian religions, which nevertheless must be recognized as the strongest of all dysgenic forces.

Christians in 389.[92] We are thus reduced to surmises, but we may at least legitimately infer that the "Aryan" religion exerted a great attraction on the other races in the vast and multi-racial Persian Empire, and that the more intelligent and ambitious members of those races adopted the official religion as a means of identifying themselves with the dominant culture, much as in recent times Chinese, Hindu, and other Orientals adopted Christianity to facilitate their relations with us. On the other hand, we can assume that the Persians, who formed the ruling aristocracy and enjoyed certain privileges (e.g., exemption from most taxation) that were not extended to other Aryans, wisely favored politically a religion that provided some bond of unity between the widely different peoples under their rule and encouraged loyalty to their empire. The Persians, like the British in India, admitted natives to fairly high administrative offices in the various provinces; it would have been only reasonable for them to favor, perhaps exclusively, natives who had adopted the religion of their conquerors and thus shown a possibly sincere desire to be assimilated into their culture.

We must also take into account the moral appeal of Zoroaster's religious confection. He had made Ahura Mazda command conduct that was of the highest social utility, and, especially in its emphasis on manly courage and speaking the truth, corresponded to the code of honor for which the Persian aristocracy was famous.[93] And pru-

---

92   The Christian rabble, led by an especially disgusting theologian, Theophilus, Patriarch of Alexandria, destroyed the Serapeum, in which the central part of the great Library had always been located, and which appears to have escaped serious damage in the earlier riots and insurrections that so frequently occurred in the city, most commonly incited by the huge colony of Jews. The date for the act of atrocious vandalism is also given as 391 in some sources. After the Christians, there was probably nothing left for the Moslems to destroy when Amr took the city in 640; the famous and oft-repeated story of the Arab commander's destruction of the Library seems to have been invented by Bar-Hebraeus, a Jew and Christian bishop, around 1270. We may especially regret the loss of the writings, whether genuine or spurious, that were probably attributed to Saena, a successor of Zoroaster who is mentioned in the *Avesta* and is said to have trained a hundred disciples, and of the works of the evidently eminent theologian Ostanes, who is said to have been a favorite of Xerxes and is credited with a work entitled *Oktateuchos* in its Greek translation. Ostanes, by the way, is cited with approbation by one of the earliest Christian writers, Minucius Felix (26.11). Next to Zoroaster, he was the most celebrated Zoroastrian sage, and the numerous references to him in the Greek and Latin writers are collected by Bidez and Cumont in *Les Mages hellénisés*.

93   The ethics of the old Persian nobility, and particularly their insistence

dent governors, whatever their personal opinions, would naturally encourage the practice of a system of psychic magic by which the lower races could be converted to a spontaneous obedience to the laws that sustain the order and domestic peace of a civilized society. There is an obvious analogy to the belief, long cherished in the modern world, that Christianity could abate and control the racial proclivities of Negroes and other savages.

The creation of equality among human beings by religious magic has another aspect, social rather than specifically racial. It obviously carries with it an implication of the "classless society" that so fascinates the votaries of the atheistic derivatives of Christianity today, exciting their *Schadenfreude*, which they call "social justice." This aspect of the religion must have appealed strongly to the "weak and downtrodden,"[94] the proletariat, the very dregs of every society. Although, as we all know, the complexity of human genetics and the vicissitudes of human fortune not infrequently produce men of talent and merit from among the poor (and likewise produce biped pests from among the wealthy), it is a simple and obvious fact that the dregs of a population naturally sink to the bottom in every orderly society, and that disaster can be the only result of the modern mania for perpetually stirring up an "open society" so that the dregs on the bottom will become the scum on the top.

---

on always speaking the truth, greatly impressed the Greeks — so much so that Xenophon made Cyrus the hero of his didactic novel, although he himself had narrowly escaped death at the hand of Tissaphernes, a Persian of noble ancestry and a model of treachery and perfidy. To be sure, Xenophon concludes the *Cyropaedia* with a chapter on the corruption and degeneracy of the Persian aristocracy in his time, when, he says, no one would trust them. Religion, as usual, seems to have done little good to their morals.

94   The phrase is taken from the modern Parsee whom I cited above, who notes that Zoroastrianism had the same appeal as the later Christianity. He, however, confuses two quite different things, the religion's appeal to social dregs (such as the Jewish rabble who supply the apostles, etc., in the "New Testament") and its appeal to women, who are not necessarily weak or of low social strata. He could have drawn a contrast between Zoroaster's religion, which did give females equality (in theory, at least) and Christianity, which, in the cult that finally attained power, regarded them as inferior and potentially dangerous creatures, and some of the Fathers speak of the "imperfect animal" in terms that suggest a wish to anticipate the Moslem doctrine that women, being without souls, would not survive to plague men in Heaven (where Allah would provide much superior replacements, the *houris*, a happy idea that did not occur to the Fathers, who saw no use for females outside Hell). But perhaps Anatole France was right when he remarked that women were properly grateful to Christianity: It made them a sin.

It is particularly regrettable that we have no means of knowing when the egalitarian fallacy, which is certainly present in Zoroaster's own *gathas*, was first logically extended to a practical application to social organization, but we may be sure, I think, that the revolutionary potential of the superstition was perceived long before our earliest record of it. Under the early Sassanids, the Mazdakites, a numerous and popular sect, preached the "social gospel," reasoning, like many Christian sects and their ostensibly secular derivatives (e.g., Marxists), that since all men have been created equal, they must be made equal in income, social status, and perquisites (e.g., access to the more desirable females). They anticipated modern "Liberals" and other communists by specifically advocating taxation as the means of making everyone equal. This pious idea appealed strongly to Kavades, who found his treasury almost empty and, like modern governments, found the "underprivileged" an admirable excuse for robbing his subjects. His successor, the great Chosroës, finding himself well-established in power with a loyal army, decided that the Mazdakites were not orthodox Zoroastrians, and proved his point by having all of them hanged (he was averse from shedding blood unnecessarily), unless other methods of practical theology were more convenient. Mazdakites who escaped the extermination in 529 doubtless became discreet, for we hear no more of them, but communism was as inherent in Zoroastrianism as it is in Christianity and it reappears in the ninth century in the sect ("brotherhood") of the Khorrami, who flourished in old Atropatene and Media, the regions wherein Zoroastrianism was always strongest, and who represented the last stand of their religion against the Moslems, who finally suppressed them.

Like all "revealed" religions, Zoroaster's invention blighted the minds of all who succumbed to its meretricious and vulgar attraction. It substituted faith, an emotional and irrational conviction, for intelligent observation and reason. It was a baneful deterioration from the relatively reasonable polytheisms it replaced, which did not really fetter and paralyse the brain. In the Graeco-Roman world, for example, the Aryan mind perceived that the human species had to be the product of some kind of evolution. As every reader of Lucretius's magnificent poem well knows, the basic principle that determines the survival or extinction of animal species was well known, and the evolution of civilized man from lower, less human stock was recognized, as was the determining factor, the ability and will to civilize themselves. With just a little imagination and journalistic

123

exaggeration, one could see in a passage from a play by Moschion (probably fourth century BC) an adumbration of the evolution of our species from the anthropophagous *Australopitheci* to Greek civilization.[95] Even before Democritus, intelligent men saw that the notion of a special creation of human beings by some clumsy god was nonsense, and thinking men tried to account for the existence of our peculiar form of animal life by reasoning logically from such data as were available to them, reaching, in the fifth century BC, hypotheses more rational than anything known in Christianized Europe before the nineteenth century.

For the exercise of intelligence, Zoroaster's "spiritual" confection and all the "revelations" that have been modelled on it substitute an inherently preposterous story on the supposed authority of a Big Daddy who knows everything, since he created it, and tells us, so that the poor in spirit will never have to distress themselves by trying to stimulate as much of a cerebral neo-cortex as they may have in their skulls. So we have the silly story about the twins, Masi and Masani, which is, however, more plausible than the idiotic Jewish story about Adam and his spare rib, which, incredible as it seems *a priori*, the Christians tried to make themselves believe and seem for centuries to have succeeded in attaining the necessary degree of imbecility. And even today we are afflicted with the chatter of pip-squeaks who, having received some technical training in colleges, have the effrontery to call themselves "scientists" and demand to peddle the moldy old hokum in the schools as "creationism," an antidote to reason. And I sadly observe in passing that they do not have even the good taste to pick out the most reasonable creation myth of which I know: The first human beings were fashioned from clay by the divine sculptor, Prometheus, who, however, did much of his work by night, after he returned from a drinking party with the other gods on Olympus, with the result that his bleary mind and unsteady hand produced the woefully botched work that we are.[96] From the activity

---

95 The text may be found in Snell's *Tragicorum Graecorum fragmenta* and in the *Oxford Book of Greek Verse*; there is an English translation in Volume III of W.C.G. Guthrie's *History of Greek Philosophy* (Cambridge University, 1969).

96 This creation myth is in *Phaedrus* (IV.15 and 16); it could be original with him. Another explanation of one of Prometheus's blunders is in a well-known Aesopic fable, No. 240 in B.E. Perry's *Aesopica* (University of Illinois, 1952). Our polytheistic religions had many creation myths, of course, but everyone was sensible enough to know that they were only myths, and anyone was free to invent a new one. Incidentally, the yarn about Eve and the loquacious snake may well have been suggested by a common motif in ancient

of these nuisances one can estimate the devastating effect of Zoroaster's hallucinations or cunning on our race; "the curse remains" and "deep is its desolation."

In the sixth century BC, Xenophanes of Colophon, whom we mentioned earlier, fully understood that if men wish to improve their lot in life, they can depend only on themselves, not on supernatural beings they imagine in moments of idle fancy. And that realistic understanding of our position in the world was held by good minds so long as the Graeco-Roman world remained Aryan, disappearing only when the Roman Empire had been so polluted by the influx of Orientals and the degrading myths dear to their irrational mentalities that the great edifice of civilization inevitably crumbled down into the barbarism of the Dark Ages. The debasing and emasculating superstition concocted by Zoroaster made men dependent on remote gods or the angels and devils that were perpetually swarming about them, and such vestiges of intelligence as men retained had to be devoted to manoeuvring among the invisible and impalpable spooks or to theological logomachies about figments of the imagination.

The whole world went mad, and men wasted and ruined their lives and the lives of innumerable contemporaries in a phrenetic attempt to reserve for their suppositious ghosts a suitable abode in a dream-world, "out of space and out of time."

Civilization is more of hope and striving than of attainment, and the best that we can achieve is fragile and at the mercy of unforeseen catastrophies and, no doubt, the deplorable vagaries of our own species; it is, at best, a small clearing in an encompassing and constantly encroaching jungle; it may be that it could not long endure under any circumstances, but one thing is quite certain: It is incompatible with "revealed" religions and their howling dervishes.

God's House

When a residence is sold these days, the new owner almost always makes changes: He has it painted another color, he has the interior redecorated and installs new furniture, he may remove a partition

---

genre-sculpture: A girl looks longingly at a delicious apple hanging on the bough of a tree about which a snake is coiled. The point of the charming composition is obvious, but a Jew would not have understood it. For one such work of sculpture, dating from the third century BC, see the *American Journal of Archaeology*, XLIX (1945), pp. 430 ff.

between small rooms or divide a very large room, he may have the kitchen remodeled, and he may make other alterations to suit his taste or convenience; but the fabric of the house, its foundations, its beams, and its walls, remain unchanged.

The foregoing description, condensed and summary as it was, will have sufficed to show that the Christians today are living in Zoroaster's old house. It has been remodeled here and there, but the fabric remains as it was built, twenty-six centuries ago.

The essentials of the newer cult are all in Zoroaster's invention: the Good God and the Bad God; their armies of angels and devils; the contested partition of the Universe between Good and Evil; the Holy War for One World of Righteousness; Heaven and Hell and even Purgatory (*Misvan Gatu*); and the apocalyptic vision of cosmic strife that will end only in a decisive last battle between the hosts of the Lord and the hosts of Satan, which will be followed by the Last Judgement and the end of Time, after which nothing can ever change again. All human beings sprang from a divinely-created original pair, whose descendants, equal in ancestry, are made equal by Faith in the Good God, who fathered and sent into the world a Virgin-born Saviour to reveal his will to mortals, whose sins and merits are accurately recorded by the celestial bookkeeping system in preparation for the Last Judgement, when, incredible as it seems, they will be resurrected, so that, so to speak, they can enjoy the life everlasting in their own persons. The Zoroastrians, by the way, explain that when the time comes, Ahura Mazda's zealous agents will find and reassemble every particle of the man's flesh, which was eaten and digested by birds of prey centuries or millennia before; Christians attempt no explanation, but in most churches they still recite the Apostles' Creed (forged at the end of the fourth century and subsequently revised), affirming that they believe in "the Resurrection of the Flesh," but they probably never think of what they are saying.

We could add numerous details of Christian doctrine that were devised by the *Magi* in the various Zoroastrian sects: confession of sins (*paitita*), penance and absolution (*barasnom*), ceremonial Last Suppers of bread and wine, observance of the twenty-fifth of December as a divine birthday, and many others, including even terminology, such as use of the title 'Father' to designate a priest.[97]

Zoroastrianism and Christianity, however, are not identical, with only a change of names and a few minor details. The remodeling has

---

[97] Many of these details Christianity took from the Mithraic cult, of which I give a brief account in Appendix II.

introduced two really striking differences. When Zoroaster emerged from the Virgin's womb, he laughed to signify that life is good and should be enjoyed, and although the *Magi*, with the normal concern of holy men for their professional emoluments, devised all sorts of sacraments, rites, ceremonies, and religious obligations to keep their customers at work for them, the religion never lost a decent respect for human nature. The first woman had been the twin sister of the first man, and no Zoroastrian ever thought of a woman as an "imperfect animal" with an insatiable lust for sexual intercourse, "an inescapable punishment, a necessary evil, a natural temptation, a desirable calamity, a domestic danger, a delectable detriment, an evil of nature, painted with fair colors."[98] No Zoroastrian ever had the Christians' morbid obsession with sex or thought he or she would conciliate a ferocious god by thwarting and perverting their own nature and natural instincts or, for that matter, by inflicting discomfort and pain on themselves in an orgy of masochism. No Zoroastrian ever thought that it would be holy to stop the reproduction of our species and leave the world uninhabited. No Zoroastrian was ever infected with the insanity that, for example, made Jerome run out into a desert so that he wouldn't see any of the "evils of nature," and made Origen castrate himself to appease a god's hatred of mankind. No Zoroastrian's mind was ever haunted and distracted by an incubus of imaginary guilt, an Original Sin inherited from a man and woman who had discovered that their creator had equipped them with sexual organs he forbade them to use.[99] No Zoroastrian intelli-

---

98   The quotation is taken from Reverend Mr. Montague Summers' translation of the famous *Malleus maleficarum* (London, 1928; Dover reprint, 1971), one of the most impressive monuments of Christian theology. There were many editions of the original in the fifteenth, sixteenth, and seventeenth centuries and a copy of one or another is likely to be found in any good library, but the Latin is even more painful than the English version.

99   The Semites' disgusting and obsessive hatred of sex is so repugnant to healthy Aryans that even fear of the terrible god could drive them only to a grudging attempt to obey him, and many must have privately thought what the author of *Aucassin et Nicolette* dared say: That he would rather go to Hell with fair ladies and cultivated men than to a Heaven infested with fat monks and uncouth saints. An occasional gleam of humanity appears even in the most orthodox Scholastics. Thomas Aquinas in his *Summa theologiae* went so far as to decide sexual intercourse must have been exquisitely delightful for Adam and Eve in Eden, where she was yet uncursed with menstruation and the threat of pregnancy, and I should not be surprised if the "Angelic Doctor," who presumably looked forward to bliss after his Resurrection, had not in his own mind

gence was ever so perverted that he felt guilty for living, maddened by morbid obsessions that are sexual in origin, but, by an even fouler perversion, may be diverted into a maudlin guilt because he does not share the squalor of the lowest strata of society or does not sufficiently degrade himself to satisfy the enemies of his race and of his own progeny.

Equally startling is the Christian remodeling of the Good God. Ahura Mazda is a strictly just, honest, and impartial deity: He has ordained certain rules of righteousness for all mankind, and his servants keep a strict account of each individual's obedience or disobedience. Yahweh, on the other hand, is a god who early conceived an inexplicable partiality for a miserable tribe of swindlers and robbers, who pleased him by observing strange taboos, sexually mutilating their male children, and defecating and urinating in the ways he likes to watch. Having created the world, he spent the greater part of its existence in abetting his barbarous pets as they preyed on more civilized people, and he was their confederate as they swindled and robbed their victims or stole a country they wanted by massacring all the men, women, and children, and even their domestic animals. He even tampered with the minds of kings so that he would have an excuse for inflicting on their subjects every sadistic torture he could devise for the delectation of his favorites. And having been the accomplice of the world's parasites for centuries, he unaccountably changed his mind and sent them his only begotten son so that they would kill him and thus give him an excuse for breaking his bargain with them. It is no wonder that Christians so constantly talk of their "fear of God" — who wouldn't fear a deity so capricious, ruthless, and unscrupulous?

No unprejudiced observer could fail to conclude that Zoroastrianism was not changed for the better when it was remodeled by its new owners.

It remains for us to account for the spiritual deterioration in the subsequent chapters of this book.

A judicious reader may inquire why the Zoroastrian religion, if so markedly superior to its successor, so declined that it now engages the faith of only a small colony of about 120,000 Parsees whose ancestors found in India a refuge from Islam. That is one of the historical questions that can be answered without qualification or uncertainty. The primary cause is obvious: In Heaven, as on Earth, nothing

---

held the heretical hope that True Believers, having been definitively Saved, could brighten up eternity by enjoying the delights of a new Eden.

succeeds like success, and failure is the cause of failure.

Although Zoroaster's invention was a "universal" religion and sent out missionaries to preach its gospel to all the world, it became the official religion of the vast and mighty Persian Empire and Ahura Mazda's fate became inextricably entwined with the fate of the Persian King of Kings. Had Xerxes' huge navy and army been victorious at Salamis and Plataea, the True Faith would have followed the Persian warriors over Europe, much as Christianity later followed the British regiments throughout the world. It is even possible, I suppose, that we should be Zoroastrians today, worshipping a god represented by an eternal flame on the altar of each community, and pestered by "creation scientists," who would try to prove to us that Darwin was wicked to doubt that Ahura Mazda created Gayamart so that he could engender Masi and Masani, the ancestors of all mankind. But I doubt it: Gods, like men, become senescent, and even if they are immortal, if they are too busy or slothful to answer their votaries' prayers and supplications for a few centuries, they have only themselves to blame when they are supplanted by younger and yet untried immortals.

The spectacular defeat of Xerxes must have shocked the True Believers: Ahura Mazda had failed to keep a promise made through his consecrated *Magi*, so there were only the painful alternatives: Either holy men can be mistaken, or Angra Mainyu was more powerful than his great and good adversary had anticipated. The crisis did not come, however, until 334-330, when Alexander the Great, who worshipped the foul fiends, overran the whole Persian Empire, the Holy Land that was dedicated to the service of Ahura Mazda, who had been either unwilling or unable to defend his own righteous nation. Zoroastrianism became the religion of peasants, barbarians beyond the borders, and old fogies, who clung to the discredited god and traditions that had suddenly become obsolete.[100]

If Alexander had lived to turn his attention and his Macedonian phalanges to Europe, or if the Greeks, who built their cities throughout the former Persian Empire and overawed their new subjects as much by their incontestable cultural superiority as by their invincible arms, had not had our race's fatal lack of racial consciousness and had not steadily weakened themselves by miscegenation, excessive tolerance, and interminable civil wars, it is possible, I suppose, that the irrational faith and fanaticism of a "revealed" religion would have been permanently discredited — but I doubt it. As it was, the

---

100   See Appendix II below.

Greek nations of Asia so declined that they, one by one, fell under the rule of virile barbarians from Scythia, the Parthians, and Ahura Mazda had another chance. Since the Romans, also afflicted with the Aryans' folly, preferred to fight each other rather than extend their empire far into Asia, Zoroastrianism, in various more or less diluted forms, recovered its prestige, and under the Sassanids, the great Chosroës, whose theology was guaranteed by his loyal army, restored the Zoroastrian orthodoxy by forcing the *Magi* to codify their Scriptures and creed, while his hangmen convinced heretics of their doctrinal errors. But alas, when the hordes of Islam, virile Arabs exalted by faith in their new deity and by the rich plunder he bestowed on them, attacked Persia, Ahura Mazda remained idle and once again proved himself an empyreal *roi fainéant*. He had muffed his last chance to be a great god, and he had to be content thereafter with the impoverished veneration of a few incorrigibly obstinate votaries.

Buddhism

Gautama, who was later called the *Buddha* ("enlightener"), is said to have been an Aryan princeling in the part of India that lies at the foot of the Himalayas and is now called Nepal. He is reported to have had the distinctive mental trait that makes us distressed by the sight of suffering and sorrow — a racial characteristic that may become a morbid sentimentality in persons who do not charge their reason with strict surveillance of their emotions. In the late sixth century BC, he elaborated a profoundly pessimistic and atheist philosophy that was, in many ways, strikingly similar to the modern systems of Schopenhauer and Hartmann.[101] It was essentially a

---

101   If we assume that Gautama formulated a logically coherent philosophy, such as the Aryan mentality demands, his doctrine may be reconstructed with some confidence from the *Milinda-panha* (which purports to be a dialogue between a Buddhist sage and Menander, the Greek King of Bactria and the Punjab, c. 140 BC; translated by Rhys Davids in Volumes XXXV and XXXVI of the well-known series, "Sacred Books of the East," Oxford,1890-94) and the canonical *sutras* (pronouncements attributed to Gautama) that do not contradict one another. I shall try to state it as concisely as possible:

The phenomenal world is a succession of empty phantasmagoria, for nothing in the Universe is permanent. The world is change, and the discreteness of things and events is an illusory appearance produced in the mind of the spectator. Thus causality is a fiction, for cause and effect are inseparable parts of a continuous mutation. And man himself, for all his vain pride in his own personality, is

repudiation of religion, denying the supposed dichotomy between matter and spirit on which is based belief in the efficacy of worship, prayers, sacrifices, and austerities. He thus negated the claims of the professional holy men, the Brahmins, to power and superiority, thus in effect abolishing the social structure of four primary castes, in which the *fakirs* had placed themselves at the top.[102] Gautama

---

likewise a mental fiction, for he too is an unremitting mutation: *Omnia mutantur, nos et mutamur in illis*. All life, consciousness, experience is pain; this world of ceaselessly changing phenomena is a gloomy labyrinth in whose blind mazes a trapped humanity wanders, to be devoured endlessly, again and again, by the Minotaur of suffering and death. The clue to this labyrinth is knowledge, for humanity, blinded by the evanescent and insubstantial phantasms of pleasure and hope, is the victim, not of circumstances or destiny, but of its own will-to-live, its ignorant desire for life. Since the soul is merely awareness of a flux of phenomena at a given instant, there obviously can be no reincarnation of an individual, but Buddhism assumes, although it nowhere clearly explains, that the will-to-live is an unconscious force which, as in Schopenhauer's philosophy, may undergo a certain palingenesis and thus engender new being. Suicide, therefore, would be self-defeating, since a desire for death is simply an inversion of a desire for life, and that desire will, paradoxically, by palingenesis give rise to another flux of sensations. It follows that the highest wisdom is to destroy in mankind this dread force, the primordially blind and baleful will that produces life and all its manifold misery. And when the last member of our wretched species dies, then shall mankind cease from troubling; then shall the Earth be at peace at last.

Gautama's psychology and epistemology are certain. There is nothing in the documents that corresponds to my last sentence, which will have reminded the reader of Flammarion's manly acceptance of an inevitable future in which a frozen and lifeless Earth will still circle sluggishly in the gloaming around a dying Sun. But that last sentence is surely implied by (a) Gautama's belief that his doctrine is for all mankind and (b) his insistence on the avoidance of all sexual relations and hence, of course, of reproduction.

What Gautama meant by *nirvana* has been endlessly debated in India and in our time. The word obviously means what happens to the flame when a lamp is blown out. I think it simply means 'annihilation,' as Western scholars once agreed in taking it to mean. The religious sects claimed that it meant only the extinction of desire in our minds, and since the horrendous mass of religious texts in Pali and Sanskrit was, in large part, edited and published, many scholars — doubtless the majority — came to agree with them.

102   We do not know how fully the caste system was developed in Gautama's time nor can we estimate how strictly it was enforced in the numerous states of India, which doubtless differed greatly among themselves, but it is certain that the Brahmins everywhere asserted their monopoly of religious rites and hence their right to live at the expense of others, as holy men always do. We should not underestimate this aspect of early Buddhism: The doctrine that all human beings

also denied the traditional values of Aryan warriors and the ruling class to which he belonged; he saw them as vain and futile in the light of the terrible truth that what is best for man is never to have been born.

In an age of lost illusions, when the old beliefs of Aryan man were crumbling under the impact of more exact knowledge and rational criticism, and in an age of political frustration, when many Aryans must have felt themselves mired in the ordure of a multiracial society, Gautama's counsel of despair must have appealed to many thoughtful men, but it could never have charmed the masses. It had a social value that must have been recognized by many rulers and administrators, who must have been pleased to see thus checked the impudent pretenses and parasitism of the holy men, and who must have welcomed an ethical system which, by deprecating all human desires and ambitions, cancelled the motives of every form of violence and crime.

Gautama's philosophy, perhaps inevitably, fell into the hands of votaries, whose minds were more emotional than logical; of professors, who began to quibble about details and argue about definitions and interpretations, making what had been logically simple and lucid obscure and complex; of popularizers, who in turn began to simplify and distort to gain the assent of the commonalty; and of social reformers, who recognized an avenue to influence and emoluments. Buddhism was finally ruined by its success. The great Emperor Asoka, after brilliant conquests, became a pacifist and a Buddhist around 260 BC, and although he regarded the philosophy as an ethical doctrine, he made it the official religion, using the resources of his vast empire for works of charity, endowing schools, hospitals, monasteries, and hospices for the convenience of travellers, and erecting *stupas* to mark the sites made holy by some legendary association with Gautama or his early disciples. He sent out missionaries to preach the new Salvation to all the world, including, according to his inscriptions, the lands around the eastern Mediterranean, which were all ruled by Greek dynasties.

The atheistic philosophy was converted into a religion, and it is a nice irony that Asoka, before his death, had to convene a council of Buddhist luminaries in the vain hope of reconciling doctrinal differences. Gautama was converted into a Saviour, complete, of course,

---

were equal in the universal wretchedness of mankind had the deplorable effect of destroying such sense of racial cohesion as the Aryans had left, but that was, so to speak, the price paid for breaking the clergy's stranglehold on society.

with an immaculate conception and virgin birth,[103] and tales of how he had resisted the temptations of an evil god, who had vainly tried to avert the salvation of mankind. What had been a philosophical principle that we must divest ourselves of all property to free ourselves from the illusion that life is worthwhile became a doctrine of salubrious poverty that spawned hordes of monks, assembled in huge monasteries, and of itinerant mendicants whom we may call friars by a valid analogy. What had been an attempt to establish truths by logic became a system of unreasoning faith (*bhakti*) and the spring of orgiastic emotions. The religion was equipped with all the grotesque paraphernalia of superstition, including immortal souls, gods, devils, heavens, hells, miracles, prayers and other magic spells, relics, and hierarchies of priests absorbed in the business of vending holiness to suckers who craved absolution from the sins they confessed — which were many, since some professionals had classified sins under 250 rubrics! And, naturally, the religion became a chaos of competing sects, each vending the only True Gospel, and collectively providing a spectrum of human folly, a wilderness in which one may find almost any variety of bizarre belief.[104] For example, although Buddhism in general admits women and has nuns as well as monks, and some of the sects even recognize a number of female Saviours, the religion, like Christianity, regards women with suspi-

---

103   There are a few slight variations in the standard story about virgin births. The Buddha's mother, Maha Maya ("The Great Illusion"!), a wife who had remained a virgin until she was forty-five, was impregnated by a "reflection" cast on Earth by his celestial father, and she bore the divine child by a kind of miraculous Caesarian section, for he burst through the side of her abdomen, which was then instantly healed. The precocious infant at once announced that he had come to save the world from the devils, and he took seven long steps towards each of the four cardinal points to show that he was going to save all mankind. He was an old hand at the salvation-business, for that was his five-hundredth incarnation on Earth, and the Buddhists soon started scribbling *jatakas* as facilely as the Christians later composed tales by martyrs and other wonderments. The *jatakas* were the true histories of the earlier incarnations of Gautama or other Buddhas. Buddhists, however, as befits Orientals, are more patient than Christians: The final salvation of mankind will be accomplished by a Buddha who will appear, in terms of our calendar, in 5,655,524 AD.

104   What happened, of course, was that all the superstitions spawned in a multiracial society were imported into the new religion, with a few clever theological twists and adaptations and some additions. It would be otiose to go into the complex details. One thing is certain, that holy men believe that unemployment in their business would be very bad for society, and they always find means of averting it.

cion as potential dangers. That, however, is not true of the Tantric sects, in which some of our addle-pated contemporaries want to see "the highest expressions of Indian mysticism." These sects hold that males and females are equal, except that women are more equal than men, who must seek sanctity in gynaeolatry carried to what some may think extreme lengths. One of their gospels, the *Candamaharosana*, for example, informs us that "Buddhahood resides in vulva."

We may be certain that if poor Gautama had indeed had powers of prophetic foresight, he would have sworn himself to perpetual silence and kept secret the conclusions to which he had come. He cannot be blamed for the religion that was perpetrated in his name[105] — much less for its pervasive influence on others.

There was a certain Aryan strength in Gautama's cosmic negation.[106] It requires fortitude to reject life and to believe that all the things that we instinctively prize and desire, such as health, bodily vigor, sexual love, beauty, culture, wealth, learning, intelligence,

---

[105] I cannot call to mind a volume that covers all the varieties of Buddhism and its very numerous sects, past and present, but an adequate outline of the principal tendencies in the religion may be found concisely in the English version of Maurice Percheron's *Buddha and Buddhism* (London, Longmans, Green, 1957). I have noted that his sympathy with the religion did not prevent him from admitting at one point (p.40) that Gautama's doctrine was quite different, a briar that did not bear the fragrant roses of "spiritual" superstitions.

[106] It is true that the distinctively Aryan spirit is a strong affirmation of life, a determination to live to the utmost, "to live, though in pain," and to be undaunted by suffering and sorrow — to confront tragedy unafraid. It is the high code of aristocratic honor that makes Achilles choose valiant deeds and an early death, that makes the Viking hero go to his doom in this world as unflinchingly as his gods will fight their last battle in the foreordained *Götterdammerung*. "The honorable end is the one thing that can not be taken from a man," said Spengler. And Nietzsche summarized the Aryan code in one sentence: "To die proudly when it is no longer possible to live proudly." For the essence of this code, so much hated by Christians, is the aristocrat's pride in his own self-mastery and indomitable will: it makes Gunnar defiant to the end, even in the snake-pit, and appears in Byron's *Manfred*: "He mastereth himself, and makes / His torture tributary to his will." Note, however, that the aristocrat's pride is in the integrity of his own personality. If he were convinced by Gautama's psychology, which so markedly resembles modern theories of a "labile psyche," he would refuse to be only a flux of sensations, and would be numbered among those of whom Glanvill said, "Certainly, could they have been put to their choice whether they would have come into being upon such terms, they would rather have been nothing forever." And, by the way, the state of being nothing, of being like the light of an extinguished lamp, is precisely what Gautama meant by nirvana.

and even our own individuality are all empty illusions, and that the greatest good is annihilation. It requires even greater fortitude to accept that belief together with its obscure and dubious corollary, which denies us the immediate release of suicide and imposes on us the painful necessity of dragging out an existence in which we reject everything that healthy men desire and for which they live. That is to endure a death in life. Whether there is truth in that cosmic negation is a problem that each man must solve by his own powers of reason, and a problem that only men of great courage will consider at all.

The rejection of life, however, becomes a cowardly evasion when a perverse superstition enjoins it as a means of appeasing or pleasing a god whom we must believe, by an act of faith, to have promised that if we frustrate every instinct of healthy men and women, he will reward us after death with a blissful life of eternal idleness, which, by an even greater miracle, he will somehow prevent from becoming an infinity of boredom. If we abstain from sexual intercourse to avoid inflicting on others the curse of life and all its miseries, we are behaving rationally and even nobly, if the premise is correct; but if we frustrate our normal desires to please the caprice of a god who presumably endowed us with our instincts to inflict on us the pain of frustrating them to avoid being tortured by him eternally — a god, moreover, who is not even generous enough to help mankind to a speedy extinction, but wants it to reproduce itself and to preserve even its tares and monsters to provide his consecrated dervishes with plenty of business — we have become the cringing slaves of a mad master. If we declare that the manifest differences between races and between the individuals of every race become, for all practical purposes, infinitesimal in comparison with the vast futility of all human life, we are affirming a hope for the annihilation of all species of anthropoids capable of suffering or even of all species of animals that have sentient life; but if we believe that equality is enjoined by a god who so desires a mindless faith that he cherishes idiots and wants us to destroy every form of superiority except clerical wiles, we are simply contriving suicide for our race and a living hell for our descendants.

The Buddhist religion consummated the ruin of India by abrogating the caste system so long as it was dominant, but we are here concerned only with the aspects of the superstition that were contributed to Christianity.

Gautama's philosophical argument for not reproducing our species was debased into a notion that complete celibacy and total abstention from sexual intercourse was in itself righteous and meritorious, generating the "spiritual values" that are part of all holy men's stock in trade. His depreciation of all forms of property as representing and stimulating the will to live that must be stifled before it creates more misery was parodied in a notion that poverty was in itself a proof of spiritual superiority. The union of the two notions naturally spawned a horde of religious mendicants, whose supposed sanctity entitled them to live at the expense of their spiritual inferiors, who were so gross that they earned their own living and engendered children to support the next generation of pious beggars.

Originally, the Buddhist *bhiksu* was a man who, having "slain the five senses" and destroyed in himself "the illusion of individuality," divested himself of all property except a distinctive mantle of coarse cloth dyed to a dark Turkey red (*kasaya*, later changed to show sectarian differences), a bowl in which to collect the food he begged, and a staff, and then, having shaved all hair from his body, he began a perpetually itinerant life (*pravrajya*). The mendicant friars found or were given for shelter at night huts (*viharas*), which, however, eventually became monasteries endowed by the pious, elaborate and wealthy establishments that provided such ease and comfort that their *bhiksus* forgot to continue their peregrinations and can more properly be described as monks, although Buddhism did not make the Christians' sharp distinction between mendicant friars and cloistered monks.

Buddhism was already waning in India when Hsüan Tsang made his pilgrimage to the land in which his religion had been born, but he found 10,000 *viharas* in Bengal alone; some of these were, no doubt, fairly small and simple buildings, but some were huge edifices that each accommodated more than a thousand ascetics.

The Buddhist ascetic, having "slain his five senses," had to keep them dead, and for that reason he was forbidden to touch a human being, least of all a woman. In one of the finest of the Sanskrit dramas, a Buddhist friar comes upon a woman who has been strangled and left for dead. He can, of course, pour water on her and fan her to revive her, but when he assists her to arise, she must grasp a vine that he holds out to her.

While it flourished in India, Buddhism was not fanatical, and its monasticism was therefore more humane (and perhaps less corrupt) than the Christian version, for the *bhiksu* was never bound by irrevocable vows. I cannot forbear to mention Bhartrihari, one of the most charming (and least translatable) of the lyric poets in Sanskrit. As his verses show, he was an elegant and polished gentleman who indulged with refinement in all sensual pleasures until satiety brought a craving for tranquillity and leisure for meditation. He is said to have oscillated between the royal court and a Buddhist monastery, and finally to have become so aware of his own fickleness that when he renounced the world once more and entered a monastery, he ordered his coachman to wait outside. His conduct was doubtless thought bizarre, but it illustrates the humanity that Buddhism never lost in India. There could have been there no parallel to the tragedy of Martha Dickinson's "Father Amatus, — cloistered young." As the Buddhist institution was carried westward and imitated by Semites, it naturally acquired a savage fanaticism that was transmitted to Christianity.

Tapas

Before leaving India, we should perhaps mention another element that is sometimes thought to have had an influence on Christianity.

Ayrans (and some other races, notably the American Indians) instinctively admired the spiritual strength and fortitude of men who can bear intense physical pain without flinching and without yielding to the normal physical reactions. The ability stoically to endure pain always arouses admiration, but it can usually be exhibited only in some worthwhile undertaking, such as war or comparable situations, as, for example, by the justly famous and honored C. Mucius Scaevola. In post-Vedic India, however, admiration for such fortitude was distorted into the doctrine of *tapas*, the belief that by simply enduring pain inflicted upon himself a man automatically acquired a spiritual (i.e., supernatural) power. We should particularly note that *tapas* produces such power by a kind of natural law, which operates independently of the wishes of the gods and is not in any way affected by the motives of the man who practices the austerities.

The power of *tapas* is illustrated by the story that is exquisitely retold by Lafcadio Hearn in his *Stray Leaves*: Two evil princes, determined to obtain ascendancy over even the Thirty-three Gods, practice austerities on a mountain top, remaining absolutely motionless, standing on their great toes only, and keeping their eyes fixed upon the Sun. After many years their self-mortification gave them such divine power that the weight of their thoughts shook the lands, as by an earthquake, and the mountain smoked with their holiness. They were thus able to destroy cities and make deserts of populous lands. (The world and the gods were saved only by the creation of Tilottama, the most beautiful of all women.)

Appendix I: Ahura Mazda

IN MY highly condensed summary of the Zoroastrian religion, I have assumed that when Zoroaster tells us there is only one supreme god of good, he means what he says, and that when he gave to that god an unprecedented name, Ahura Mazda, he coined that name for his deity to show that his god differed from all gods previously known.

Ahura Mazda, therefore, is his invention. It goes without saying that Zoroaster's theopoeic imagination would have been influenced by what he knew of the gods in vogue in his time, and that if some of those gods had traits which suited his ethical purposes, those particular traits would reappear in the god whom he fashioned, to the exclusion, of course, of traits of which he disapproved. Very limited similarities can therefore be discovered, but Zoroaster refers to his god only by the name Ahura Mazda, and common sense tells us that he devised a new name for his god precisely because he wanted to show that his god was fundamentally different from all others.

My conclusion, however, differs substantially from what you may find in references to Zoroaster that are based on the work of some very recent scholars, who read into what Zoroaster said (so far as this can be determined from the *gathas*) elements of the old Iranian religion as they have reconstructed it, largely on the basis of the Sanskrit *Vedas*, a few references in the *Avesta*, and the lucubrations of the Pahlavi theologians, of whom the earliest must be many centuries later. I feel obliged, therefore, to defend my position as briefly and perspicuously as I can.

The two major works of modern erudition are:

1. Marijan Molé, *Culte, mythe et cosmologie dans l'Iran ancien: le problème zoroastrien et la tradition mazdéenne* (Paris, 1963 = *Annales du Musée Guimet*, Bibliothèque d'études, t. 69). Dr. Molé is primarily concerned with the late Pahlavi writings, from which he quotes copiously and from which he tries to reconstruct, "à la lumière de la phénoménologie religieuse moderne," not the actual creed of Zoroaster so much as "l'image que se font les mazdéens de leur Prophète," using texts of which the earliest cannot be earlier than the seventh century (AD). This is a very learned and valuable work, but may be misleading, if one does not bear in mind how much time and how many vicissitudes of history intervened between those writings and the presumed date of our text of the *Avesta*, which itself includes and

expounds the *gathas*, which are very considerably earlier and which are the only texts that can be supposed to report some approximation of what Zoroaster actually said. That the late writings in Pahlavi preserve vestiges of the early theology may be granted, but how far they are separated from Zoroaster and from the time of the Persian Empire may be judged from the fact that the name of Ahura Mazda has been corrupted to Ormazd (Ohrmazd, Ormuzd, Ormizd, etc.) while the name of Angra Mainyu has been corrupted to Ahraman/Ahriman or Enak Ménok.

2. Mary Boyce, *A History of Zoroastrianism*, Vol. I (Leiden, 1975 = *Handbuch der Orientalistik*, I. Abteilung, VIII. Band, I. Abschnitt, Leiferang 2, Heft 2A). The very learned lady's work will be completed in four volumes, but only the first, which deals with the time of Zoroaster, need concern us. Her work is the most thorough treatment of the subject known to me, and forms part of what is likely to be the standard reference encyclopaedia for many decades. Some of her interpretations differ widely from those given by Dr. Molé, but fortunately these are matters of detail which we need not discuss here. The crucial questions are, one, the identity of Ahura Mazda; two, the significance of *ahura*; and, three, Zoroaster's conception of certain Indo-Iranian gods.

I shall divide my three main points into numbered sections.

I

We are told, on the basis of some similarities and much theory, that Zoroaster's god was really Varuna, one of the numerous gods mentioned in the the hymns of the two early *Vedas*,[107] and we are even given a linguistic reconstruction of what Varuna's name would have been in Avestan, if he had ever been mentioned in the *Avesta*. The identification is based on two considerations: Varuna is one of the several gods who are given the title *asura* in the Vedas (a point that we shall discuss below), and some aspects of Varuna, as he is depicted in the *Vedas*, resemble attributes of Zoroaster's god.

It is true that in one hymn of the *Rigveda* (4.42), Varuna and Indra define their respective spheres of authority, and the former rep-

---

107 The oldest hymns in the *Rigveda* are by far the earliest expression of the primitive Aryan religion; the *Atharvaveda* is later, but still very early. For our purposes here, it will suffice to say that both must be considerably earlier than Zoroaster. I am not so temerarious as to try to determine precise dates for their composition.

resents himself as the deity of law and order, of what is morally right, and so resembles Ahura Mazda, while Indra, a god whom Zoroaster particularly reprobated and denounced by name, says that he is the patron of the aristocracy that delights in war and poetry. It must be noted, however, that the two gods appear in the hymn as friendly colleagues in the pantheon, and there is no hint of rivalry between the two, neither showing the slightest disposition to trespass on the other's divine territory. Varuna does boast that he is the greatest of the *asuras* (whatever he may mean by that) and his will (i.e., law and order) is obeyed by other gods, which no more proves his supremacy than Zeus's notoriously numerous affairs with mortal women prove that Aphrodite, who inspires the sexual desires of gods as well as of men, is supreme on Olympus, where Zeus, Poseidon, and all the other gods who indulge in erotic and amatory adventures obviously obey her will when they do so. Varuna says no more than that the gods, who have an orderly society of their own, thus accept the social principle he represents.

Some aspects of Varuna do appeal to the religiosity that was formed by Zoroastrianism and its derivatives. Moderns are apt to be unduly impressed by the "spirituality" of such hymns as *Atharvaveda* 4.16, in which Varuna is credited with knowing every man's inmost thoughts and also with maintaining (unnecessarily?) an army of invisible spirits who, like Hesiod's thirty thousand agents of Zeus, report on all the actions of men; and *Rigveda* 5.85, in which the worshipper begs Varuna to forgive his sins, if ever he sinned against a "loving man" (i.e., a man's 'best' friend, with whom he has an especially close and intimate relationship; there is no implication of homosexuality) or wronged a brother, friend, comrade, neighbor, or even stranger. Christians like to think such ideas were wonderful discoveries made by their deity many centuries later, and are usually perplexed or angry when they find that Jesus was a late-comer in the field of moral exhortation.

Very well, but let us not forget to balance such traits against others that were also attributed to Varuna. Take, for example, a hymn in the *Atharvaveda* (3.25) by a man who wants the gods to make a woman love him so that he can take her away from her parents and home. He very reasonably asks Kama (the god of sexual love) to inspire her with a burning desire for his embraces, but then he asks Varuna and Mitra to brainwash her, so that she can think of nothing else and will have no will of her own and thus cannot refuse to elope with him. Can we imagine a Zoroastrian's asking Ahura Mazda to help him seduce a woman? If not, then Ahura Mazda is a fundamentally different god.

II

Zoroaster called his good god Ahura Mazda, and the second of these words means 'illustrious, bright' (and was consequently used a few decades ago in the United States to designate an improved kind of electric light bulb), and 'bright' always suggests 'wise' when applied to persons. The new god was 'the brilliant *ahura*,' and an *ahura* is a great supernatural power, i.e. a god. Avestan *ahura* is obviously a dialectical form corresponding to the Sanskrit *asura*, which is applied in the *Vedas* to some of the gods honored in them.

Now the generic word for 'god' in Sanskrit is *deva*, which becomes *daeva* in Avestan, and Zoroaster, by his drastic and epochal *Überwertung*, transformed all the *devas* into evil beings, the servants of Angra Mainya, so that in his language *daeva* means 'devil,' a foul fiend whose worship must be suppressed.[108] He vehemently denounces veneration and even respect shown to such agents of pure evil, and while he singles out for special obloquy Indra, who was the equivalent of Odin for the Aryans of India, he certainly includes in his irate reprobation all the other *devas* of whom he knew and, by implication, all the gods of whom he had never heard. Recent scholars have argued, however, that while Zoroaster damns all the *devas*,

---

108 When Zoroaster made *daeva* a word denoting utter evil, he was, in the vernacular phrase, cutting it fine, for he had to retain the obviously cognate word, *daena*, usually translated as 'religion,' as a term for a praiseworthy activity. The Avestan *daena* becomes *den* in Pahlavi and forms part of the extremely common term for Zoroastrianism, *Veh Den*, i.e., "the Right Religion." In Avestan, however, some learned perplexities could be avoided by translating *daena* as 'spiritual' and supplying from the context either 'things' or 'nature' as the accompanying noun. In some contexts the word does mean a reverence for spiritual matters, but in others it must designate the 'spiritual nature' that a man creates for himself by righteous or sinful conduct as he passes through life. In the Zoroastrian eschatology, which must be Zoroaster's, the soul of the dead man must go to the Cinvato Bridge, where it is judged: the True Believers pass over the bridge to Heaven, but the wicked (including, of course, all infidels) slip from the bridge and fall into the abyss of Hell. How this happens is explained in several ways, but a common explanation is that the soul is accompanied by its *daena*, which is hypostatized as an attendant maiden or female *genius*; if she is righteous, she sustains him as he walks across the very narrow bridge, but if she bears the accumulation of his evil deeds, her weight, as she clings to him, causes him to lose his footing and fall to his terrible doom.

he makes an exception for the gods who are called *asuras* in the *Vedas*, since he calls his own god an *asura*.

The generic word for 'god,' *deva*, seems originally to have meant 'shining one, bright being,' presumably with special reference to the bright sky, while *asura* seems to mean 'lord', although its derivation is uncertain.[109] So the question is: In the old hymns of the *Vedas* (and hence in Zoroaster's understanding) was *asura* a word that designated a kind of being different from a *deva* or was it simply an epithet like *aditya*, which was applied to various gods without implying that they were a special class of being?

Although *asura* seems most frequently applied to three gods in the old Vedic hymns, Dyáus, Váruna, and Mitrá, it cannot be shown that any generic distinction is intended. There is certainly no indication of antagonism or rivalry. I have already mentioned the hymn in which Varuna and Indra as friendly colleagues define their specialities in the celestial faculty. The gods who are called *asura* are included in the *visve devah* ('all-gods,' i.e., the pantheon). And in the hymns, the gods who are often called *asura* are worshipped by the same rites and by the same priests as the other gods. Of the three gods to whom the term is commonly applied, Dyaus becomes the Greek Zeus but fades out of the Indian pantheon in later times; Mitra likewise fades out, but appears in the later Zoroastrian cult as Mithra; but Varuna continues to be worshipped as one of the Thirty-Three Gods and is assigned jurisdiction over the ocean (he is the Hindu equivalent of Neptune) and is the Regent of the West (i.e., one of the four *Lokapalas*, the gods who preside over the four cardinal points of the compass and foreign lands that lie in the indicated direction).

Obviously Zoroaster intended *asura* to mean something radically different from *deva* when he applied it to his god, but having decided to call the latter 'brilliant,' he needed a noun that would take the place of *deva* and his choice was limited. I can think of only two available alternatives. The Sanskrit *aditya*, 'heavenly being', would have suggested the vague Vedic myth of a goddess, Aditi, who was their mother, and if Zoroaster's god was to have existed from all time, he couldn't have parents. The word *bhaga* (Avestan *bagha*, Old Persian

---

109   A common etymology derives the word from *Ashur* (*Assur*), the Assyrians' name for their country, their capital city, and its tutelary god; it would thus have designated the gods of an enemy nation, which would explain the later use of the term *asura* that I shall mention shortly — but why would the Aryans have applied the word to their own gods? It is possible, of course, that we have two words of entirely different origin that came to be pronounced alike and so confused.

baga) seems originally to have meant 'giver of gifts, bestower of good fortune,' and was, like the English 'lord,' a term applicable to both human and supernatural beings. It does mean 'god' in Old Persian and so was applied to Ahura Mazda, but Zoroaster would probably have had a different sense of the word's connotation; it occurs very frequently in the *Rigveda* (e.g., 3.62.11) as an epithet of the god Savitr, who, whether or not he is to be identified with Indra, was presumably a *deva* in Zoroaster's opinion, and the word also occurs at least once (10.85.36) as the name of a god who evidently presides over marriages to assure the prosperity of the wedded couple, thus providing another connotation Zoroaster would have wished to avoid. So far as I can see now, *asura*, meaning something like 'lord,' a word not associated with any one earlier god and not connected with any attribution of genealogical descent, was about the only word connoting divinity that Zoroaster had at his disposal.

What causes the trouble, of course, is that in post-Vedic Sanskrit the word *asura* does become the generic name of a race of supernatural beings who are the enemies of the Indian gods, although it must be carefully noted that the gods who are called *asura* in the early Vedas never appear among the *asuras* of the later myths. It is hard to say how *asura* acquired this different meaning.[110] I have toyed with the idea that Zoroaster really caused it, that what we find in India was the reaction of the Hindu Brahmins to his attack on their *devas* as evil beings and his attempt to supplant them with an *asura* of his own creation. We all know how holy men react to a threat to their business, and the reaction would have been violent even among the common people, if the early Zoroastrians were as active in trying to promote godliness with swords as their traditions suggest or even if the Hindus were pestered by missionaries.

In the later Hindu theology, it is an axiom that the *Asuras* are the enemies of the gods, just as the numerous races of demons are the enemies of mortal men. Most of these demons, who are chiefly conspicuous in the literature because the Aryan heroes slay so many thousands of them, obviously represent the alien races of aborigines whom the Aryans encountered in India when they invaded that sub-continent or later.[111] One could accordingly think of the *Asuras*

---

110   One explanation is given in the preceding note. Another possibility is that *asura* was originally a word of very wide meaning in its application to supernatural beings, as are some comparable words in English: The average Christian does not, in his own mind, connect his Holy Ghost with the innumerable ghosts who haunt houses and gibber in the night to scare foolish women.

111   This is most clearly seen in the *Dasas*, who are a race of demons but

as foreign gods, although that does not necessarily follow. I think it worthy of note that the *Asuras* are anti-gods, not devils, and they retain their dignity in the best Sanskrit literature, a cultural amalgam in which distinctively Aryan elements long survived, so that they are treated with the respect that our race accords to valiant enemies.[112] But I see no reason for reading into the very early hymns of the *Vedas*, and hence into Zoroaster's consciousness, a meaning of the word that is attested only much later. I therefore reject the views of many contemporary scholars.

For what interest it may have, I add the conjecture that the transformation of the concept of *asura* may have been facilitated by a kind of religious evolution that is of some interest in itself. The Vedic gods became commonplace and, so to speak, were becoming worn out, since even pious votaries must eventually have come to suspect that they importuned in vain deities who could not answer their prayers. As the Brahmins consolidated their lucrative monopoly of religion, they subordinated the old pantheon, often called the "Thirty-Three Gods," to the newer and greater divinity of a Trinity — Brahman, Visnu, and Siva. And, oddly enough, the Brahmins shared some of Zoroaster's animus, for they particularly exerted themselves to denigrate Indra, who had been the Aryan god *par excellence*, and reduce him to the status of a second-class god, who, while retaining a limited jurisdiction in his own heavenly principality, sins and is punished for his sins by a superior power. The professional venders of Salvation vented on Indra their venomous hatred of the Aryan

---

obviously represent the dark-skinned aborigines, since the word always retained the meaning of 'slave' or 'Sudra.' The *Raksasas* may originally have been Mongolians, whose characteristically slant eyes were exaggerated into the vertical eyes of the demons, while their yellow complexion was supplemented by other colors. The *Pisitasins* (*Pisitasas*) were obviously anthropophagous native tribes before they became ghouls. The *Pisacas* were barbarians who had a language capable of literary expression; I have often wondered who they may have been.

112 For one example, see above. It is true that *Asuras* appear in some myths as destroyers, but they are never degraded to mere devils. In the *Kathasaritsagara*, for example, we are twice told the story of the *Asura* Angaraka, father of the most beautiful woman in the world. She, smitten with love for King Mahasena, eventually betrays her father, as libidinously impulsive as Scylla, who betrays Nisus in the Vergilian poem, but until she does, Angaraka slays Mahasena's police officers and, in the guise of a great boar, ravages the countryside, but he does so, we are told, because a divine curse forced him to become a *Raksasa* to expiate a sin. That preserves the purity of his daughter's praeternatural lineage and saves the dignity of the *Asuras*.

aristocracy — an animosity that may also have been racial, as we surmised earlier.

Indra was left in possession of his own special heaven, Svarga, which is the highest paradise accessible to those who have not become "pure mind." It is the Hindu Valhalla, to which Indra welcomes the souls of warriors who have died in battle, and it is also a heaven worth attaining, for it abounds in all luxuries and sensuous delights, from magic trees (*kalpapadapa*, etc.) that produce whatever is asked of them, to the radiantly beautiful *Apsarasas*, who are the courtesans of heaven. But poor Indra was reduced to an almost comic figure, for he was taught that even a god of his rank must respect the sanctity of holy men. There is, for example, an Hindu analogue to the well-known story of Zeus and Alcmene: Indra impersonated Gautama, a great sage, and thus seduced Ahalya, the sage's wife, but Gautama, a holy man who had acquired great spiritual power by his piety, cursed the amorous god, whose body was accordingly covered with one thousand miniature representations of the female sexual organs, and the disgraced god had to hide in shame until the holy man was finally persuaded to relent and change the stigmata to eyes. Indra, who had once been the Aryans' *pater hominum deorumque*, even became guilty of the most horrible, abominable, and almost unspeakable of all sins: He accidentally killed a Brahmin! He fled in terror to the end of the Earth and hid among the lotus blossoms that float on the waters of the abyss, and he remained in hiding, trembling, until Brhaspati, the Priest of the Gods, by sacrificing many celestial horses in the *asvamedha* rite and performing many other powerful liturgies and invultuations, finally cleansed the terrified god of his awful crime. In India, the clergy entrenched themselves in power even more ingeniously than their counterparts in the West.

III

We are told that Ahura Mazda was not Zoroaster's only god, because he "must" have admitted the worship of certain gods supposedly favored by his contemporaries, since they (e.g., Mithra) turn up in the pantheon of later Zoroastrian sects. Now I think it would have been odd indeed if Zoroaster not only forgot to mention the favored deities, but invented the six *Ameša Spentas* as the immediate subordinates of Ahura Mazda and the only ones he mentions. There is no mention of Mithra in any *gatha* or other text that could conceivably go back to the time of Zoroaster, who very frequently mentions his six great archangels. Miss Boyce tries to read Mithra into two words (*mazda ahurañho*) in a line that could be ancient. The grammatical relationship of the two words is puzzling and the text is probably defective or corrupt. But however that may be, if you had a text that constantly invokes Yahweh and constantly appeals to Gabriel, Michael, Ithuriel, Raphael, and other archangels, but never mentions Jesus, would you believe that when the author wrote "god & co." in one line, he intended thereby to express his veneration of Jesus? As for the common argument that Zoroaster must have permitted the worship of Mithra because he does not specifically forbid it — well, I shall not be so unkind as to comment.

I cannot think the question important. If Zoroaster did, perchance, accord grace to a few of the supposed Iranian gods, he made them subordinate to the six great archangels. Miss Boyce admits (p. 192) that "the core of Zoroaster's new teachings" was his claim that "in the beginning... there was only one good God... namely Ahura Mazda," who created the six archangels to help him in the war against Angra Mainya. It would follow, therefore, that any Iranian gods that Zoroaster may have exempted from his general damnation of all other gods were created by Ahura Mazda (or the archangels) as spirits (*yazatas*) subordinate to the six and therefore subordinate in a second degree to the supreme god.

Miss Boyce admits (p. 255) that Angra Mainyu, the supreme god of evil, is entirely Zoroaster's invention, and that he made all the Vedic *devas* into devils (Avestan *daevas*), the creations and servants of his one supreme god of evil. If Zoroaster permitted a few Iranian gods to serve his good god, that does not alter in the least his great and enormously important innovation, the transformation of the whole world into one divided between two gods, one of pure good and the other of pure evil, with all (or almost all) of the gods previously worshipped by men, no matter how fair and gracious they were, made the malignant servants of the god of pure evil and therefore the enemies of all righteous men, who are thereby obligated to convert or exterminate every worshipper of those gods.

That, I submit, was an epochal innovation and a disaster to the civilized world — a cataclysm of which we still suffer the terrible aftermath.

Appendix II: Later Zoroastrianism

SINCE one of the later Zoroastrian sects exerted a great influence on early Christianity, some mention of it in these pages seems called for.

A first-rate theologian always wants to rise and shine by devising some novel twist or application of doctrine, and it is safe to assume that in the time of the Persian Empire, many an ambitious *Magus* tried to make himself prominent. But we do not know what checks there were on heresy. We do not know how the *Magi* were organized, by what discipline they maintained a reasonable uniformity of dogma, or whether they could make the usual appeal to the "secular arm" in cases of contumacy. In the history of all religions, a heresy is a doctrine disapproved by theologians who are "orthodox" because they have the power to enforce their opinions, especially when their orthodoxy is guaranteed by the police and hangmen. When those indispensable guardians of the True Faith are lacking or ineffectual, the usual result is a schism and an enormous waste of ink and papyrus or paper. But it would be temerarious to guess either that religion evolved normally in the Persian Empire or that it did not.

There is some evidence that the religion's centre of gravity shifted to Babylon at some time after the Persian conquest. In that large and opulent city the *Magi* would have come into contact with Semitic superstitions, especially the cult of the god Marduk, and it is only reasonable to assume that they urged or applauded the action of Xerxes when he desecrated the god's temple and confiscated his huge effigy, reportedly of solid gold. They came into contact (assuming that there was no earlier relation) with the city's large and wealthy colony of crafty Jews, but we do not know in what ways the Jews tried to exploit them. The Zoroastrian holy men in Babylon also found themselves in the very capital of one of the world's oldest and most lucrative superstitions, astrology. It was, furthermore, a superstition which at that time, and indeed for many centuries thereafter, could plausibly claim to be a scientific observation of the real world.[113]

---

113   In antiquity, the fallacies of most of the astrologers' hocus-pocus were apparent to good minds long before Carneades and the Academics systematically demolished the hoax, but, as Cicero had to concede in the *De divinatione* (II.43.90), there was one argument for planetary influences on human life that could not be dismissed or refuted, so that candid and objective students, such as Diogenes of Seleucia (whom Cicero quotes *ad loc.*), had to concede to astrology a considerable element of probable truth. It has always been a matter of common observation that the children of one man by one woman, if not identical twins,

The premises of Zoroaster's religion, and indeed of most religions, should exclude astrology, but it is a poor theologian who cannot make his Scriptures say whatever he deems expedient. It would be interesting to know to what extent astrology penetrated the doctrines of the presumably orthodox priests in the Persian Empire, but all that we know is that the Chaldaean astromancy was taken up by the *Magi* who were operating in the Greek cities along the Mediterranean and who, if we conjectured rightly above, gave their Saviour's name the form in which it is now familiar.

The preaching of Zoroaster's gospel to all the world was interrupted by one of the climacteric events of history, the conquest of the Persian Empire by Alexander the Great and the consequent Greek

---

always differ from one another, and often differ radically, not only in physical characteristics, such as features, stature, and figure, but also in temperament and mentality, although they receive the same nurture and the same education. The great differences between the offspring of one pair of parents, observed in circumstances that excluded all suspicion of adultery and even between the children of a brother and sister (as in Egypt or among the *Magi*) had to be explained by the operation of some variable factor, and before the genetic processes that ineluctably determine innate qualities were scientifically determined in our own time, the significant variables seemed to be the times of conception and birth, and hence astral influences, since observation would quickly exclude such factors as weather and the seasons. The alternatives were 1) unperceived causes, 2) metempsychosis, and 3) special creation of individuals by a god or gods who artistically avoided duplication in their handiwork. The first of these was simply a confession of irremediable ignorance and the third was fantastic, leaving, for all practical purposes, the second; and the hypothesis that there were invisible and impalpable souls that could accumulate in successive lives experiences they could not remember was, objectively considered, much less likely than the hypothesis that some influence from the planets, invisible as the influence of a magnet on iron is invisible, acted on the foetus in the womb from the very moment of conception. Thus the abilities and characters of men and women were to some extent, and perhaps almost entirely, determined by the planetary influences before and during birth; and character within certain limits does determine an individual's fortunes. This opened the door for a claim by the soothsayers that the planetary influences which had determined character could throughout life exert at least some influence on the being they had formed. Before the modern science of genetics, there was a real problem, and we should not feel for all consideration of astrology in antiquity the contempt that we feel for the practice of it today, when it is simply a notorious imposture on the gullible and superstitious. It is not remarkable that the astrological racket has become so lucrative today: Minds that have been so sabotaged that they can believe in the equality of races can believe in anything.

colonization of Asia from the Mediterranean to the borders of China and from the Caspian Sea to the Ganges. From its status as the official religion of a mighty empire, Zoroastrianism suddenly fell to the abject position of being only the faith of conquered peoples, discredited by the crushing defeat of its pious monarchs, and abandoned by a large part of its former adherents because they had lost faith in an impotent god, or because they recognized the cultural superiority attested by the conquerors' military superiority, or because they saw the advantages of joining the victors, or even because they had adhered to Zoroastrianism only because it was fashionable. To the *Magi*, it must have seemed as though the end of the world had come, and we may be certain that they then began to devise the theology that explained the catastrophe as the result of some bargain between Ahura Mazda and Angra Mainyu whereby the latter was granted a stipulated period of dominion.[114]

Zoroastrianism was eclipsed, but it would be an exaggeration to say that it went underground. There was, of course, no persecution, no opposition to it, no official disapproval of it by the Greeks, who were too intelligent and civilized to be susceptible to the fanaticism and pious delirium excited by "universal" religions. What happened was that the better part of the population spontaneously recognized the superiority of Greek civilization and adopted it, including its incomparable language, its elegant culture, and the Aryan attitude toward religion. It must not be forgotten that the dominant part of the

---

114   The most generally accepted explanation was that at the very beginning of time Ahura Mazda established a preordained chronology and a series of epochs during which Angra Mainyu was to be dominant. The first era ended when God sent Zoroaster to restore righteousness, but the schedule called for a relapse into sin until, at the end of the next period, one of Zoroaster's belated sons would be engendered by the miraculous process we described earlier. This notion reappears, of course, in the various Christian doctrines that Yahweh had allotted to Satan a certain period of prosperity, but the Christians do not commonly suppose a bargain between the two gods. In the common version of the Gospel of Thomas, that apostle encounters the snake that seduced Eve in the Garden of Eden and compels him to restore a dead man to life by sucking out the venom with which he killed him, and the snake, infected by its own deadly poison, swells up and bursts, but not before complaining that Thomas is destroying him before the end of his allotted time; similar complaints are made by devils whom Thomas coerces by what they regard as a "tyrannical" violation of their rights, but it is never explained who did the allotting of time. It would have been embarrassing to admit that the good god was directly responsible for the successes of the evil god and also embarrassing to admit that he was powerless to prevent them. That is the inescapable dilemma of all ditheisms.

population of the Persian Empire was composed of Persians, Medes, and other Aryans, the racial kin of the victors and therefore sharing their basic racial instincts.[115] I can imagine that many a cultivated Persian had only to become acquainted with Greek literature and philosophy to free himself from the hariolations of a "revealed" religion and to enjoy kicking the Salvation-peddlers from his door. As for the non-Aryan subjects of the former empire, they had new masters to conciliate and to exploit.

The Greeks built Greek cities throughout the lands Alexander had conquered, and Greek became the language of all persons who had any pretensions to culture. Aramaic, the Semitic langaage which had been the *lingua franca* of the Persian Empire, became largely the language of illiterates, spoken by the Semites among the ignorant peasantry of the countryside and the mongrel or alien proletariat that formed the most debased social stratum of the cities. Ahura Mazda, his name modernized to Horomasdes, lost his universal empire and became just a commoner in a supernatural world already crowded with a plethora of gods. His gospels could not be marketed in polite society: fanaticism had become uncouth. The *Magi*, who had been God's terrestrial representatives and the authorized salesmen of eternal life and *post mortem* beatitude, were reduced to the status of the swindlers who pose as "evangelists" and "psychics" in our society. They had to adapt their sales-pitch to their customers, the ignorant

---

115   It is extremely odd that even so diligent a scholar as Tarn should have overlooked this obvious fact and attributed to Alexander an itch for race-mixing and a universal brotherhood of mongrels. The plain fact is that Alexander encouraged intermarriage only between his followers and high-born Persians, who were of pure or relatively pure Aryan ancestry. Not being stupid, Alexander would have perceived that fact, if he did not already know it, from their features and bodily conformation; their language, furthermore, was Old Persian, which did not differ from Attic, Ionic, and Doric Greek very much more than did some of the epichoric and contaminated dialects of Greek that may be inspected in A. Thumb's *Handbuch der griechischen Dialekte*, revised by Kieckers and Scherer (Heidelberg, 1932-59). What Alexander proposed was nothing more radical than marriage between Anglo-Saxons and Irish or between Germans and northern Italians. There is no evidence at all to support the entirely gratuitous assumption that Alexander would have favored racial miscegenation. Propaganda that he had done so was concocted in the centuries that immediately followed his death, probably by Jews. One audacious forgery was a purported letter from Aristotle to Alexander advising him to interchange the populations of Asia and Europe to produce a mongrelized One World; it is now extant only in an Arabic translation. See S.M. Stern, *Aristotle on the World State* (Oxford, Cassirer, 1968), in which you will also find copious references to the Jews' exploitation of the hoax.

and gullible, and their skill in tricks of prestidigitation, psychological impostures, and applied chemistry gave the word 'magic' to all modern languages.

During the period of Greek dominion, however, alien superstitions seeped upward from the multi-racial soil on which the Greek society was built in Asia, thus providing a confirmation of Günther's hypothesis, which we mentioned above. The Aryan's lack of fanaticism makes him tolerant of alien superstitions, and it is supplemented by what we may call a geographical relativism in religion, which we commonly so take for granted in the modern world that we overlook it.[116] It does startle us, however, when we first encounter it in the ancient world, where it usually takes the form of a theocrasy that, at first sight, seems to us incredible. We, habituated to Christian dogma and its pretensions to know the "truth" about its triple deity, simply gasp when we first see Herodotus give to the Egyptians' cow-headed Hathor the name of the Greeks' gracious and beautiful

---

116   We usually read Chaucer's greatest poem when we are young:
When that Aprile with his shoures soote
The droghte of Marche hath perced to the rote, . . .
Then longen folk to goon on pilgrimages.

The pilgrims are taking a vacation to enjoy travel through the vernal countryside. But why do they go to Canterbury, "the holy blisful martir for to seke"? Isn't Thomas à Becket up with Jesus in his paradise somewhere above the clouds? Or is he still in his tomb in the Cathedral? The pilgrims are glad of an opportunity to be out on the open road, and naturally refuse to worry about such nice points in theology. Many years ago, I visited the famous shrine at Guadalupe Hidalgo and chance permitted me to converse with a cultivated lady of Spanish ancestry who had come from Guadalajara, halfway across Mexico, to solicit a favor from the Virgin. She admitted that there were shrines of the Virgin in Guadalajara, and she agreed that the Virgin was the same Virgin everywhere, but she was nonetheless convinced that the Virgin at Guadalupe would do things that the Virgin wouldn't do in Guadalajara. Our feeling for religious geography is stronger than the abstractions of dogma. Many men and women go to Lourdes and are healed of psychosomatic maladies by the strong emotions that are excited by their inner conviction that the Virgin will perform there miracles she is unwilling or unable to perform elsewhere, even though she must now be looking down on the Earth from an abode far above it. The Virgin at Lourdes is as efficient as was the goddess Sequana at her shrine, which was uncovered by archaeologists some years ago, but the polytheist who journeyed to Sequana's temple nineteen centuries ago did so quite logically: She was a local goddess and, though invisible, resided where she was worshipped. You couldn't expect her to leave home and come to you, so you naturally had to go to her. Her therapeutic powers were very great, no doubt, but all her powers were limited to the small area that belonged to her.

Aphrodite. To us, who believe in neither, that seems a profanation; it did not to Herodotus, who identified them as aspects of a single *numen* in whose existence he was willing provisionally to believe. When we first read *Iphigenia in Tauris*, we wonder why Euripides' fellow Athenians did not accuse him of the most outrageous blasphemy against Artemis when he portrayed that fair maiden as the barbarously sanguinary goddess of blood-thirsty barbarians. That puzzles us until we realize that a Greek was willing to regard an alien deity as the equivalent of the traditional Greek god from whom he or she least differed, and to believe that, if supernatural beings did exist, since they were by nature unknowable, the exotic gods might well represent the same religious concepts as adjusted to a radically different culture of radically different human beings in a remote part of the world.[117]

A striking and fresh verification of Günther's hypothesis is provided by the current excavations at the site of a great Greek city at the confluence of the Oxus and the Kokoha in the northeastern corner of Afghanistan, three thousand miles from Greece.[118] The city is probably Eucratidia, one of the many cities founded by Greek colonists in the then fertile land of ancient Bactria. The Greeks, who, for several centuries, civilized that distant land, may have weakened themselves by miscegenation, although their rulers, as shown by the portraits on their coins, were handsome Aryans to the end. The Greeks of Bactria certainly weakened themselves by almost incessant wars against their fellow Greeks, the Seleucid Empire, from which they had declared independence, and the Greek kings of India, who were determined to remain independent of Bactria if they could not conquer it. The Greeks further weakened themselves by some civil wars in which, we may be sure, the lower races profited at the expense of their Greek masters. Thus the Greeks and civilization in Bactria eventually succumbed to hordes of barbarians who poured in from what is now part of China. The excavations show, however, that to

---

117   This intelligent attitude was, of course, favored by the diversity of their own gods which posed the questions that Cicero noted in the last book of the *De natura deorum*. There are, for example, five different stories about the parentage and birthplace of Minerva: Does this mean that there actually are five homonymous goddesses? If not, why not? A Christian theologian, accustomed to making Trinities, would have had no difficulty in making a Quintity out of Minerva, but he would have been laughed at. A polytheist would have reasonably asked the theologian how he knew and such impertinence always sends holy men into fits.

118   See the report in the *Scientific American*, CCXLVI #1 (January 1982), pp. 148-159.

the end the Greeks kept and cherished their elegant language and their incomparable literature; they maintained their distinctive institutions, such as gymnasia, so repugnant to Oriental vulgarity and prudery; they ingeniously adapted their architecture to the climate of a region in which stone suitable for building was rare; and, significantly, the only evidence of cultural miscegenation is in religion, the few divinities thus far found are all patently non-Greek, and thus far no inscriptions have been found to tell us what names they were given. The chances are that Greeks thought of them as local varieties of their own gods.

The *Magi*, in a world grown so evil that their incomes had dropped drastically, had to adapt their Glad Tidings to the market. They, no doubt, still had customers among the peasantry and the urban proletariats, both, alas, impoverished. Astromancy, which even good minds had to accept as possible, was, of course, a staple for which there was always a fair demand. But Zoroastrianism really survived in heresies that would have made Zoroaster speechless with horror. The Greeks would listen to no nonsense about a supreme god who had made devils out of all the amiable and companionable gods of the whole world, but they were quite willing to believe that Zeus was also Horomasdes in inner Asia. Why not? He was Amun in Egypt, and it was only reasonable that he would seem different to a different people.

The Great Heresy

One consequence of the Greek conquest of Asia was that Zoroastrianism survived in bastard cults that would have given its founder apoplexy.

A very good example is the spectacular monument, which has partly survived the depredations of two millennia, on the high mountain which the Turks call Nemrud Dag, close to the upper course of the Euphrates and about 365 miles east-southeast of Ankara.[119] There, as close to heaven as men could climb, Antiochus I of the small buffer kingdom of Commagene, who claimed both Alexander and Darius as ancestors, erected, on both sides of an artificial hill added to the summit, colossal statues of his gods, who wear Oriental robes and Persian headdress above features that are portrayed in the

---

119 A concise account of the monument with excellent photographs may be found in an estimable periodical published at Zürich, *Antike Welt*, Sondernummer 1975.

Greek style and which, if viewed apart from their accoutrements, could pass as Greek. One of the two principal gods, who sat in majesty, looking out over the wide valley below, is a fusion of Zeus and Oromasdes (= Ahura Mazda), bizarre as that seems to us. The second, equally august, is a blend of Apollo, Helios, and Mithras[120] (with a bit of Hermes thrown in for good measure). The three assistant gods are equally hybrid.

We need not smile at this example of religious bastardy nor amuse ourselves by imagining what execrations the great monument would have evoked from Zoroaster, who had taught that we should worship only Ahura Mazda and represent him only in aniconic form as fire, the pure element that is the essence of divinity. The shrine, despite the Greek camouflage given it by Antiochus, is late Zoroastrian and even included a massive altar on which the sacred flame could be kept burning. Antiochus, a relatively petty king who, under Roman patronage, ruled his client kingdom from 64 to 38 B.C., undoubtedly spoke a fairly pure Greek and would have stared uncomprehendingly at a text in Old Persian, Avestan, or Aramaic; what he himself believed, we have no means of knowing, but it is most unlikely that he was fooled by his own pretenses. He knew that kings should hedge themselves about with divinity, and that it was expedient to associate himself with the Zoroastrian religion, which had been revived by the Parthians after the collapse of Seleucid (i.e., Greek) power in Asia.[121]

---

120   "Mithras," with the terminal "s," is the later form of the god's name, and was the one used in the Mithraic cults which eventually became so notable in the later Roman Empire. — Ed.

121   Antiochus I of Commagene was doubtless a cultivated man, who could not repudiate Greek culture or ignore the gods traditionally associated with it. His kingdom was a buffer between the Roman Empire on one side and on the other the aggressive Parthian Empire, whose greatest king, Mithridates VI Eupator (a votary of Mithras, as his name indicates), had waged a series of bloody wars with the Romans from 88 to 66, when he was finally defeated decisively by Pompey and fled to his territories in the Crimea, where he committed suicide. The Parthian power was still formidable, as Crassus was to learn at Carrhae. It is likely that the greater part of Antiochus's multiracial subjects were given to some form of Zoroastrianism, so that his theocrasy was obviously a political necessity. Scholars differ in their estimates of the extent to which it may have been his own invention. In an extant inscription, he affirms that when his body is placed in the tomb he has prepared for it (and which archaeologists have not yet found), his soul will ascend to Heaven to join the other gods. The gods, however, neglected to give him advice that would have saved him from making a bad guess during the Roman civil wars that followed the assassination of Julius Caesar.

To the southeast of Nemrud Dag may still be seen, stripped of its once lavish ornaments, a remarkable shrine that was probably built and excavated by Antiochus for an annual commemoration of the miraculous birth of the Son of God, Mithras, who, like the later Jesus, was born in a cave,[122] saluted by choirs of rejoicing angels, and first adored by understandably-amazed shepherds. Mithras, however, was born an adult, so that his Epiphany immediately followed his Nativity as he emerged from the maternal cave.

The shrine was a large cave in the side of a mountain. A wide terrace was built up in front of it, and the entrance made an arch in walls covered with sculptured reliefs and inscriptions, which have long since disappeared. From the floor of the cave, engineers sank a

---

122   It is well-known, of course, that in the early form of the Christian myth, preserved in the several recensions of the Gospel of James, purportedly composed by the brother of Jesus (who should have known!), Jesus was born in a cave. This was the story known to the early Fathers of the Church, including Tertullian and Eusebius, and the latter, in the biography of Constantine that he concocted to spread the fiction of that emperor's "conversion" by the miracle of "*in hoc signo vinces*," implied that Constantine had built a church in front of the sacred cave. Until recently a cave was, and perhaps it still is, exhibited as the scene of the Incarnation to gawking tourists who visit the Church of the Nativity in Jerusalem. All this suggests that the shift of the scene to a house in Matth. 2.11, and to a stable in Luc. 2.7, were late retouches of the tales, introduced when it was thought best to play down the story about the *Magi* and Zoroaster's Prophecy. One can see why it was thought desirable to minimize similarities to the Nativity of Mithras, but one cannot imagine why the Fathers did not make the stories in the two gospels agree before incorporating them in their anthology. The only explanation seems to be sheer carelessness on their part. In the gospels of James, one of the gospels attributed to Matthew, and others, the Nativity in a cave is logically accounted for, since Mary is overtaken by labor pains when she and Joseph are in a desert, some distance from the nearest town. A very amusing example of theologians' carelessness may conveniently be found in the two Latin *Infancy Gospels* edited by M.R. James (Cambridge, 1927). Both gospels are obviously the work of holy men who are fixing up the story to suit their somewhat different tastes. In both tales, Mary, her husband, and her stepson are walking to Bethlehem, and since Mary is far advanced in pregnancy, she has to walk very slowly. Joseph therefore goes ahead to the town and, since he cannot find room in an inn, picks out an empty stable and prepares it for Mary. In both versions Mary finally arrives under the care of her stepson, who explains that she had frequently to stop and rest on the way, but in one version she then dismounts from an ass! In both versions, Joseph takes her into the place he has prepared, which, by an editorial miracle, is suddenly transformed into a cave! The stable becomes a cave within the space of a printed page in both versions, thus giving us a measure of the retentiveness of evangelists' memories.

tunnel, at an angle of 45° downward, into the mountain for 520 feet and enlarged it to a room of considerable size at the bottom. In all probability, the shrine was used for a reënactment of the Saviour's Epiphany, doubtless at the rebirth of the Sun on the twenty-fifth of December, after the winter solstice. In the room at the bottom, Antiochus probably performed religious rites to renew his own participation in divinity, put on suitable garments to impersonate Mithras, and manifested himself, probably at the dramatic moment of sunrise, on the terrace as the *theos epiphanes*, suggesting to the assembled worshippers that he was, if not a reincarnation of Mithras, at least the Saviour's divinely-appointed representative on Earth. He was doubtless adored by shepherds, who had been carefully rehearsed in their rôle, and received the plaudits of a multitude assembled from far and wide to witness the iterated miracle, which must have stirred their pious hearts.[123] The choirs of angels (*fravasi*) had unfortunately to be omitted from the performance, but it may be that Antiochus had suitable background music provided in the ceremony by which he convinced the common people that he was indeed the Vicar of God on Earth, hoping, of course, that the True Believers were too ignorant and stupid to perceive that he, in his relatively constricted domain, was only the vicar of whatever Roman general held the proconsular imperium in Asia.

Besides doubling for Mithras in the annual celebration of the Nativity, Anitiochus had himself portrayed in the favorite pose of most Oriental kings, tête-à-tête with his god. He and Mithras, both stalwart figures in Persian dress (loose trousers and tunic) stand facing one another and joining their hands, doubtless sealing an agreement with a handshake. Antiochus is distinguished by his crown, Mithras by the rays of the sun, which appear behind his Phrygian cap. The two appear as equals: Antiochus was not a megalomaniac, just a good politician. He also had himself portrayed as shaking hands with Ahura Mazda, who remains seated on his throne, since

---

123 The priests must have had their part in the ceremony, of course, but it is hard to guess what it was. The *Magi* cannot have brought gifts, for there is no precedent for that act in the Mithraic myth, according to which it is the shepherds who bring the first fruits of their flocks and fields as gifts for the new-born god, and the *Magi* do not appear on the scene at all, since they were first given the glad tidings of Salvation by Zoroaster, long afterwards. Mithras was the Divine Mediator (a title later given to Jesus in the "New Testament") between the Creator and his creations, but the priests had, as usual, acquired a monopoly of mediation between men and the Mediator, so they cannot have been left out. Only *Magi*, for example, could tend the sacred fire, which keeps demons away.

the supreme god is entitled to that social precedence. That preëminence, however, was threatened by two developments in Zoroastrian theology that we must mention here.

Some earnest theologians were evidently puzzled by the coëxistence of a supreme god of good and a supreme god of evil. It did not seem right for the former to have created the latter, for a respectable god really should not be so stupid as to create, whether voluntarily or by inadvertence, an implacable adversary as powerful as himself. The problem, like the equivalent one in Christianity and similar religions, is insoluble, of course, but it was felt that it would be less objectionable to make the divine antagonists brothers, so a father was created for them out of the concept of time (*zurvan*). This primordial god, Zurvan, later Zervan, was commonly called, in Greek and Latin, Aeon or Cronos (i.e., Saturn, but the name was confused with Chronos); originally conceived as hermaphroditic and thus able to engender children by himself, he was eventually depicted as a nude male figure having wings and the head of a lion, and having a serpent coiled many times about his body. Needless to say, this theological device merely pushed the dilemma one step farther back: Who was Zervan's daddy? And for that matter, since his sex is unmistakable in most representations of him, where did he find a mama for his boys when he was the only being in the whole Universe? And why did Zervan fecklessly or maliciously engender an evil son to hate and strive to destroy his good son, to say nothing of raising Hell on the Earth that the good son was going to create? As in all religions, the answer, of course, is that it is damnably wicked to bother theologians with embarrassing questions. You must have Faith.

Zervan, however, created another difficulty that even oodles of Faith could not completely overcome. It was fundamental Zoroastrian teaching that after the Resurrection of the Dead and the Last Judgement, the triumphant Ahura Mazda would put an end to time, and if Time was his father, that would be patricide. One could, of course, give the standard explanation that this was a "mystery" that the human mind must not think about, but the doctrine was so fundamental in Zoroastrianism that the paregoric did not always work. When the Christians grabbed the idea of a Resurrection and Last Judgement, they were content with the phrase, "time shall be no more," without trying to understand it. In Zoroastrian eschatology, however, the distinction between time and eternity must be understood. Time is what causes the distressing state of affairs in the world, in which it produces change, happenings, events and thus creates history. Time is thus the fatal flaw in the world that permits the powers of evil to afflict mankind. After the Last Judgement, therefore, Ahura Mazda will abolish it and restore the Universe to its state of timeless perfection, and since perfection admits of no change, that will be an eternity in which nothing can ever happen again. Just how the good can enjoy this bliss and the wicked can suffer exquisite torments if they are as changeless as marble statues is not explained.

Zervan virtually replaced Ahura Mazda, who was thus reduced to a mere link between his Father and his Son, and one can see why many *Magi* did not hold with the innovation. The Zervanists flourished, however, until c. 531, when the "orthodox" Magi got the ear of Chosroës (Khosrau) I, the greatest of the Sassanian kings of Persia, who ruled that the Zervanists were heretics. Since there was no question about the loyalty of his army, he and God were clearly in agreement on that theological point.[124]

---

124 Chosroës had already proved his infallibility as a theologian by exterminating the Mazdakites, a numerous and popular sect that had been his father's favorites. To save his subjects from future mistakes, Chosroës authorized his orthodox *Magi* to compile an authoritative text of the *Avesta* and gave it his approval, which, naturally, carried great weight. This is the version that was the basis of the text that we now have.

Chosroës protected the Christians in his domains, even after many of them were caught in an unsuccessful conspiracy to replace him with his son. He may have been influenced by the consideration that almost all of the Christians in Persia were Nestorians, whom his principal enemy, Justinian, the pious Christian emperor in Constantinople, was eager to exterminate. One of Chosroës's acts is greatly to his honor and should be remembered. In 529, Justinian closed the "university" in Athens to extirpate the last, degenerate vestiges of Greek philosophy; the seven Neoplatonist teachers there, deprived of a livelihood and probably attracted by the talk about "social justice" in Persia during the ascendancy of the Mazdakites, migrated thither in 531, perhaps with the illusions that made unintelligent "intellectuals" flock to Russia after 1918. Chosroës welcomed them, but they were naturally disappointed by the discovery that Persia was not an earthly paradise and probably by the discovery that the hangmen had just corrected the Mazdakites' theological errors. When Justinian in 533 negotiated with Chosroës a treaty for "eternal peace" (it did last almost seven years, which is about par for such treaties), Chosroës insisted on a clause which provided that the seven Neoplatonists were to be permitted to return home and live thereafter without molestation from the pious. One of the seven was Simplicius, who later wrote the well-known commentaries on Aristotle and Epictetus that have preserved for us important fragments of Greek philosophers whose works were subsequently lost. We are therefore indebted to the Zoroastrian "tyrant" for both information and an example of concern for humane scholarship.

Poor God was squeezed from above and below, for his Son, having become the Saviour of mankind and the god who must be contacted for favors, reduced him to a mere figurehead in most of the Zoroastrian denominations, including the Zervanists and others. Mithras' votaries early provided him with an indubitably immaculate conception, having him born from rock of a sacred mountain, and gave a distinctive explanation of his work as the Saviour. He slew the Cosmic Bull, and if I understand the ambiguous references aright, it was from this bull that he obtained the "eternal blood" that was shed for the Salvation of mankind.[125] The blood may originally have been thought to be the hallucinatory drug *haoma* but the common tradition reported that Mithras and his companions drank wine at the Last Supper, when they celebrated the completion of his work of Salvation; and when his votaries assembled for the love-feasts at which they celebrated that Last Supper, wine was the soteric blood. Mithras either was the Sun or the hero who delivered the Sun from darkness or the hero who conquered the Sun and made it attend to its business. The theologians disagreed about that rather important article of Faith, as may most readily be seen from the very large number of votive inscriptions in Latin, many of which are to "Mithras, the Invincible Sun," while as many others regard Mithras as the companion of that Sun.[126] The latter conception is in agreement with the usual form of

---

125   An inscription, unfortunately mutilated, in the Mithraeum beneath the church of Santa Prisca on the Aventine in Rome, is a prayer to Mithras containing the praise, "*nos servasti eternali sanguine fuso.*" Professor Schwertheim, in the issue of *Antike Welt* that I cite below, quotes a late and odd Mithraic text in which Mithras says: "He who does not eat of my body and drink of my blood, so that he partakes of me as I am [thereby] commingled with him, will never attain Salvation." I think this must be an heretical idea in Zoroastrianism, for there is, so far as I know, no other evidence that the votaries of Mithras thought of their holy suppers as theophagous, with the cannibalistic implications of the Christian imitation of them. Their Last Suppers commemorated, and hence doubtless imitated, the sacred meal at which Mithras and his assistants, celebrating their victory over the powers of evil, partook of bread and wine, the bread being made from the wheat that sprang from the spine of the slain Bull, and the wine from the grapes that sprang from the Bull's blood. The Mithraic concept of redemption by blood appears in the *taurobolia* so frequently celebrated by the religious in the waning Roman Empire: They were cleansed of their sins by the blood of a bull that was slain in obvious imitation of Mithras' slaying of the Cosmic Bull.

126   The dedications usually give the name of the god in the dative, so we have "*Soli Invicto Mithrae*" as opposed to "*Soli Invicto et Mithrae.*" I cannot say offhand which form is the more common. In sculpture representing the great Tauroctony, the side panels, if they include Helios, sometimes show him clasping

the myth that Helios was the coadjutor of Mithras in the struggle to save mankind from the powers of darkness and that he even saved Mithras by carrying him safely over the demon-infested ocean; after their victory the two celestial companions and their assistants shared the sacred repast we have mentioned, and faithful Mithraists imitated it in their holy suppers, which were a pledge of their comradeship and reciprocal affection in their common struggle against the evils of the world. The third interpretation comes from a supplemental myth to the effect that soon after he was born, Mithras was attacked by the jealous god of the Sun, but overthrew him in a wrestling match, forced him to do homage, and compelled him to traverse the heavens and shed light on the world regularly. Mithras crowned his defeated rival with the radiance that the Sun has had about his head ever since and gave him the right hand of friendship, thus forming an alliance that both have ever since loyally observed. This myth, obviously, was devised to prove that Mithras had subdued and annexed the Babylonian Sun god, Shamesh, who is known as Shemesh to readers of the "Old Testament" in the common English version.[127]

We cannot enter into the intricacies of the Mithraic theology, but may note a curious detail which may show some propensity to trinitarian thinking. In most of the sculptural representations of him, Mithras is accompanied by two figures whose names, of uncertain

---

the hand of Mithras in friendship and sometimes as kneeling humbly before his new master.

127   The name of the god is Samsu in theophoric names from the time of Hammurabi (including that of his son and successor), and Šamšu on the tablets from Mari, and the latter form is the more common generally. The pronunciation of the Hebrew equivalent in the second and first centuries BC is shown by the spelling in the Septuagint, but the Greek alphabet at that time had no means of distinguishing between s and š. The Babylonian god was undoubtedly the hero of the legend about a praeternaturally strong man, who is called Samson in the Jews' adaptation of the myth. The strong man's name admittedly means 'of the Sun, solar' in Hebrew, as it doubtless did in the Babylonian original, i.e., 'son of the Sun.' In the Hebrew myth, he was born and buried near the temple of the Babylonian god (Beth-Samus), and the Jewish tale of his miraculous birth with celestial annunciations and influence, as in the later tale about Jesus, is probably an expanded amplification of the Babylonian account of the birth of a hero who, like Enkidu, fell a victim to the wiles of a prostitute. Students of religion may speculate endlessly and dispute about whether or not the Mithraic tale about the Cosmic Bull was ultimately derived from the Babylonian tale of the heavenly bull that was slain by Gilgamesh and Enkidu as an offering to Shamash or was a natively Aryan idea suggested by the well-known Aryan regard for cattle, which has now left a conspicuous trace in Hindu superstition.

derivation and meaning, are Cautes and Cautoptes, and who are commonly called the *dadophori* because they are carrying torches; one has the torch elevated, while the other holds it reversed. They look like replicas of Mithras and doubtless represent aspects of him (the rising and setting Sun?) that were explained to the Faithful in the prolonged instruction they were given before they were initiated into each of the several degrees of the cult, for it had become a "mystery religion," in imitation of the Eleusinian and other early Greek mysteries.

As is well known, since Mithras was born in a cave, the Mithraea, the "churches" of the cult, had to be located underground, and if no natural cave was conveniently available, an area of ground was excavated and roofed over, a fact which accounts for the partial preservation of so many of the *spelaea*, since the Christians, when they took over, were content to desecrate a shrine and then build one of their churches on top of it to make sure that the Devil's magic would remain permanently buried and inaccessible. A normal Mithraeum would accommodate only thirty or thirty-five worshippers at one time,[128] and there can be no doubt but that the size of a congregation was deliberately limited to ensure that its members were truly united as comrades, feeling the close fellowship and reciprocal trust and affection that were so large a part of the cult. One may think of an analogy to the "lodges" of the Masons and perhaps other basically religious "fraternal" societies of the present day.

The Mithraic worship was exclusively for men. Their wives went to the temple of the Magna Mater (a development of Cybele), which was usually located just across the street for their convenience and, being entirely above ground, was usually effaced completely by the fury of the Christians when they were at last able to take over. There was necessarily a close alliance between the cults of Mithras and the Magna Mater, of which the details escape us, and there was to some extent an interpenetration of the two theologies. As numerous inscriptions attest, women could indulge in a taurobolium and have their sins washed away by the magical blood of the bull who was slain in memory of the Cosmic Bull and whose blood was doubtless believed to be charged with religious efficacy by a kind of simple

---

128 A Mithraeum into which a hundred votaries might have crowded has been found in Rome, but, so far as I know, it is exceptional. Many Mithraea could have accommodated only twenty or so celebrants without intolerable crowding. Whether a given Mithraeum was used by more than one congregation of Brethren is an open question.

transubstantiation. They were also acquainted with the use of holy water for ritual purification, and one or two scholars have guessed that the Magna Mater might have been thought of as corresponding to the Anahita of the divine trinity recognized by Artaxerxes in the springtime of the religion.

The reader will have observed an impressive religious evolution. We begin with a religion in which Ahura Mazda, represented only in aniconic form by the sacred fire, is the only god to be worshipped, and there is no hint of a suggestion that he might have a son.[129] In the Mithraic cult, the Son has, for all practical purposes ousted the Father, who survives only as a link between Zervan and Mithra, so that it would have been easy to dispense with poor old Ahura Mazda without a significant change in the cult or even its theology, and the sacred fire has been replaced by sculpture, some of it of fair quality, and such rites as Last Suppers.

The reader will also have observed that in the course of our discussion of Mithraism we moved from Persia to the Roman world. That was because it is only in the latter that we have any secure information about it.[130] It almost certainly arose in or near the old Persian territory, and it could most easily be explained as a heresy of a heresy. It retained the theology of the Zervanists, and so must be an offshoot of that cult, showing an even greater devotion to the Son of God and perhaps adopting a new religious organization, limiting membership to male proselytes who were willing to form groups comparable to the lodges of modern religious clubs, such as the Masons, and to

---

129   I dealt with this point in Appendix I.
130   An admirably concise and handsomely illustrated account of Mithraism in the Roman Empire by Dr. Elmar Schwertheim forms the 1979 Sondernummer of the well-known journal of general archaeology, *Antike Welt*. Good photographs show many of the best-preserved Mithraic sculptures and, what is not common, portraits of two *Magi*, in which historians of art may see an anticipation of the style of Byzantine religious paintings. Also shown is a trick arrow, one of the devices used to make simpletons gawk in pious awe; it is, of course, an anticipation of the device now commonly used on the stage and in the cinema when it is desired to show a man slain by an arrow or sword through his body. For the English reader, there is a compendious account in the translation of Franz Cumont's *The Mysteries of Mithra*, which is available in a Dover reprint. A series of scholarly volumes devoted to Mithraism is in course of publication at Leiden as part of the collection of *Études préliminaires aux religions orientales dans l'empire romaine*. The inscriptions are collected in the *Corpus inscriptionum et monumentorum religionis Mithriacae*, edited by M.J. Vermaseren. For a basic bibliography of other works, see the notes to Dr. Schwertheim's long article.

proceed through several degrees of initiation, learning and memorizing fresh "secrets" at each stage, to full membership.[131]

After the gradual revival of Zoroastrianism under the Parthians, the Zervanists, as we have already said, flourished in the old Persian territories as one of the Zoroastrian sects until Chosroës ruled them heretical. We have, so far as I know, no information about the Mithraic sect that we have described in the same territory, and that suggests that it was either a relatively minor sect or underwent considerable modifications for export. Given the limitation of our sources, however, that is not necessarily true. I have often thought that the Mithraic cult, in the form in which we know it, would have particularly appealed to the Parthian aristocracy, whose special devotion to Mithras is attested by their use of such common names as Mithridates. They were officially Zoroastrians and maintained *Magi* at their courts to keep the sacred fires alight and provide holiness when needed, but they were so negligent in their observation of the Zoroastrian proprieties that the Zoroastrians of the Sassanid period regarded them as little better than infidels. They, like the Mithraists of whom we know, had so little godliness that they never felt a yen to persecute and kill *ad maiorem gloriam Dei*. So marked was this lack of zeal among the Parthian aristocracy that Professor Tarn remarks that "one gathers the impression that they thought all religions useful, none material; what mattered to a man was his horse, his bow, and his own right arm." But perhaps that goes too far. Would not their chivalry have found a religious satisfaction in a kind of mystery cult that formed them into small congregations of comrades, bound together by a kind of military sacrament, for the worship of the heroic Son of God, who had subjugated even the Sun, and who was ever ready to fight evil? The speculation appeals to me, but I know of no evidence to confirm or even bolster it.[132]

We first hear of the Mithraic cult in Cilicia early in the first century

---

131   Masonic rituals and the bizarre myths about Yahweh, Solomon, Hiram, and a trio of malefactors, Jebulo, Jebula, and Jebulum, may be found in the Reverend Mr. Walton Hannah's *Christian by Degrees* (London, 1964) and *Darkness Visible* (London, 1966). The myths are said to be understood symbolically, rather than literally, by the adepts, but Christians are exercised over the question whether the symbols are compatible with their religion.

132   To my mind, a Parthian origin is suggested by the fact that the proselyte could advance through seven degrees of which the fifth was "Persian." (The sixth was "Messenger of the Sun," i.e., Mithra, and the seventh was "Father," i.e. a consecrated priest.) This corresponds to the respect that the Parthians had for the Persians over whom they ruled.

BC. So manly a religion had an obvious attraction for military men, and it is believed, no doubt correctly, that it was spread throughout the Roman world by Roman soldiers, to whom it offered a double chance of immortality: A man's soul, which had come down from Heaven to be imprisoned in the flesh, could, if he had sufficiently kept it pure from falsehood and evil in this life, ascend directly to heaven, perhaps a sequence of seven heavens, when he died; otherwise, as in Christian doctrine, his soul would sleep until the final Resurrection, when it would rejoin his reconstituted body for the Last Judgement, after which, if found worthy, he could dwell in God's Paradise, or if found stained with ineradicable evil, he would be annihilated, since the cult did not have the sadistic urge that made Christians hope to see unbelievers and sinners tortured with the utmost of fiendish ingenuity forever and forever.

To Zoroastrians who preserved any knowledge of the religion that had been proclaimed by Zoroaster, Mithraism must have seemed a shockingly wicked perversion, even more ungodly than the Zervanism from which it had sprung. If there were Mithraists in Persian territory in the time of Chosroës, they undoubtedly vanished with the Zervanists. The great king undertook to restore and enforce an orthodoxy based on what had survived, or was assumed to have survived, of the old Zoroastrian scriptures. To Zoroaster, *mithra* seems to have been only a noun meaning 'compact, agreement,' but Mithra as a spirit of some sort was mentioned in the *Avesta* and he was too firmly established to be expunged, but the orthodox *Magi* quickly cut him down to size. The Father returned in glory to his old supremacy.

It is a nice irony that Christianity, which was a remodeled Zoroastrianism, also borrowed many of its trappings and decorations from a Zoroastrian heresy with which it had to compete in its formative years.

About the Author

Dr. Revilo Pendleton Oliver (1908-1994), Professor of the Classics at the University of Illinois for 32 years and one of the leading philologists of his time, read eleven languages, including Sanskrit, and for more than half a century wrote scholarly articles in four languages for academic publications in the United States and Europe.

Oliver was also the possessor of a penetrating intellect — and a scintillating wit unequaled by any writer, though the great H.L. Mencken may have come close.

Dr. Oliver was born in Texas in 1908, and was an undergraduate at Pomona College, California. He obtained his doctorate under the tutelage of the highly respected Classicist William Abbot Oldfather at the University of Illinois. His first book was a copiously annotated translation from the Sanskrit, *Mrcchakatika* (*The Little Clay Cart*) published by the University of Illinois in 1938.

During World War 2, he was Director of Research in a highly secret cryptographic agency of the War Department in Washington, DC, and was cited for outstanding service to his country. It was during his time in Washington that Dr. Oliver first became aware of the degree to which Communism — and, more importantly, the alien forces behind Communism, especially the Jewish power structure — had penetrated the American establishment and had precipitated the fratricidal slaughter of 1939-1945. He believed at the time, however, that the acts of these subversives would be quickly brought to light after the war and that an awakened nation would deal decisively and finally with its enemies. Confident in his nation's future, he continued his pursuit of the scholarship which was, next to his beloved wife Grace, his greatest love in life.

After his work for the War Department, Dr. Oliver was awarded a Guggenheim Post-Service Fellowship, and during the years 1953 and 1954 he travelled to Italy on a Fulbright Research Fellowship to study Italian Renaissance manuscripts.

Upon his return home in 1954, Dr. Oliver was alarmed at the progress made by the subversive forces in the United States, who had infiltrated both major political parties and the business establishment there — especially the media of information and entertainment. He made a fateful decision in that year to devote all his available energies to what was then called anti-Communism or Americanism or conservatism, and which is today called by its adherents Racial-Nationalism. For the next 40 years, until his death in 1994, he was a major figure in that movement, though in many ways an anomalous one.

Dr. Oliver made many notable contributions to his chosen cause: He participated in the creation of *National Review* magazine and was for years one of its principal writers; he was one of the founders of the John Birch Society; he made numerous speeches before patriotic groups including the Congress of Freedom, the Steuben Society, the Indignation Committees, the Citizens' Councils, and the Daughters of the American Revolution; and he wrote hundreds of articles and reviews for *Modern Age, American Progress, Free Enterprise, American Opinion, Christian Economics,* the aforementioned *National Review, Nation's Business, The American Mercury,* Wilmot Robertson's great monthly *Instauration,* Dr. William Pierce's brilliant *National Vanguard* magazine, and, especially, George Dietz's *Liberty Bell* magazine, where he was a regular columnist.

A collection of many of Dr. Oliver's best writings from his first decade in the patriotic movement is contained in his book *America's Decline: The Education of a Conservative.* That book also chronicles his eventual bitter disillusionment with conservatism as a political weapon for restoring America and the West.

Many of Dr. Oliver's best writings not yet collected in book form, may be read at nationalvanguard.org, the online continuation of William Pierce's print magazine, associated with the National Alliance, and at revilo-oliver.com.

Revilo Oliver stood apart — not only from his more "liberal" colleagues who accepted or welcomed the political and social changes forced upon the West after World War 2 — but also from his "conservative" and "patriot" allies who refused to see that much of the fault for our civilization's decline lay in ourselves, in the racial and societal characteristics that left us nearly defenseless against an implacable, relentless, and clever enemy. In his most striking departure from most of his conservative allies, Dr. Oliver concluded that one of the major weaknesses of our civilization was its religion, which has been, since the latter years of the Roman Empire, some form of Christianity.

Dr. Oliver was a close associate of Dr. William Pierce and Kevin Alfred Strom of the National Alliance, and was instrumental in the founding of the Alliance's predecessor organization, the National Youth Alliance, in 1969. Dr. Oliver made a short film that year, *After Fifty Years,* to promote support for the group.

More from Cosmotheist Books

- *The Jewish Strategy* by Revilo P. Oliver

    What is it about the Jews that has allowed them not only to survive as a nation-within-nations for 2,500 years, but to become the dominant power in the world today? What are their plans for us under their rule?

- *Blood Ritual* by Philip de Vier

    What is the truth about Jewish ritual murder over the centuries? Is it merely a "blood libel," a result of unreasoning prejudice? Or are some cases too well-documented to dismiss?

- *Building a New White World* by William Pierce

    The real-world, practical program of the National Alliance to save our race and build a new, progressive order in which our people can thrive.

- *Bolshevism from Moses to Lenin* by Dietrich Eckart

    A philosophical conversation between the author and Adolf Hitler on the purpose of life, struggle, race, faith, and nationhood — and the nature of the Jew. Translated by William Pierce.

- *Gun Control in Germany* by William Pierce

    Conservatives claim Hitler's Germany was against private gun ownership — a myth created to hide the fact that the main force pushing for gun control today is the Jewish power structure. This book shows that gun laws were actually *relaxed* under National Socialism, which was very much in favor of its citizens owning and using firearms.

- *The Turner Diaries* by Andrew Macdonald

    Written by Dr. William Pierce under the pen name Macdonald, this is the book that the censors have banned again and again. *The Turner Diaries* is a searingly violent action novel of a new American — and ultimately worldwide — revolution against the forces which are killing our race.

- *Hunter* by Andrew Macdonald

    Another powerful novel of race and revolution written by William Pierce, even more radical in its ideas and explicit in its life-and-death action than *The Turner Diaries*.

- *Serpent's Walk* by Randolph Calverhall

    Written for the National Alliance by the great fantasy writer M.A.R. Barker under the pen name Calverhall, this is an intellectually-stimulating action novel in which Hitler's warrior elite — the SS — didn't give up their struggle for a White world when they lost the Second World War.

- *The Lightning and the Sun* by Savitri Devi

    A work about the historical inevitability of cultural decay and rebirth, written by one of Adolf Hitler's most devoted admirers. Savitri Devi couches her arguments in metaphor, using "lightning" to refer to forces of destruction and "sun" to refer to building in accordance with Nature's eternal laws.

- *Which Way Western Man?* by William Gayley Simpson

    During his long lifetime, William Gayley Simpson was both a philosopher and a careful observer of our civilization and its dominant faith. An exceptionally deep thinker, he traced the sickness that overtook the White man's world in the 20th century to its roots in Jewish-derived religion and social movements.

- *The Best of Attack and National Vanguard* by William Pierce, *et al.*

    Every editorial, article, and feature of lasting value from Dr. Pierce and his associates' early public writings is in this classic, large-format, long out-of-print book, reproduced from all 85 of the original *Attack* and *National Vanguard* tabloid newspapers from 1970 to 1982. This book has been described as a "university education in 216 pages," and it has been said that if a man is capable of being radicalized, reading this book will do it.

- *Cosmotheism: Religion of the Future* by William Pierce (with Kevin Alfred Strom and Fred Streed)

    Dr. William Luther Pierce's Cosmotheism is not a revealed religion, but is instead what he called a *natural* religion: It rejects all of the claimed supernatural "revelations" which find their way onto shining golden plates or ancient scrolls, instead having its basis in the realities of Nature that our eyes — and the investigations of science — have confirmed. In the drama of the evolution of life from non-living matter, and of higher and more conscious beings from lower forms of life, William Pierce sees a path of purpose and destiny for us.

- *The Fame of a Dead Man's Deeds* by Robert S. Griffin

    The only biography of Dr. William L. Pierce; written with sensitivity and objectivity by a man who lived side-by-side with Dr. Pierce and came to know him deeply.

Audio Recordings

- *The Turner Diaries* audio book read by William Pierce

    This unabridged ten-hour MP3-CD presents *The Turner Diaries* as read by the author, Dr. William Pierce. Digitally remastered in excellent, high-fidelity sound.

- *The Power of Truth* series; an ever-expanding library of recordings of classic *American Dissident Voices* radio programs

    Some of the most powerful oratory you will ever hear are the broadcasts of William Pierce; the spoken word can explain and inspire in a way that the printed word cannot match; 20 programs on each CD.

Get these and other materials by visiting
COSMOTHEISTCHURCH.ORG

www.ingramcontent.com/pod-product-compliance
Lightning Source LLC
Chambersburg PA
CBHW071848070526
44583CB00016B/1594